Where There Are
Asians,
There Are
Rice Cookers

To the late Takashi Nakano

In a 1971 postcard to his seven year-old daughter, he wrote,
"I'm in Hong Kong, in the southern part of the Chinese mainland.
It's a free port and the shops sell products from all over the world."
The truth of this observation did not sink in until some 30 years later.

Hong Kong, circa 1971.

Where There Are
Asians,
There Are
Rice Cookers

How "National" Went Global via Hong Kong

Yoshiko Nakano

香港大學出版社
HONG KONG UNIVERSITY PRESS

Hong Kong University Press
14/F Hing Wai Centre
7 Tin Wan Praya Road
Aberdeen
Hong Kong

© Hong Kong University Press 2009
First published 2009
Reprinted 2010

ISBN 978-988-8028-08-5

Secure On-line Ordering
http://www.hkupress.org

British Library Cataloguing-in-Publication Data
A catalogue record for this book is available from the British Library.

Printed and bound by Condor Production Co. Ltd., Hong Kong, China

Contents

Acknowledgments

This manuscript is the third incarnation of a project that started life in 2002. In 2003, along with two of my colleagues in the Department of Japanese Studies at the University of Hong Kong, Kirsten Refsing and Dixon H. W. Wong, I co-authored a Chinese book entitled 由樂聲牌電飯煲而起：蒙民偉和信興集團走過的道路 [*Selling Japan in Hong Kong: William Mong and the National Brand*]. The book's focus was William Mong, his life and management style.

Its second incarnation was as a Japanese version of the book. One of the lessons we learned from writing about National's successes and struggles in the Hong Kong market was that we would need to localize our product: we could not simply take the Chinese book, translate it, and expect people in Japan to read it. Therefore, Dixon Wong and I conducted additional interviews, undertook supplementary research, and I completely rewrote the manuscript. In 2005, the two of us published *Onajikama no Meshi* [*Eating Rice from the Same Pot*], focusing on the partnership between Matsushita Electric and Shun Hing. The book has been favorably reviewed by various Japanese publications including *Yomiuri Shimbun, Asahi Shimbun*, and *Nikkei Business*.

When looking to adapt our material for an English version, Dixon Wong and I decided that further emphasis should be put on how National rice cookers went global via Hong Kong and how the sections I had written should be expanded. I therefore took on the project on my own. As a result, this book deviates greatly from the earlier Chinese version and does not discuss Shun Hing's management style at any length. Instead, it follows the basic structure of the first six chapters that make up the Japanese version. I completely rewrote the last two chapters to focus on the transnational flow of rice cookers, and revised, adapted, and updated wherever I felt it necessary to do so. While William Mong remains the main character, this is not in any sense a conventional biography. It is the story of how a Japanese manufacturing giant, working hand in hand with a Hong Kong Chinese entrepreneur, learned to localize its rice cookers for the global market.

I sincerely thank Dixon Wong and Kirsten Refsing for their generosity in allowing me to base my writing on their materials. Dixon was the one who first made me aware that the National rice cooker could be considered an icon of modern living. It had played a far more important role in Hong Kong than anyone familiar with the company's products in Japan could ever have imagined. His insights into the manner in which Japanese culture has been assimilated into Hong Kong society remain the backbone of this book. Kirsten, who left HKU to become Dean of Humanities at Copenhagen University, suggested that we needed to look at Mong's family background to understand his drive and versatility. Her work became the basis for Chapter 2, in which I discuss how anxiety fuels Hong Kong entrepreneurs.

In the seven years it has taken me to collect the data and write the manuscript for this book, I have received assistance from countless people in Hong Kong and Japan. In Hong Kong, I am grateful to William Mong and his staff at Shun Hing Group, who generously shared their stories and photographs. Naturally, he was concerned about my portrayal of his life, but he agreed that I could publish this manuscript without any prior review or approval necessary on his part.

In Japan, employees at Matsushita Electric Trading and Matsushita Electric Industrial (now Panasonic), both active and retired, contributed many anecdotes about their dealings with Mong and other business associates around the world. I feel privileged to have recorded their pioneering efforts to globalize National/Panasonic appliances. Staff in two Panasonic units tirelessly responded to my persistent inquiries for data and archival materials: the Hong Kong Team in the Sales Office for China and Northeast Asia, and Panasonic Home Appliances Company's Cooking Appliances Business Unit, previously known as Matsushita's Rice Cooker Division (1958–2002) and Cooking Systems Division (2002–06). I also received valuable assistance from the children of employees involved in National's localization projects. Sadayoshi and Ryuzo Sakamoto, two sons of National's first director of the Rice Cooker Division, provided photographs of their father's 1960 fact-finding trip to Hong Kong and Bangkok.

I would also like to thank the Toyota Foundation for funding the project "Japan in Hong Kong: Systems of Production, Circulation, and Consumption of Culture," which was led by Dixon Wong and ran from 2000 to 2001. As part of the project, we collected Japan-related advertisements that had appeared in Hong Kong's Chinese-language newspapers from 1945 onwards, and these provided the starting point for our subsequent research into rice cookers.

In 2003, I was made an Asia Leadership Fellow by the Japan Foundation and the International House of Japan. The award involved a three-month stay in Tokyo, during which I had the opportunity to continue my research and interview several Matsushita employees, both in Tokyo and Osaka. Exchanges with other Fellows from all over Asia also led to some interesting discoveries, such as the one that many Bhutanese professionals had forgotten their country's traditional method of preparing rice because they all used rice cookers purchased in Singapore. Their stories reinforced my belief that the rice cooker has transformed the lives of people across Asia.

In line with its transnational theme, the project involved interviews and materials in Japanese, Cantonese, and English. I am grateful to the Faculty of Arts at the University of Hong Kong for granting me time away from my teaching duties to work on this version of the book. Georgina Challen edited my English manuscript with her usual meticulousness and great care. I also received editorial advice and translation assistance from my current and former colleagues in the Department of Japanese Studies, Takemichi Hara, Peter Cave, Chan Cham-yi, and Andrew MacNaughton, as well as from Clare Vickers and Shirley Lok. Izumi Nakayama provided welcome editorial assistance and brought clarity to the structure of the narrative.

My students in the Department of Japanese Studies at the School of Modern Languages and Cultures acted as research assistants at various stages of this project, translating texts, conducting library research, identifying potential Hong Kong interviewees, and locating decades-old rice cooker advertisements. They are Natsuko Fukue, Samuel Young, Lily Yao, Janice Ng, Milton Chu, Amanda Chiu, Janas Lao, and Joyce Leung.

This long list of acknowledgements only goes to show that this account of "How 'National' Went Global via Hong Kong" owes much to the contributions of others, just as the Japanese Rice Cooker Division benefited from the insights of its associates throughout Asia.

March 2009
Hong Kong

A Note to the Reader

Over the past five decades, many of the brand, company, and division names, as well as job titles mentioned in this book, have undergone significant changes. To avoid confusion and retain the authentic feel of the period, I have used the names and terminology that were in common use at the time.

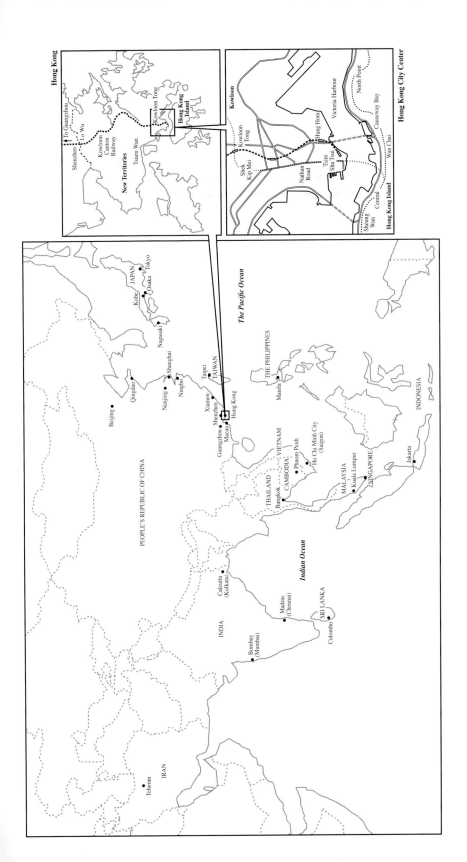

Introduction
We Are Not That Poor Any More

Where there are Asians, there are rice cookers. According to one estimate, some 43 million units were sold worldwide in 2006.[1] The electric rice cooker has to be one of the "Made in Japan" products that has had the most impact on the lives of Asian people. And yet the story of its globalization has not received much attention. In the United States, the rice cooker is basically a niche product for hyphenated Americans, often dismissed as a never-to-be-opened wedding gift. In Japan, it is not exactly glamorous either: when the automatic rice cooker was first introduced by Toshiba in 1955, it immediately became a hit. Its success, however, was overshadowed by that of the "Three Sacred Treasures"— the television, washing machine and refrigerator—that were considered the true icons of modern Japanese living.[2] In comparison, the rice cooker was seen as a minor, though useful, appliance targeted at housewives (*okusan-yōhin*).[3]

In 1960s Hong Kong, the National brand rice cooker was held in much higher regard and embodied the aspirations of an emerging middle class for a better quality of life. It enjoyed elevated status and took pride of place in the kitchens, and even living rooms, of many Chinese households. Following my move to Hong Kong from Washington, DC, in 1997, along with four of my colleagues in the Department of Japanese Studies at the University of Hong Kong, I became involved in a project called "Japan in Hong Kong." The project set out to examine the assimilation of Japanese culture into Hong Kong society. To my surprise, the National rice cooker kept coming up as one of the first Japanese products to be embraced by the city's residents. In the 1960s, the sweet smell of steamed rice assured many first-time rice cooker owners that they were "not that poor any more."

The gap between perceptions of the rice cooker in Hong Kong and Japan was intriguing. After learning that the person who had laid the foundation for the success of the National rice cooker in Hong Kong was not a Japanese *salaryman* but a Chinese entrepreneur, it seemed important to document this domestic appliance's transnational flow and to highlight the contributions of the Asian men and women who had made it possible. This story of "Made in Japan" is based on oral history interviews with forty-three individuals from Hong Kong and Japan, supplemented by archival research. Memories can sometimes be unreliable and fade over time, so it was vital to record them before they were lost altogether.[4]

For most Japanese, the rice cooker has traditionally played only a minor, if any, role in the success story that is "Made in Japan." As in the case of Sony founder Akio Morita's autobiography, *Made in Japan*, the story typically starts with the transistor radio—the first shining star that earned the Japanese electronics industry the most dollars in the 1950s—and leads to automobiles, Walkmans, and Pokémon. The globalization of these products is usually presented as the result of heroic efforts on the part of Japanese men: how diligently their project teams worked, how their products created a sensation in the United States, and how their endeavors enriched the Japanese economy.

But is this the only way to tell "Made in Japan" stories? What if we look at this globalization process not as a Japanese commercial victory but as the result of a three-way interaction between Japanese manufacturers, local distributors, and consumers? What if we expand the scope of inquiry from the United States to Asia and look at how products have crossed borders? What if we consider not only the economic impact these products have had on Japan but also their social impact on consumers in other countries? Once we begin to shift our perspectives, the rice cooker emerges as a star in Asia, where over ninety percent of the world's rice crop is grown.[5]

Hong Kong played a vital role in the globalization of the rice cooker. It was the place that the National team first established its procedures for modifying Japanese rice cookers to suit international consumers, long before the process of "localization" had acquired its name. Unlike more universal electronic appliances like televisions and refrigerators, or even the Walkman, subtle product adjustments were essential to the successful localization of the rice cooker. Rice is deeply cultural and a source of comfort, pride, and occasionally chauvinism.[6] To ensure that it would appeal to international consumers, the rice cooker team had to adapt the rice cooker to accommodate diverse varieties of rice and a wide range of recipes.

As early as 1960, the National rice cooker team began to develop an Asian version of the Japanese original, in collaboration with William Mong Man-wai (蒙民偉), later known in the Chinese-speaking world as the "King of Electrical Appliances." The son of ethnic Chinese parents born and raised in Nagasaki, Japan, Mong is not a physically imposing man, but no detail escapes his eagle eye and he is ready to seize any business opportunity that presents itself. He was born in Hong Kong in 1927, the same year Matsushita Electric Industrial's founder, Konosuke Matsushita (松下幸之助), came up with the brand name National to market his battery-powered bicycle lamp, in the hope that it would one day be used nationwide.

Matsushita Electric Industrial (now Panasonic) is today one of the world's largest consumer electronics empires. In 2007, its annual net sales totaled US$77 billion worldwide, half of which was generated outside Japan.[7] The company's two main brands—National, used for home appliances, and Panasonic, used for audiovisual products—have become household names in Asia. Against Hong Kong's panoramic skyline, the name Panasonic, in four-storey-high, gleaming blue letters, illuminates Victoria Harbour.

In 2003, the President of Matsushita Electric Industrial, Kunio Nakamura, paid tribute to Mong at a cocktail reception held to mark the fiftieth anniversary of his company's partnership with Mong's Shun Hing Group (信興集團). "It is no exaggeration to say that Mr Mong was the driving force behind our international sales expansion," he told the 1,000 assembled guests. Nakamura went on to illustrate how Mong's efforts were instrumental to Matsushita's globalization efforts:

> When we look back to half a century, we did not have the know-how to grow our business internationally, and we had hardly any products suitable for sale in overseas markets. In 1954, Mr Mong placed his first order for thirty vacuum radios directly to our factory, and we exported them to Hong Kong. Since then, we have received numerous suggestions on how to develop products for the Hong Kong market. Our company has tried its best to accommodate these requests, and through this process our [international] product lines have become more competitive.
>
> In those early days, when we came up with new products for export, most of the first shipments were destined for Hong Kong.[8]

Following the establishment of his relationship with Matsushita, William Mong, the archetypal Hong Kong entrepreneur, quickly became involved in product planning and was able to develop new markets thanks to his versatile linguistic skills, cultural awareness, and extensive use of transnational networks. As a result of interactions with Mong and other partners in Asia, Matsushita Electric expanded the range of its early export products from radios to electric fans, rice cookers, and refrigerators, and today Hong Kong continues to be an ideal test market for its latest digital products. Their collaboration has proven particularly fruitful where rice cookers are concerned: of all the brands, National/Panasonic remains the most successful in global market reach.

Hong Kong has long played a vital role as the gateway to both China and Chinese diasporas around the world. A free port whose favorable customs regulations enabled the easy flow of goods into and out of the city, Hong Kong became a focal point for the re-export of appliances at a time when protectionist trade policies were the norm. Japanese appliances not only stayed in the territory, but many followed Chinese traders, travelers, and migrants—to the Philippines, Indonesia, and the Middle East in the 1960s, to China after it adopted its Open Door Policy in 1979, and to Canada and Australia in the late 1980s. Both smaller appliances, like rice cookers and transistor radios, and larger ones, like television sets, readily crossed borders and traveled along Chinese family and business networks to other parts of Asia and to Asian diasporas, in ways that were beyond what any Japanese salaryman could ever have imagined.

This book presents a different approach to the success story of "Made in Japan" products in Hong Kong and beyond, adopting multiple perspectives rather than a single Japanese one. It tells how a Japanese manufacturing giant, working hand in hand with a Chinese entrepreneur, learned to localize its appliances for the global market and, transcending national boundaries, brought modern Japanese convenience to the city's emerging middle class.

The Sweet Smell from the Rice Cooker

This story starts in Hong Kong with the Wongs, a working-class family who bought their first National rice cooker in 1967.[9] Prior to that, the only electrical product they possessed was a small National radio.

During the summer of 1967, China was in the grip of the violence and turmoil brought about by the launch of Mao's Great Proletarian Cultural Revolution the year before. In Hong Kong, only a few miles from the Chinese border, loudspeakers installed by the Bank of China at its headquarters in the center of the city starting blaring out Maoist chants in Mandarin. The Communist anthem, *Dongfang Hong* (The East is Red), echoed ominously throughout the Central financial district on Hong Kong Island. In retaliation, the British colonial government placed several even larger speakers near the Bank of China building to try and drown out the communist propaganda by playing Cantonese opera at full volume.[10]

In May, an industrial dispute flared up at a Hong Kong artificial flower factory in Kowloon. Laid-off workers picketed the factory building and clashed with police. The anger felt by many local Hong Kong residents over their treatment at the hands of the colonial government came to a head and boiled over into violent protests. Rioters threw stones at Government House and set buses on fire, leading the government to impose a three-day curfew. Star Ferry and tram services were suspended. These events sparked off full-blown riots that gradually spread to other parts of the city.

For the following seven months the situation in the territory remained extremely tense. Free-to-air television broadcasting did not start until November of that year, and Japanese transistor radios, available from most of the city's electrical appliance shops, were in unusually high demand. For many, this was the only way to find out what was happening on the city's streets. There were over 8,074 reports of homemade bombs being planted around the city by leftist protesters. As many as one in seven actually went off, usually with a loud bang and emitting thick clouds of smoke. By the time the riots subsided, at the end of 1967, fifty-one people had died.[11]

Like many Hong Kong residents unable to leave their homes, the Wongs spent hours listening to news of the riots on the radio.[12] The four-member family lived in a single room in an apartment in Wanchai (灣仔), on Hong Kong Island. The space was so small that they had to lie almost on top of each other to sleep, an unpleasant experience during Hong Kong's hot and humid summer nights. There was not even an electric fan.

This was a time of hardship for many local residents, who often had to endure appalling living conditions. It was fairly common for the whole family to be crammed into one room in a two-bedroom apartment. The landlady lived in the other bedroom, and they all shared a living room and tiny kitchen. The father was a repairman at the city's telephone service provider, Cable and Wireless, and he was paid a fixed monthly salary. Yet, as soon as he received his paycheck, he would gamble most of it away on the horses, and the family was having a hard time making ends meet. To supplement their income, the mother decided to become a part-time cleaner in an office building.

A clay pot (center) for cooking rice in a 1960s Hong Kong kitchen.
Courtesy of Sadayoshi Sakamoto

Then, their landlady purchased a mysterious-looking pot that could cook rice without fire. In those days, the most common way of cooking rice or congee (rice gruel) in Hong Kong was in clay pots heated over a gas or charcoal stove. The landlady was so proud of her new acquisition that she put it in the shared living room rather than in the kitchen. The Wongs' son, Bill, a primary school student at the time, was intrigued, wondering how rice could possibly be cooked without fire. He recalls:

> "At that time, the rice cooker was a symbol of conspicuous consumption, so she put it in the living room to show it off."[13]

When the landlady switched on the rice cooker, Bill sat down beside it and looked through the glass lid as the simmering rice filled the room with its warm aroma. Bill could actually see the rice as it cooked, thanks to an ingenious glass viewing pane installed by the manufacturer.

> "I was amazed," he recalls. "So many years have passed, yet I still clearly remember the moment, the water evaporating and the sweet smell of rice."[14]

Bill, now a Hong Kong civil servant, smiles as he remembers the day when he was nine, and the Wong family had finally put aside enough money from their living expenses to buy their first rice cooker:

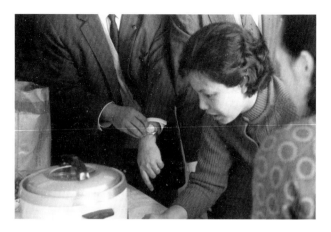

Seeing the rice cooker at work for the first time. Hong Kong, 1960.
Courtesy of Sadayoshi Sakamoto

"The feeling was quite special, because it was the first electrical appliance we had at home besides our radio. We finally had the money to buy it. The feeling was 'we are not that poor any more'."[15]

For working-class families, the rice cooker was an icon of modern living, and one which, if they worked hard, they could some day afford to buy. In 1960, the number of National rice cookers imported into Hong Kong stood at just 100 a year; seven years later, in 1967, annual sales had increased to over 100,000. By the time US President Richard Nixon visited Beijing in February 1972, as a prelude to the normalization of diplomatic ties between the United States and the People's Republic of China, the Japanese rice cooker had become a standard appliance in most Hong Kong homes.

Bill's generation, too young to remember that Japanese appliances had once been considered cheap, unreliable substitutes for Western appliances, was witnessing the emergence of a new Hong Kong middle class.[16] At that time, almost half the city's working population was employed in the manufacturing industry, and the biggest employers were garment factories. The "Made in Hong Kong" label, however, was not restricted to clothes, and Hong Kong factories soon began assembling all kinds of goods, including electrical appliances. The daily lives of Hong Kong's working class started to change dramatically. According to an article that appeared in the city's leading English language newspaper, "by 1971, well over half the households had an income above HK$600 a month against just over HK$150 in 1966."[17]

After purchasing a rice cooker, next on the list for most Hong Kongers was a television set, followed by a refrigerator, radio cassette player, and washing machine. Japanese electrical appliances gradually became an indispensable part of modern living in Hong Kong.

Japanese Dramas on Hong Kong Television

In 1969, when Bill turned eleven, his mother bought a black-and-white television set. This was just two years after the disruption caused by the Hong Kong riots and the start of free-to-air television broadcasting.

> At that time, my mother was worried I might turn into a triad member, you know, join a street gang. I was never at home, always going to the park to play football or basketball.[18] There were always triad gangs hanging around the basketball court, as playgrounds were good places for them to recruit new members.
>
> My mother thought it was dangerous for me to play outside. So, she used TV to make me stay at home. But then again, she also worried if I spent too much time watching TV.[19]

For this reason, Bill's mother chose a JVC television set. It looked like a cupboard with double doors that could be closed to block off the screen completely and could even be locked. Japanese television sets were the only ones to incorporate doors into their design and therefore were very popular with Hong Kong parents. Bill's mother had the key and could control the amount of time he spent watching television.

Bill had many favorite television programs, but the one he looked forward to the most was a variety show called *Enjoy Yourself Tonight* (歡樂今宵). It had singing and comedy and was on every weeknight at 9:30. It was modeled after *The Ed Sullivan Show* on CBS in the United States. Just as *The Ed Sullivan Show* had provided a platform for budding stars such as Elvis Presley, The Beatles, and Mary Tyler Moore, *Enjoy Yourself Tonight* served as the launch pad for Cantonese-speaking talents. And the laughter the show generated united the territory's residents, almost half of whom were immigrants from various parts of China with few shared memories.

Other television programs he enjoyed were the cult British series *Thunderbirds* and the Japanese drama *V is Our Sign* (Sain wa V) about a girls' volleyball team. This drama celebrating the "can-do spirit" had been translated into Cantonese as 青春火花 (Youth Sparkle), and was a smash hit in the territory.

> I think it was showing at 8:00 p.m. on Sundays. I still remember some elements of the story, what they had to do to win the games, the jealousy among the teammates. I remember the music from the theme song too.
>
> After this, more and more Japanese TV drama series [that featured sports] were broadcast: *A Beautiful Challenger* (紅粉健兒), which was about bowling, and *Sugata Sanshiro* (柔道龍虎榜), which was about Judo wrestlers. But *V is Our Sign* was the first one.[20]

V is Our Sign became popular in Japan in 1969, five years after the Japanese women's volleyball team won gold at the 1964 Tokyo Olympic Games. A year later, in 1970, it had made its way onto Hong Kong television screens. Hong Kong's first free-to-air television station, Television Broadcasts Limited (TVB), had started broadcasting in 1967 but, up until the mid-1970s was unable to produce a sufficient amount of homegrown content to fill up its schedule. The channel was especially short of television dramas to broadcast in the station's prime-time weekend slots. Chinese-language dramas tended to be like mini-movies rather than programs with a single narrative stretched over several episodes. In addition, many of them were produced in Mandarin rather than Cantonese, the language used by the majority of local Hong Kong people.

To fill the air time, Hong Kong imported drama series from Japan and the United States. As far as the Japanese television shows were concerned, their premises often revolved around sports competitions, and they were usually dubbed into Cantonese, making them accessible to local audiences. TVB had two channels: the Chinese-language channel, Jade, which most Hong Kong people tuned into, and the English-language channel, Pearl, which served Hong Kong's Chinese elite and expatriates. Japanese dramas, *anime,* and children's programs were shown on the more popular Jade rather than on Pearl. In other words, these Japanese shows were foreign, but not too much so, and struck a chord with Hong Kong Chinese audiences.

The local sponsor of *V is Our Sign* was Mitsubishi Electric's Hong Kong agent. By sponsoring the popular Japanese television program, the company aimed to boost sales of its television sets in the territory. During the 1970s, it was quite common for Japanese electrical goods manufacturers, such as Mitsubishi Electric, National, and Toshiba, to sponsor prime-time programs in Hong Kong. For example, Sharp sponsored a television singing contest that was shown on Wednesday nights. The program's title incorporated the company's name, *The Night of Sharp* (聲寶之夜) and, of course, the winner's prize was supplied by Sharp.[21]

On December 6, 1970, the day the first episode of *V is Our Sign* was broadcast on TVB, Mitsubishi Electric took out an ad in one of the local Chinese-language newspapers promoting the program and, naturally, the company's latest television set:

Mitsubishi Electric Trading Limited 5th Anniversary Celebrations

Two Special Offers

1. We are the proud sponsors of the color television series *V is Our Sign.* From the 6th of this month, the show will be broadcast every Sunday night from 8:00 to 8:30 p.m. on TVB Jade.

V is Our Sign tells the story of a women's volleyball team whose members overcome all obstacles and unite for victory. The series is shot in a truly innovative style, and is full of the passion and vitality of youth. This new show will provide entertainment for the whole family, young and old alike. Make sure you get the best picture quality: watch it on a Mitsubishi TV set.

2. To thank you for your custom, we are offering 300 16-inch TV sets at a very special price. Don't miss out. Installment plans also available.

(*Sing Tao Daily*, December 6, 1970)

Although the television set featured in the newspaper ad was a color one, in 1970, the total number of color television sets imported into the territory stood at approximately 1,800, versus 126,000 black-and-white sets, a ratio of 70 to 1. At the time, about half of Hong Kong's households owned a black-and-white television.

What's more, the television set pictured in the advertisement had only a sixteen-inch screen. Telefunken, a West German high-end electrical goods manufacturer, owned the patent for the PAL color encoding system adopted by Hong Kong.[22] When Japanese manufacturers first sought to enter the PAL system market, Telefunken would not grant them permission to start producing television sets with anything larger than a twenty-three-inch screen. This, however, ended up working in the Japanese companies' favor as far as Hong Kong was concerned, as the small-screen Japanese sets were better suited to the cramped living conditions of many of the city's residents.[23]

In 1963, before even the advent of TVB and free-to-air broadcasting, when the only local channel was the subscription cable station *Rediffusion Television,*[24] compact and affordable Japanese televisions already ranked first in number of sets imported into Hong Kong. This was just the beginning. By 1970, Japanese televisions accounted for seventy-eight percent of the total number of sets imported into Hong Kong.

It was still, however, the dream of most Hong Kong consumers to own a big-screen European-brand TV. Unfortunately, television sets manufactured in Europe, where the climate was dry, were not ideally suited to Hong Kong's subtropical weather. In late spring, when the humidity is at its highest, condensation runs down the walls, and Victoria Peak disappears behind a thick curtain of fog. At this time of year, the picture of the big-screen European-made sets flickered and lacked definition. "Made in Japan" televisions, in contrast, because they were made to withstand Japan's rainy season, remained unaffected.[25]

In the early 1970s, Hong Kong families would gather around their small-screen Japanese television sets during prime time, to watch Japanese television dramas. These were much more popular among young people than were the Chinese-language series, whose storylines were often drawn from Chinese literary classics and shot on a studio soundstage. Lavish martial arts epics or court dramas featuring ladies clad in sumptuously embroidered Chinese dresses were far removed from the life of ordinary Hong Kong people.

V is Our Sign, although set in Japan, was a story about ordinary young people. Young women, armed with determination and an indomitable spirit, overcame extraordinary difficulties to reach their goal. This storyline in many ways reflected Hong Kong's own situation. Bill's generation, however, thought that many of the underlying messages in *V is Our Sign*, such as giving one's all and never giving up, were very Japanese:

> "The theme was very Japanese. Whatever it takes, they have to win the competition. Effort after effort. They will put themselves on the line. This is different from the Chinese. We Chinese tend to be humble."[26]

In fact, in Japanese eyes, it was young Hong Kong people like Bill who were to be admired for their perseverance and dedication in overcoming adversity and raising their standard of living.

The young people of Bill's generation, born between the late 1950s and the early 1960s, worked extremely hard to improve their economic situation and that of their family. Children who did well at school went on to receive the higher education that had been denied their parents, with the aim of eventually securing well-paid, white-collar employment. Those who did not distinguish themselves academically toiled in manual jobs and dreamed of running their own businesses one day. Gradually, their hard work started to pay off and, thanks in part to the remarkable growth of Hong Kong's manufacturing industry, they began to bolster the ranks of the city's new middle class.[27]

A Refrigerator in the Living Room

When Bill turned twelve, in 1970, his family moved to another apartment in the same Wanchai neighborhood. One day, a salesperson came to the door and asked if they would be interested in purchasing a refrigerator on an installment plan.

> A salesman came to my home. He showed us pictures of different [refrigerator] models. No down payment was necessary. We had to pay back [the total amount] within a year or a year and a half. That was very common. Nowadays, if you buy a car, you pay by installments, but back then, you used monthly installment [plans] to buy a refrigerator.[28]

After some deliberation, the family decided to buy a Sanyo refrigerator. Bill and his sister were over the moon. They had a ready supply of cold water and, of course, ice, which, when shaved and covered with sweet red bean paste, made a good dessert. They also liked dissolving Robertson's instant jelly powder in hot water and putting the liquid in the refrigerator to solidify. Bill's favorite was the yellow pineapple-flavored jelly.

> "It was a thrill for us kids," he recalls. "Water magically transformed into a dessert. It was like an experiment in science class."[29]

The Wong family, who had purchased a refrigerator earlier than many of their neighbors, was truly proud of its new acquisition, as it symbolized their new social status.[30]

> At home, we put our rice cooker in the kitchen, not the living room. But when we bought a refrigerator, we put it in our living room, to show it off. Many other families did the same in those days.[31]

It was not just a case of the kitchen being too small to accommodate such a large appliance but also of the family wanting to display the new refrigerator for visitors to admire. When they opened the fridge door and took out some ice to welcome their guests with a cool drink of water, it gave them a tremendous sense of satisfaction.

After the launch of free-to-air television broadcasting in 1967, television ownership in Hong Kong skyrocketed. The import of household refrigerators, however, grew at a much slower pace. It had started as early as the 1950s but was mainly for restaurants and expatriates: refrigerators remained a luxury item that few could afford. For most housewives, not having one meant shopping twice a day, once in the morning and once in the evening. They would go to wet markets to buy fresh meat, fish, and vegetables.[32] Cuts of pork dangled from thick metal hooks, and cages of live ducks and chickens lined the narrow alleys. In the freshwater fish section, there were dozens of frogs jostling each other and live prawns jumping out of their tanks. Dead fish were cheap; for Hong Kong people, the freshness of the ingredients was paramount. Even today, comments such as "fish has to be steamed straight from the tank," or "if chicken isn't freshly killed, the flesh holds too much water" are commonly heard.

By the time *V is Our Sign* made its debut on the small screen in Hong Kong, the rate of refrigerator ownership in the territory was still growing at a much slower pace than that of television sets. It was not just that they were expensive but also that many people in Hong Kong continued to believe that meat, fish, and vegetables kept in a refrigerator were not as fresh as those bought straight from the market. While they might have realized that keeping food in the refrigerator prolonged its shelf life, they preferred to go to the market twice a day. As the rate of ownership began to increase, however, the refrigerator began to change the daily routine of Hong Kong people, especially women.

When Bill turned fourteen in 1972, he left school and started looking for a job. He had just completed his first year of junior high. In Hong Kong, compulsory junior high school education was not implemented until after 1978, and it was therefore very difficult for working-class children to progress more than a year or two beyond primary school.[33] Teenagers had to contribute to the family's living expenses, something they could not do by reading books.

There were plenty of factories willing to employ teenagers. In 1972, forty-six percent of the territory's industrial workforce was engaged in the booming textile industry; electronics assembly factories were also thriving. That year, Hong Kong surpassed Japan to become the world's biggest toy exporter.[34] Bill's mother, however, was hoping Bill could acquire a skill that would be useful in starting his own business in the future, instead of just working on an assembly line.

> I don't think I was a good student, and nobody really pushed me. My mother probably thought, "He is not interested in studying, so give him a chance to learn the skills to become a carpenter or house painter.[35]

In the end, Bill's mother took him to a typewriter repair shop in the neighborhood and asked the owners to take him on as an apprentice. The shop repaired Underwood typewriters, which were produced in Spain, and employed about twelve workers. It occupied two flats on the third floor of a residential building. In fact, the studio did not just repair typewriters but also collected used Underwood typewriters for parts, which the workers re-assembled to make "new" typewriters for sale at bargain prices.

Bill's first salary was HK$200 a month. On Children's Day in 1975, a local newspaper carried an advertisement for one of Hong Kong's oldest department stores, Wing On, enticing shoppers with the offer of a free Japanese action figure:

> Wing On Department Store
>
> Gives Away Masked Rider Action Figure
>
> Between April 1st and 6th, buy HK$50 worth of children's clothes, shoes, socks, toys or stationery, and get a Masked Rider action figure worth HK$12.50 for free.
>
> April 4th Children's Day
>
> (*Overseas Chinese Daily*, April 1, 1975)

"Spend HK$ 50 and get a Masked Rider action
figure for free."
(*Overseas Chinese Daily*, April 1, 1975)

Power Rangers did not take off in the United States until the 1990s. But by the mid-1970s, Japanese children's shows were already mainstream in Hong Kong, and rubber-suited Japanese superheroes like Kamen Rider (Masked Rider; 幪面超人) were idolized by Hong Kong children.[36]

Bill had also grown up with the Japanese Ultraman and Kamen Rider shows, but he could only dream of shopping at such posh department stores. Whenever he managed to set aside a few dollars from his salary, he would take a twenty-cent bus ride to *Dai Dat*

Dei (大笪地), which literally means "big patch of land." This was a large reclaimed area on the Sheung Wan (上環) waterfront, located in the northwest of Hong Kong Island, where a vibrant night market that sold everything from food to clothing operated until midnight.

> There were lots of really cheap things like pirated music tapes and plenty of delicious, MSG-laden food. The nickname for the night market was the "Poor Man's Night Club."[37]

Bill could purchase tapes featuring current Billboard top ten hits for HK$5 a piece. Of course, they were bootleg versions. At that time, there were many shops selling compilations of current hits. As tape recorders became more popular and affordable, some music shops in Wanchai offered to dub a customer's favorite songs for a few dollars. This service was against the law, but it was popular.[38]

After two years of training at the typewriter repair shop, Bill resumed his junior high school education. He was keen to continue his studies and wanted to be able to speak English. He listened to British singer Daniel Boone's "Beautiful Sunday" over and over again on the cassette player his mother had bought him. Listening to American and British pop turned out to be useful for improving his English skills. In 1979, Bill successfully passed the entrance examination for Baptist College and enrolled in courses that were taught in English. He was the first, and only, member of his family to receive a tertiary education. The family did not buy a single new electronic appliance for the duration of his time at college.

A Housing Complex with a Drain

When the Japanese still referred to washing machines, black-and-white televisions and refrigerators as "The Three Sacred Treasures," the washing machine was the most accessible. In 1959, for example, 33 percent of Japanese urban families owned a washing machine, 23.6 percent a black-and-white television set, and 5.7 percent a refrigerator.[39] In Hong Kong, however, washing machines lagged well behind the two other "treasures" in sales. In 1975, 43 percent of Hong Kong's 4.4 million residents lived in public housing.[40] Apartments were not equipped with any kind of wastewater drainage facility. Furthermore, bathrooms and kitchens were small. Although manufacturers had produced a washing machine that could fit under the kitchen sink, it took up a lot of space in already tight living conditions.

Illegal immigrants from mainland China continued to arrive in large numbers. There were border checkpoints, of course, but if people somehow managed to evade police patrols and make their way along country roads into Hong Kong's urban areas, it was relatively easy for them to obtain a residency permit. This lenient immigration policy was called the "touch-base policy," and it remained in place until October 1980, nearly two years after Deng Xiaoping launched China's Open Door policy.[41]

Public housing estates, which started as resettlement estates for squatters, were full of newly arrived mainland Chinese families. These public housing rooms did not have their own kitchen or bathroom, let alone a drainage facility. Each floor had just two communal water taps, and there was therefore nowhere to install a washing machine. Even in private apartment blocks, toilet, shower, and kitchen facilities were often shared.

These harsh living conditions were part of what had incited residents to rise up against the Hong Kong authorities. Following the riots of 1966 and 1967, the colonial government was compelled to implement measures that would improve the living standards of the great majority of Hong Kong's working-class population.[42] In the 1970s, under the governorship of Sir Murray MacLehose, the government launched its Ten-Year Housing Program and began development on several new towns, built in the suburbs, away from the overpopulated urban areas. Modern high-rise housing complexes started springing up all over the place. This time, each flat came with its own bathroom, kitchen, and drainage facilities, making owning a washing machine no longer impossible.[43]

In 1983, when Bill graduated from college and joined the civil service, his family moved to a housing complex in the suburbs of Tsuen Wan (荃灣), one of the new towns developed by the colonial government in the New Territories. The new apartment was more spacious than their previous one, and it came with a drain, meaning that the family could now install a washing machine. Bill went to an electrical appliance shop and finally decided on a Sanyo twin tub model, one tub for washing clothes, the other to spin dry them. He liked its green color, and the price was slightly lower than that of the other available brands. In 1970, his family had paid for their refrigerator in installments; this time, however, thirteen years later, Bill could afford to buy the washing machine outright.

> He recalls, "We did not have to buy it on a monthly installment plan because our spending power had greatly increased."[44]

> Bill's mother was finally released from the drudgery of washing clothes by hand.

Becoming a Hong Konger through Japanese Appliances

As Hong Kong became more affluent, more and more Japanese home appliances were imported into the territory. The surging sales of Japanese home appliances served as a barometer of the city's growing affluence. One of the authors of an earlier Chinese-language version of this book, Dixon H. W. Wong, offers a unique theory regarding what Japanese modern appliances and consumer culture have meant for Hong Kong and its people. Wong, a native Hong Konger who witnessed the rise of the modern Hong Kong lifestyle, argues that Japanese appliances facilitated the process by which "Chinese people" developed a second identity as "Hong Kong people."[45]

In 1975, four out of ten of the city's residents had been born on the Mainland.[46] Among those who had fled the turmoil of Guangdong (廣東) or Fujian (福建) Province and barely made it across the border into Hong Kong, there were some who had left their home with painful reluctance. Many elderly people in particular were unwilling to think of Hong Kong as a permanent place of abode, preferring to see it as just a temporary refuge. For those whose parents and siblings remained across the border, mainland China was still considered home.

Hong Kong, however, offered a modern living environment and appealed to a younger generation aspiring to join the ranks of the middle classes. The more young people modernized their lifestyles by purchasing Japanese home appliances, the more they felt they were distancing themselves from being "Chinese" or "Mainlanders" and establishing a dual and overlapping identity as "Hong Kongers." As their perception of themselves began to change throughout the 1970s, it seemed almost as if they were living on a completely different planet from that of their relatives who had stayed behind in China.

Just a few miles across the border, in mainland China, their cousins' homes did not have an electric rice cooker, let alone a television set.

Chapter Topics

Over the following seven chapters, National (now Panasonic) rice cookers take center stage, ably supported by an ensemble cast of "Made in Japan" star products including radios and televisions, so-called "white goods" like refrigerators and washing machines, and "health-care products" like lounge massage chairs. These supporting players provide a historical context to the story of how rice cookers went global via Hong Kong.

Chapter 1 describes how the National rice cooker team and William Mong worked together to adapt Japanese rice cookers for Chinese consumers. It opens in 1959, the year Mong imported his first twenty-four rice cookers from a National factory in Osaka. It goes on to detail the sales tactics that Mong and his associates employed to introduce this unknown invention to Hong Kong citizens. As early as 1960, Mong campaigned vigorously for changes in design to accommodate local tastes, which led to him personally carrying bags of rice from Hong Kong to Japan and taking part in grueling taste tests. The National team kept an open-minded approach to cultural divergences, willingly going beyond the limitations of a single Japanese interpretation.

Mong's success as an intermediary between the business cultures of Hong Kong and Japan can be attributed to three main characteristics: his versatile linguistic skills, cultural awareness, and ability to capitalize on transnational networks. Chapter 2 considers Mong's family background and chronicles his rise to become the "King of Electrical Appliances." Mong, the son of an ethnic Chinese merchant born in Nagasaki (長崎), grew up in Hong Kong as a subject of two empires, Britain and Japan. He went on to receive a rather unusual education in Hong Kong, mainland China, and Japan.

In Chapter 3, Mong, the Hong Kong entrepreneur, takes on Matsushita, the Japanese manufacturing giant, at a time when anti-Japanese sentiments were still rampant in

Hong Kong. In 1954, the company's founder, Konosuke Matsushita, personally, and without any written agreement, entrusted Mong with the exclusive rights for the sale and distribution of National products in Hong Kong. The chapter describes Mong's attempts at localizing Matsushita's star product at the time, the classic vacuum radio, and the encounters with his Japanese salaryman counterparts that ensued. It reveals Mong's attention to detail, his high expectations, both of himself and others, and how he made use of Chinese transnational networks to expand his market.

Chapter 4 looks at Hong Kong's growing importance in Matsushita's plans for market expansion during the 1960s: as a showcase for National appliances; a test market for new export items, including refrigerators and washing machines; and a gateway to Southeast Asian markets that remained off-limits for political or economic reasons. A free port whose favorable customs regulations enabled the easy flow of goods into and out of the city, Hong Kong became the Japanese manufacturer's strategic base at a time when protectionist trade policies were the norm in many other parts of the world. At the same time, Mong's business sense had not gone unnoticed, and a National competitor tried to entice him away from Matsushita.

Chapter 5 describes the transnational flow of appliances from Japan to mainland China via Hong Kong from 1979 to the end of the 1980s. By the time China opened its doors to Hong Kong "compatriots," the majority of Hong Kongers were already enjoying the benefits of modern appliances like rice cookers and televisions. New policies allowed Hong Kongers entering China to carry one television per person per year as a gift to the relatives they had left behind. Mong and his associates took the initiative and negotiated with the National factory in Osaka to create a model that would work in China. Along with three other manufacturers, they also introduced the innovative "pay in Hong Kong; pick up in China" system that enabled Hong Kongers to provide their relatives with the comforts of a modern lifestyle without the trouble of having to carry the goods on a tiring and crowded journey across the border.

Chapter 6 returns to rice cookers and discusses how they followed Asian migrants, students, and businessmen to Asian diasporas in Europe and North America. In 1979, National's all-male rice cooker team began to recruit female rice specialists who became known as "rice ladies." Their research led to the development of new models that prepared more flavorful steamed rice and Cantonese congee. The versatile model was so valued by Hong Kongers that, when they began to immigrate to Canada, Australia, and other countries after the signing of the Sino-British Joint Declaration in 1984, many took their rice cookers with them. In the meantime, hyphenated Asians in the United States, Canada, and France made use of existing ethnic distribution networks to promote rice cookers alongside bottles of soy and fish sauce.

The final chapter details how the National/Panasonic rice cooker team applied the interactive approach to localization that it established with William Mong in Hong Kong to other markets worldwide. As early as 1967, the team developed a model for Iran with the help of an Iranian taste advisor. As it continued with its localization efforts, the team stuck to the deceptively simple principle of asking local distributors and consumers for their input, respecting local tastes, and even embracing the highly creative uses the rice cooker has sometimes been put to. In 2001, the team went beyond just listening to local opinion and it hired two Thai "rice ladies", who were given free rein to develop localized models. They went on to create a rice cooker that incorporates a cake-baking function.

1

Let's Take Our Rice Cookers to the World
Adapting Japanese Rice Cookers for the Chinese Consumer

Mong makes a point to Sakamoto at a cooking demonstration
for National agents in Osaka, 1967.
Courtesy of Shun Hing Group

Eight million rice cookers. Placed side by side, they would form a 2,400- kilometer-long chain stretching from Osaka to Hong Kong.

Since 1959, the year William Mong began importing National automatic rice cookers to Hong Kong, his company, Shun Hing, has sold more than 8 million units in a city with a population of only 7 million. This equates to approximately ten percent of the total number of National rice cookers manufactured in the world. One might say that the rice cooker was the first "Made in Japan" product to be embraced by the people of Hong Kong. National was one of the first brands to introduce rice cookers to the city and remains the number one choice for Hong Kong consumers, with nearly sixty percent of the market share.[1] Many Hong Kong citizens therefore automatically associate rice cookers with the National brand.

> Even back in the days when we lived in poverty, if we thought of buying an electric rice cooker it had to be "National." To us, "National" *meant* rice cooker. I wouldn't dream of buying a different brand now.[2]

Lily Choi was three years old in 1960, when she immigrated to Hong Kong from Fujian Province in China. Her father left for the Philippines to work at a friend's factory, and little Lily remained in Hong Kong with her mother in a rented room in a North Point (北角) apartment that was home to several other immigrant families from Fujian. Their living conditions were basic: the only electrical appliance in their room was a reading lamp, and they shared the kitchen with four other families. In the evening, Lily's mother would light their portable gas stove and cook congee in a clay pot. Lily explains why they had to eat congee:

> "You need two cups of raw rice to make steamed rice, but if it's congee, you need only one cup of rice. Congee is far more economical!"[3]

The main dish was also simple: fermented *tofu* or canned pork with fried green vegetables. Lily's mother rented the top shelf of the landlord's refrigerator and stored their leftovers in the limited space.

In 1967, when Lily was in the first grade, free-to-air television broadcasting was launched in Hong Kong, and a family on Lily's floor bought a television set. Some early television owners were known to charge the neighborhood children who gathered around to watch their set a few cents for the privilege, but the family on Lily's floor was generous. As their living room was not large enough to accommodate visitors, they turned the television screen to face the front door, which they kept open, so that children could see it from the hallway. Lily and her friends brought their chairs and watched *kung fu* movies and *anime* through the metal screen door.

After class, Lily went home to help her mother with her piecework. Her mother supplemented the money her husband sent from the Philippines by sewing sequins onto sweaters. Lily, with her small hands, would first lay out the tiny sequins according to the elaborate design they had been provided with, and then her mother would sew them on. Whenever they needed an iron for the sequined sweaters, they had to rent the landlord's, who charged them a half-hour's "electricity fee" every time they wanted to use it. As soon as their thirty minutes were up and the cord was unplugged, they would hurry back to their room with the iron, which was still hot, and try to press as many things as possible until it turned completely cold. When the sequin piecework ran out, Lily's mother reluctantly took on jobs assembling artificial flowers, the famous "Hong Kong flowers." The end result was beautiful, but the assembly work was troublesome: it littered the room with tiny bits of plastic, and a strong chemical smell lingered for days.

Lily was sixteen before she finally saved up enough money to buy her family their first rice cooker. She went from store to store to make sure she got the best bargain on a National rice cooker. According to Lily, "Rice cooker equals National; National equals rice cooker. We were programmed!"[4]

Lily now lives a comfortable life with her husband and two sons. Before the 1997 handover of Hong Kong to the PRC, she and her family moved to Australia with all their household belongings, including two National rice cookers, one large and one small. After obtaining Australian citizenship, however, the family moved back to Hong Kong, and only their elder son remains in Melbourne to complete his studies. The rest of the family lives in a luxury high-rise apartment overlooking Victoria Harbour. In Lily's kitchen, there are two National rice cookers, one for cooking rice, and the other for making congee. In the evening, their Filipino domestic helper switches on one of them, depending on whether the family wants steamed rice or congee for dinner.

Hong Kong: Showcase for the World's Best

In 1960, despite the economic hardship suffered by many of the city's newly arrived immigrants, Hong Kong, by virtue of its status as a free port, was a showcase for the world's most luxurious products and biggest brands. Most of the taxis in the city were Mercedes-Benz, and wealthy Asians came to Hong Kong to buy Rolex watches, rubies, and diamonds. The same went for electrical appliances. The world's best were all available in Hong Kong, as reflected in this newspaper advertisement for a thriving store of the time, Yiu Hing Electrical Appliances:

> We trade in all types of domestic electrical appliances from Britain, America, Germany, Italy, France, and Japan, including refrigerators, washing machines, irons, lamps, radios, and electric floor, table, and ceiling fans.
>
> (*Overseas Chinese Daily*, April 8, 1960)

For most Hong Kong citizens, having a refrigerator or washing machine at home was a distant dream. Their sights were set more realistically on purchasing an electric fan, which already meant squeezing every single dollar out of their income. As for a television set, there was no thought of owning one before 1967, the year free-to-air television finally came to Hong Kong.

In contrast to the life of ordinary Hong Kong people, the British colonial city had become the Asian showcase for the world's leading manufacturers: Hoover washing machines, General Electric refrigerators, Philips record players, and Telefunken and RCA radios. Appliances made in Japan were considered second-rate and were listed after those of Italy and France in advertisements similar to the one above. Japanese manufacturers often bought the latest Western appliances in Hong Kong and shipped them back to factories in Japan to "study" them.

Hong Kong people used to sneer at the perceived poor quality of Japanese products by making a play on words. "Japanese goods" in Cantonese is *yat pun fo* (日本貨), but with a slight change in pronunciation it becomes *yat bun fo* (日半貨), meaning goods that malfunction within a day and a half of purchase. Many Hong Kong residents still had vivid memories of the cheap Japanese flashlights sold before the war.[5] Even after

Electrical appliance ad for the Yiu Hing
store, "We trade in all types of domestic
electrical appliances from Britain, America,
Germany, Italy, France, and Japan."
(*Overseas Chinese Daily*, April 8, 1960)

the launch of Japanese transistor radios in 1955, which became popular in Hong Kong
a few years later, "Made in Japan" goods still carried a stigma, and Japanese products'
reputation for dependability was yet to come.

Memories of World War II were also a major obstacle. During the war, Imperial
Japan had occupied Hong Kong for three years and eight months, beginning Christmas
Day 1941. Many Hong Kong citizens had suffered during the occupation—and anti-
Japanese sentiment was no less virulent among the mainland Chinese refugees who had
been flooding into Hong Kong since 1945. When, in 1954, William Mong sought retail
outlets for his Japanese vacuum tube radios, the predecessors of the transistor radio, he
was often subjected to a barrage of abuse from shop owners:

> Have you forgotten about your fellow Chinese killed by the Japanese?
>
> Jap goods? Can't you even wait until the blood's dry?!
>
> Have you forgotten who it was that caused our suffering?

"I had my troubles then," recalls William Mong.[6] Indeed, in 1960, he still came across
clients with strong anti-Japanese feelings.

Mong faced an uphill battle overcoming the negative historical associations of
"Made in Japan." In 1960, when local agents of Japanese appliance manufacturers started

advertising their products in Hong Kong, they took a low-key approach, emphasizing their appliances' value for money, energy-saving qualities, and suitability for small apartments.

There was, however, one Japanese product that had managed to buck the trend and was selling well overseas. The transistor radio earned Japan large amounts of foreign currency, a national priority at the time. Thanks to its successful radio sales, Matsushita Electric's export revenues jumped from ¥3.2 billion in 1958 to ¥13 billion in 1960, the exports accounting for twelve percent of its total production[7] and the United States proving to be its most lucrative market.

A Grand Dream

The Radio Division's senior management had the United States in its sights. The dream was to have Matsushita's transistor radios, sold under the Panasonic brand, featured in the electric appliance section of New York's biggest department store, Macy's. The management believed that, unless their radios were able to win over the hearts of New Yorkers, they would never be considered first-rate by the rest of the world.

One man, however, had a different dream from that of Matsushita's elite. Tatsunosuke Sakamoto had risen from the position of lowly technician to become the director of the newly independent Rice Cooker Division. His ambition was to make the National rice cooker the choice of every rice-consuming family, not just in Japan but around the world. Born in 1909, Sakamoto joined Matsushita after completing the eighth grade and became known for setting extremely high standards both for himself and his staff. When things did not go according to plan at the rice cooker factory or on the sales front, he was quick to raise his voice, and his thick eyebrows. His subordinates were terrified of being called into his office. In 1958, at the age of forty-nine, he was appointed the first director of the Rice Cooker Division.

The Rice Cooker factory stood in Himejima (姫島), in Osaka's western suburbs, which were home to a high concentration of back-alley "cottage industries" with two or three employees apiece. The noise of chainsaws cutting through metal and the chemical smell of spray paint filled the air around the rice cooker factory which, although one of the biggest in the neighborhood, was nothing more than an old wooden building with a tiled roof and a chimney. Matsushita had acquired it from an industrial machine manufacturer and modified it to produce washing machines and blenders. The washing machine had soon become a hot item in Japan, however, and its division had moved to a bigger and better location. Thus, in 1958, the budding Rice Cooker Division had set up its operations in this "third-hand" factory.

The transistor radio factory was housed in a modern state-of-the-art facility, fully air-conditioned, with linoleum flooring. It was in stark contrast to the rice cooker factory, whose wooden floorboards squeaked as workers walked over them. In this humble factory, Sakamoto nursed a grand dream: "Let's take our rice cookers to all the rice-eaters in the world." Since at this time rice cookers were not available outside Japan, this meant building up an overseas market from scratch. But Sakamoto was convinced that anyone for whom rice was a diet staple could not fail to realize how convenient the rice cooker was. He therefore focused his attention on Asia and Asian diasporas.

Matsushita, however, was not the first company to manufacture automatic rice cookers; rival Toshiba was. Toshiba, looking to create an appliance that could cook rice conveniently and consistently, had produced the original automatic rice cooker, called it *denki-gama* (electric pot), and started selling it in Japan in 1955.[8] This compact appliance steamed rice without the need for a wood or gas stove; in other words, "without fire." It relieved housewives of the tedious task of watching over pots, and moved the daily routine of cooking rice from the kitchen to any place with an electrical outlet. It was a safe alternative to the gas stove, especially in the cramped, newly introduced *danchi*, public apartment complexes with modern facilities, usually located in the suburbs.[9] "Now you can cook fabulous rice scientifically" went Toshiba's advertising copy in 1955.[10] This was when a radio was one of the few "scientific" electrical devices to be found in the majority of Japanese living rooms. Appliances that commonly appeared in American comic strips—washing machines, black-and-white television sets, and refrigerators—were collectively known as the "Three Sacred Treasures" in Japan and belonged more to Japanese dreams than homes.[11]

When the Toshiba rice cooker made its debut, Matsushita engineers were stunned. In those days, Matsushita specialized in home appliances that were considered "light electrical machines," as opposed to the "heavy electrical machines," or industrial machines, produced by Toshiba, Hitachi, and Mitsubishi Electric. The manufacturers of "heavy electrical machines" enjoyed a higher status and attracted top university engineering graduates. Matsushita's engineers, however, made it their job to cater to people's domestic needs, and took pride in this. It was therefore seen as a disgrace that such a convenient home appliance as the rice cooker should have come from Toshiba, a manufacturer that was better known for producing industrial machines.[12] Upon learning this news, Konosuke Matsushita, president of the company, was infuriated and gave Sakamoto a hard time. Later Matsushita realized that he might have been too harsh and became concerned that the shame might drive Sakamoto to contemplate committing suicide.[13]

The Matsushita engineers were determined to come up with a better rice cooker than their competitor's. The Toshiba rice cooker was basically an electric steamer with two pots, one inside the other. It required the user to pour water into the bigger pot; the boiling water then steamed the rice that had been placed in the smaller pot. But the two-pot design meant greater quantities of aluminum went into its manufacture, which drove up the sales price; it also gave the user less control over the heat and a higher electricity bill. Sakamoto's team racked their brains: "Is this the only way to cook rice?" "Why can't we heat the rice pot directly?" "How can we cook better-tasting rice?"

By the time Matsushita set up its Rice Cooker Division in 1958, Toshiba rice cookers were already gaining in popularity among Japanese living in the United States. To capitalize on this, Toshiba ran a campaign in Japan that had advertisements designed to look like urgent telegrams from the West Coast:

"Send rice cooker STOP Japanese in America STOP"

Toshiba is overwhelmed by the number of orders for rice cookers it has received from our fellow Japanese and foreigners overseas.[14]

Clearly, the rice cooker was in demand among the Japanese diasporas. By the time this advertisement was published, however, Sakamoto's team had already launched a more advanced rice cooker model. In contrast to Toshiba's dual-pot system, National's engineers had come up with a machine that could cook rice using a single pot. They called it *suihanki* (rice cooking machine) to distinguish it from Toshiba's electric pot. In 1959, Matsushita ran an ad proudly promoting its new appliance, adopting a cute feminine tone targeted at young Japanese housewives:

The Most Advanced Rice Cooker: National Automatic Rice Cooker

The Secret of the Direct Heating System

Our rice cooker always cooks fluffy delicious rice because it heats the rice directly, the single pot sitting directly on top of the heating plate, so even though it's only 600 watts, it cooks the rice at high heat.

And all you need to do is prepare the rice. You don't have to pour water into an outer pot. Al dente rice, soft rice: you can adjust it to whatever consistency you like. And there's more.

You can steam any dish easily. And your electricity bill comes to just ¥4 for every 1.8 liters [of rice] you cook, thanks to direct heating. Just plug it into any of your electrical outlets at home.

Its high quality is also recognized in the United States. It has been given a seal of approval by [the Department of Building and Safety, City of] Los Angeles (for its dependability).[15]

In the graphics, exclamations of "Super!" and "Wow!" danced above the rice cooker as if they were steam from the pot. Although National's first overseas shipment of rice cookers was destined for the United States, Sakamoto's team decided that what they really wanted to do was take it to the rest of Asia.

Not long after this, in 1959, Sakamoto took a rice cooker and some rice to the Tokyo office of William Mong's father, Mong Kwok-ping, a long-established merchant in the Hong Kong–Japan import-export business.[16] Mong Kwok-ping did business with Matsushita, importing its carbon rods for use in batteries, and Matsushita employees looked up to him as an *oyabun*—a father figure—and often turned to him for advice.[17] Sakamoto took out the plain white-bodied rice cooker and turned it on. After a thirty-eight-minute cooking time, it switched off automatically, and the sweet smell of steamed rice filled the air.

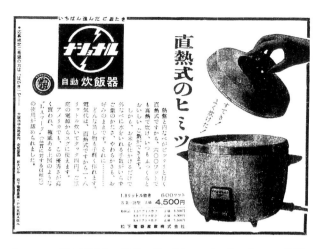

Japanese ad highlighting National's all-in-one heating element, 1959.
Courtesy of Panasonic

"Now, that's convenient!" Kwok-ping was impressed and told his son William in Hong Kong about the new appliance. William recognized its sales potential at once. An automated kitchen was crucial to leading a modern lifestyle. Replacing the butane gas stove with an electric rice cooker would be groundbreaking. "The rice cooker was revolutionary. I thought, 'this will definitely sell in the future,'" recalls William Mong. In 1959, he placed a small order of twenty-four as a trial, and in 1960, at age 32, he took the plunge and ordered 100 rice cooker units. To Mong's advantage, there was no competition from Western manufacturers, as none of them made rice cookers. Prior to this, William had had to chase after the market share held by the leading Western

The first 24 National rice cookers shipped to
Hong Kong in 1959 had a solid aluminum lid.
Courtesy of Shun Hing Group

manufacturers of radios, irons, and refrigerators, but now, for the first time, he had an original Japanese invention to sell. And it was compact enough for Hong Kong's small living spaces, where a shared kitchen was the norm. He poured all his efforts into creating a market for the rice cooker in Hong Kong.

We Have to Let People See How it Works!

In Hong Kong director Wong Kar-wai's movie, *In the Mood for Love* (花樣年華), the automatic rice cooker is portrayed as a symbol of the city's lifestyle in the 1960s. The scene is set in a Hong Kong apartment in 1962. The residents are white-collar workers: Tony Leung plays a necktie-sporting journalist, and Maggie Cheung, dressed in a Chinese silk cheongsam, plays a secretary. Her husband, who works for a Japanese trading firm, has just brought a rice cooker back from a visit to Japan. Maggie Cheung's character has brought the rice cooker along to a party with the other tenants. While everyone is relaxing, the rice cooker finishes its job, switches itself off, and the room goes wild:

> Neighbor: Is that an electric cooker? Mrs Koo, is it yours?
>
> Mrs Koo (The landlady): No, I have no idea what it is! It's Mrs Chan's.
>
> Mrs Chan (Maggie Cheung): My husband brought it from Japan. I thought it was very good, so I just wanted to show it to Mrs Koo.
>
> Mrs Koo: It switched off! It switched off! How convenient! Mrs Chan, can your husband get me one next time he goes to Japan?
>
> Mrs Chan: Sure, no problem.[18]

The movie captures the moment when rice cookers first became popular in the city, and "Made in Japan" products finally began to gain a measure of trust among Hong Kong consumers.

In 1960, most Hong Kong people cooked rice in clay pots placed over butane gas, charcoal or portable stoves, and some even used firewood. The majority had neither seen nor heard of an appliance that cooked rice without fire. The white enamel body of the rice cooker had been chosen by a Japanese designer to imitate the delicate porcelain of a rice bowl.[19] But it provoked a different reaction in Hong Kong: some thought the rice cooker was a new style of Chinese spittoon. Several Hong Kong appliance shop owners refused to stock the rice cooker because they could not tell what it did just by looking at it. And there was no free-to-air television; radio advertisements were unable to communicate how easy it was to cook rice with it. Therefore, Sakamoto, the director of the Rice Cooker Division, insisted, "We have to let people see how it works!" Starting in 1946, many Japanese had been introduced to new electrical appliances through their appearance in popular American comic strips such as *Blondie*. They marveled at, for example, illustrations of toasters, refrigerators, and vacuum cleaners. But rice cookers had no precedent in American pop culture. Sakamoto told his domestic as well as international sales teams:

> We can't make rice cookers popular without cooking demonstrations. Imagine you are seeing this rice cooker for the first time. Do you understand what it does just by looking at it?
>
> That's why it's important that we demonstrate how it works and show it does everything automatically.[20]

Mong made it his mission to let Hong Kong people see how rice cookers worked, and he and his associates launched a series of cooking demonstrations. Even when he paid a visit to his favorite Shanghai barber, he would take a few rice cookers with him. Junichi Ukita, then twenty-nine years old, was in charge of Hong Kong at Matsushita Trading. He witnessed one of Mong's barbershop cooking demonstrations when he visited the city for the first time in 1960. In those days, there were no *shinkansen* bullet trains; therefore, even Tokyo was considered a world away from Osaka. When a Matsushita employee was transferred from Osaka to Tokyo, his colleagues would gather on the platform at Osaka Station, and shout "*Banzai! Banzai!*" It was rare for a junior member of staff to make a business trip to Tokyo, let alone Hong Kong. An anxious Ukita departed Osaka with his newly issued leather-covered passport:

> It was really unusual to travel overseas in 1960. One US dollar was worth ¥360. Foreign currencies were in short supply [in Japan].
>
> Mr Arataro Takahashi, the chairman of Matsushita Trading, told me, "We can't send you on a trip around the world, but a trip to Hong Kong will be a learning experience for you. Visit Mong-san in Hong Kong and see what's going on. Hong Kong is a free market, so only the most competitive products from around the world make it to its stores. Go there and see for yourself. Compare National products against the world's best and see what sets them apart.[21]

Sakamoto introduces a group of female retailers to National's latest rice cooker. Osaka, 1961. Courtesy of Sadayoshi Sakamoto

Junichi Ukita on his first business trip to Hong Kong, 1960.
Courtesy of Junichi Ukita

Ukita was seen off at Osaka Itami Airport in the early morning and boarded a propeller plane from Osaka to Hong Kong, via Tokyo and Okinawa (沖繩). By the time he arrived, it was late at night. At Hong Kong's Kai Tak Airport, billboards advertising European brands caught his eye: Philips, Siemens, and Telefunken electrical appliances, Rado and Omega luxury watches. These products were out of reach for most people in Japan because of the government's protectionist trade policy that slapped a huge import tax on them. Hong Kong, however, was a showcase for the world's best, and Ukita could not find a single billboard promoting Japanese goods. "This place is amazing," he thought.

Then, Ukita heard somebody calling his name. It was Mr and Mrs Mong waving at him from the roof of the airport terminal.

> I was really touched. It was my very first trip overseas. Maybe it's difficult to imagine today, because millions of people fly every day, how I felt then.
>
> The Mongs came all the way to the airport to pick me up, and greeted me with, "Uki-chan!" I was truly grateful.[22]

Ukita was exhausted after the long flight and the long workdays that had preceded it. His hair was in complete disarray, prompting Mong to say to him, "Hey, I have to take you to the barber. You look like Beethoven!" So Mong took Ukita to his Shanghainese barber, San Gin Gwok (新建國), where he was a regular. When Ukita got to the barbershop, he realized that a haircut was not the only reason for their visit. Mong had brought along a few rice cookers, some rinsed rice, and a salami-like Chinese sausage called *lapchong* (臘腸). While Ukita had his hair cut, Mong plugged in his rice cookers and switched them on one by one. During the thirty-eight minutes it took for the rice to cook, customers stayed glued to their chairs, entranced by the warm and delicious aroma emanating from the pot. Mong thought that it was the perfect setting for a cooking demonstration. Ukita still vividly remembers Mong's sales pitch:

The San Gin Gwok barbershop where Mong
conducted rice cooker demonstrations
in the early 1960s.
Courtesy of Yūki Ogasawara

Mong-san would bring two or three rice cookers and start them cooking one by
one. "What's that?" the customers were curious. They had never seen anything
like this before, so they had no idea. And Mong-san would reply: "It cooks rice.
You just press the switch down, leave it to work its magic, and the rice will come
out all cooked![23]

When the barber was about to finish a haircut, Mong would open the lid and add in the
lapchong sausage. A moment later, a delicious smell would spread through the shop,
and then the rice cooker would switch itself off automatically. Mong would proudly tell
customers:

"Look at this! It's really cooked. Nobody's touched it, and it's not burnt at all. All
you need to do is leave it alone, and it does the rest."[24]

Then Mong would offer each customer a bowl of rice to taste. Plain rice alone got a
mixed response, but the rice with the sausage brought smiles and praise: "The flavor's
wonderful! It's really good." In those early days, rice prepared in a rice cooker did
not quite match the flavor of rice cooked in a traditional clay pot, but adding the
lapchong sausage masked this fact. Thus, Mong added his own personal Chinese twist
to Matsushita's sales strategy.

House Calls with Rice Cookers

Mong also made house calls. Armed with a rice cooker, rinsed rice, and *lapchong* sausages, he canvassed a massive housing complex on the Hong Kong Island waterfront, home to over 1,500 families. The North Point Estate, started in 1957, was Hong Kong Island's first public housing estate. Unlike in other, earlier public housing estates in Kowloon, the electricity supply was stable, and residents were generally better-off, white-collar workers. Mong and his staff went from door to door several times a week, demonstrating to housewives how effortlessly their revolutionary appliance cooked rice:

> "At that time there were few burglaries in Hong Kong, so everyone opened their
> doors to us. Of course, there were a few who refused to let us in, but most of them
> welcomed our demonstrations."[25]

Mong and his staff would go into the living room, plug in the rice cooker, and chat with the housewives until the rice was ready. Some could afford to place an order for a rice cooker right away. For many, though, it was still a luxury item, the smallest model serving six costing HK$98. So, the majority of people just watched the demonstration. But Mong understood the value of good word of mouth and the door-to-door approach later became part of National's worldwide sales strategy for rice cookers.[26]

Mong's company, Shun Hing, also advertised its rice cooker house calls in the newspaper. The weeks leading up to the Chinese Lunar New Year holiday, which traditionally falls between mid-January and mid-February, were the peak season for sales in Hong Kong. In January 1961, Mong put the first advertisement devoted entirely to rice cookers in the leading Chinese-language newspaper of the time, the *Overseas Chinese Daily* (華僑日報). Three step-by-step illustrations demonstrated its low-maintenance cooking process: press the button to start the operation, leave the machine to cook the rice, and open the lid when ready. The ad then went on to address the concern of many potential customers that the rice cooker might run up a huge electricity bill:

> Just three cents to cook rice: that's all each pot will cost you in electricity fees. It's
> more economical than butane gas or charcoal.

At that time, the *Overseas Chinese Daily* cost 20¢ per copy; therefore, at one-seventh of the price of a newspaper, the electricity fee was indeed low. The advertisement ended with Shun Hing offering to make house calls:

> Please write to us if you have any questions regarding how the rice cooker
> works, what the rice tastes like, or anything else. We will be happy to make an
> appointment to visit your home for a demonstration. We also hold public cooking
> demonstrations every Saturday, at 8:00 pm, on the third floor of the Hong Kong
> Daimaru Department Store. Please come and join us.
>
> (*Overseas Chinese Daily*, January 25, 1961)

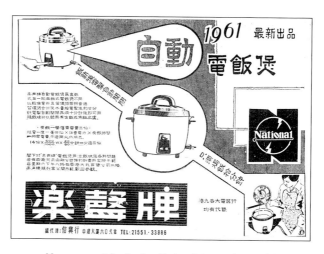

Newspaper ad for the first National rice cooker model
to be localized for the Hong Kong market. In it,
Shun Hing promotes its "house call" service.
(*Overseas Chinese Daily*, January 25, 1961)

Daimaru (大丸) opened its doors in 1960. It was Hong Kong's first Japanese department store and it attracted a more high-class clientele. But Shun Hing's product demonstrations were not confined to Daimaru. Mong and his Shun Hing staff took their rice cooker demonstrations all over Hong Kong, from outside movie theaters in the more affluent areas to unpretentious Chinese restaurants in the New Territories.

Tomi Egami, the popular host of a television cooking show and author of numerous cookbooks, also lent a helping hand. Egami was the Japanese equivalent of Julia Child. She had attended Le Cordon Bleu in Paris and introduced exotic cuisine to the public through NHK's pioneering cooking program *Kyō no Ryōri* (Today's Cooking). Egami was a Mong family friend and later became an advisor to Matsushita's Rice Cooker Division. In 1961, she visited the Hongkong Japanese Club where, using a National rice cooker, she prepared chicken rice flavored with soy sauce. Egami found that the chicken sold in Hong Kong markets was far more flavorful than that sold in Japan. Hong Kong retailers offered the juicy meat of young hens, killed fifteen to twenty days after they had laid their first egg; Japanese retailers, in contrast, sold the tougher meat of roosters and old hens that no longer produced eggs.[27] Egami gave her elegant cooking demonstration at the clubhouse and explained to the wives of elite salarymen that they should make the most of Hong Kong's wonderful chicken.

As Mong, his staff, and Matsushita colleagues visiting from Osaka persevered with their demonstrations, awareness of the rice cooker as a convenient appliance began to grow across Hong Kong. But this did not immediately translate into increased sales. One obstacle was a rumor that cooking in aluminum pots and pans could cause cancer. A book backing up these claims was published in the UK and found its way to Hong Kong.

As the rice cooker's cooking pot was made of aluminum, this negatively affected sales. Mong immediately contacted the Rice Cooker Division in Osaka. An engineer assured him that the aluminum pot was safe and that there was nothing to worry about, because baby powder used aluminum oxide as one of its main ingredients. Mong emotionally recalls, "It took a lot of effort to make National rice cookers a household name."[28]

By 1965, the volume of National rice cooker sales had increased dramatically. From the 100 rice cookers imported in 1960, the number had soared to 88,000 in 1965, and now accounted for one-half of all National rice cooker exports. In other words, one out of every two rice cookers that Matsushita manufactured for export was sold in Hong Kong.

Revamping "Made in Japan"

William Mong visited the Matsushita factories in Osaka at least once every two months. Each time, he would bring three pairs of shoes with him: the first were lace-up shoes for formal occasions, the second were waterproof shoes for rainy days, and the third were comfortable slip-ons for his factory visits. He would put on his factory shoes and spend the whole day at the production units located in the suburbs of Kadoma or Moriguchi.

Konosuke Matsushita introduced a new management style in 1933, following the relocation of Matsushita Electric's headquarters to the outskirts of Osaka.[29] He set up three divisions, each with its own product line: radios; light bulbs and batteries; and electrical components, such as wiring, plastic, and heating devices. Each division was responsible for its own factories, research and development, production, marketing, sales and promotion, as well as finance. In other words, they operated as independent "companies." This self-reliant system of accountability was truly groundbreaking in the 1930s, not just in Japan but in the world.[30] It nurtured talented and versatile executives, and, in the ensuing decades has been applied to an ever-expanding number of product lines.[31]

Looking at it from an international buyer's perspective, however, this meant visiting and negotiating with several different "companies" scattered around the Osaka suburbs. During his visits, Mong was assisted by an employee of Matsushita Electric Industry's subsidiary, Matsushita Electric Trading, who acted as his liaison. At each and every product division, Mong would insist on spending significant amounts of time on the factory floor. In this, he distinguished himself from many other foreign distributors who were content with a brief tour, if that. Some had never actually visited the factory in person, and left everything to a Japanese intermediary. Mong explains the rationale behind his visits:

> "In the early days, Matsushita tried to export products that were popular in Japan. But you can't simply export products that are popular in Japan and assume that Chinese people will pay for them."[32]

The products had to appeal to Hong Kong people and cater to their domestic needs. To this end, Mong spent countless hours at the various National factories in Osaka looking for new products and making numerous suggestions for adjustments that would cater to local tastes. And he would not leave the factory until he was totally satisfied. These lengthy factory visits were the reason why Mong needed a third pair of comfortable shoes.

Mong involved himself in everything, from design and specifications to price and delivery dates. He went on negotiating until every last detail was to his satisfaction. He was especially demanding with regard to design. Mong insisted that "The design is what first catches the consumer's eye."[33] He felt that Matsushita needed to work on this area, because their designs were often reminiscent of older Japanese appliances, which for many Hong Kong people evoked painful wartime memories or a reputation for being poorly put together. "How to revamp that image—that was our job [as foreign agents]," says Mong. He drew up a business plan, in which he mapped out his expansion strategy for the Hong Kong market and beyond. He was adamant that every detail conform to his specifications. "I want it like this," "I want it like that," he would assert in fluent Japanese, so fluent that many of the younger Matsushita employees doubted that Mong was really Chinese. The engineers would produce one prototype after another in their efforts to satisfy Mong's demands. Shoichiro Koyama, a Matsushita Electric Trading employee who accompanied Mong on various factory visits, recalls how he used to plead with him to reach a compromise:

> I would try to convince him, "Mong-san, the engineers have tried their best. Isn't this good enough?" He would say, "No!" So we had to start all over again. It was just unbelievable.[34]

Sakamoto and his rice cooker team carry out taste tests using jasmine rice from Hong Kong at their factory in Osaka, 1960.
Courtesy of Junichi Ukita

Some at Matsushita were put off by Mong's incredible energy. Some found his level of dedication obsessive. Some were reluctant to invest in products for Hong Kong, which they considered a small market. National appliances were in great demand in Japan, and it was costly to develop a metallic mold for a new design, Mong's critics therefore felt it did not make economic sense to develop a Hong Kong model. Some were enthusiastic about overseas markets but favored exporting to the lucrative American market. The director of the Rice Cooker Division, Tatsunosuke Sakamoto, however, loved working with the Chinese agent, seventeen years his junior. Sakamoto had the mind of an artisan, striving for perfection in his handiwork.[35] That Hong Kong, the gateway to Asia, had adopted the rice cooker his team had created, gave him a sense of profound satisfaction. Although in poor health, he was not a man given to compromise. These two like-minded individuals worked together to adapt the Japanese rice cooker for Hong Kong consumers, and in the process paved the way for the product's globalization, taking it to Asia, the Middle East, and Asian diasporas around the world.

A Rice Cooker with a View

The first localization project on which the National Rice Cooker Division and Mong collaborated was in 1960. This was long before the process of "localization" had acquired its name. During one of Mong's visits to Osaka, Sakamoto had asked Mong what adjustments were needed to make rice cookers desirable items in Hong Kong. Mong suggested that Sakamoto install a glass viewing pane in the center of the rice cooker's lid. The original Japanese model had a solid aluminum lid, but Mong insisted that a glass window would be useful. Rice casseroles are popular among Hong Kong

Chinese *lapchong* sausage adds local flavor
to rice cooked in a Japanese appliance.
Courtesy of Sadayoshi Sakamoto

people; they like adding Chinese *lapchong* sausage or salty fish to the rice for extra flavor. Thai jasmine rice is the most widely consumed variety in Hong Kong. It is more fragrant, has longer grains, and contains less moisture and starch than japonica rice. The juices of the sausage or fish run into the rice to make it more flavorful and moist. But these extra ingredients have to be added towards the end of the cooking process; otherwise, their flesh gets tough. Once the rice has come to a boil and absorbed all the water in the pot, Chinese cooks open the lid and add *lapchong* sausage to the rice. To get the timing right, Mong insisted, they have to be able to see inside the pot.

"Is that how they cook rice in Hong Kong?" The Japanese engineers were astounded. An age-old Japanese rice-cooking tip goes: "Never take the lid off even when your little one cries out for rice [*Akago naitemo futa toruna*]." And this golden rule applied not only to the cooking itself but also to the ten or fifteen minutes after the heat was turned off, to let the rice settle. Therefore, it was unimaginable to the Japanese engineers that anyone should want to install a glass window in the lid so as to know when to take it off. But it was debating these cultural issues that made the rice cooker team realize that the Japanese way of doing things did not necessarily apply to the rest of the world. They listened to the 33-year-old Chinese agent's suggestion, and took up the challenge of localizing the rice cooker to meet Chinese consumers' needs. And this was just the beginning of a process that continues to this very day.

Inserting a glass viewing pane was easier said than done. Experiments with a flat tempered glass insert were unsuccessful, because the pane would quickly become steamed up and was therefore no longer transparent. In addition, water drops would form on the surface and fall back onto the rice, making it soggy and affecting the taste. What could they do to prevent the pane from steaming up? Wanting to match local conditions as much as possible, Sakamoto's team experimented repeatedly with Thai jasmine rice. Finally they found a solution: they made the glass pane convex, the rounded part on the inside of the pot. The water droplets that formed on the pane would run off it and drop directly into the center of the pot, where the heat was most intense, and evaporate rapidly, without affecting the texture of the rice. The convex glass afforded a clear view of the cooking process but led to another problem: this new lid was significantly more costly than a simple aluminum one. Nonetheless, Sakamoto decided to go ahead with its mass production.

The glass viewing pane also required a design innovation. Since it was first invented by Toshiba, every single rice cooker produced had had a traditional lid with a knob in the middle. But the new Hong Kong model sported a black "bridge" handle and a white enamel body, much more stylish than the traditional Japanese version. "This is the model we will market abroad," said Sakamoto. By 1961, this international model had made its debut not only in Hong Kong but also in Singapore, Malaysia, and Thailand.

The glass viewing pane brought an unexpected benefit: it made the cooking process visible to those who had never seen or heard of a rice cooker and who had a difficult time believing that this white pot could cook rice without being put on the stove. During cooking demonstrations held to introduce the rice cooker to new markets in Asia, small

A Hong Kong ad promoting the glass
viewing pane advocated by Mong.
(*Overseas Chinese Daily*, November 3, 1962)

children in the audience would often run up to it and take off the lid to peek inside. By making the cooking process visible, the viewing pane reassured skeptical first-time users around the world that the machine did, in fact, cook rice without fire; it contributed to the popularization of the rice cooker and its eventual globalization. This original model, which National later nicknamed the "World Series," soon became an industry standard. Over 8 million units have been sold around the world, and its sales remain stable.[36] It gave rise to a new culinary culture. It also generated calls for an even more sophisticated model.

Congee: Japanese *Okayu*, Cantonese *Juk*

In 1976, National introduced the first rice cooker that could cook congee, once again at William Mong's urging. Both Japanese and Hong Kong versions of congee are soupy rice, but they vary greatly in preparation and cultural applications. Japanese *okayu* (粥) is rather plain in taste and, much like chicken soup in the West, is often prepared for the old or the sick. It is also served during elaborate breakfasts at traditional inns. It is not, however, part of the daily meal and, for this reason, it did not occur to the National Rice Cooker Division to develop a model with a congee-cooking function.

In Hong Kong, however, Cantonese *juk* (粥) is part of the daily diet. A large bowl of it is traditionally eaten at breakfast, and most Chinese restaurants in Hong Kong offer it as an alternative to steamed rice at lunch and dinner. Canteens usually have two rice cookers, one for steamed rice and one for congee. In addition, because congee soaks up a lot of water and therefore requires less rice, it is popular among working-class families and newly arrived immigrants from China trying to make their food supplies stretch as far as possible.

In 1975, the National rice cooker team was in need of a new hit item. The 1973 embargo, imposed by members of the Organization of Arab Petroleum Exporting Countries (OAPEC) on oil exports to nations that supported Israel, had driven up the price of aluminum, iron, and other materials used in the manufacture of rice cookers. As a result, production costs went up by forty percent, and sales were badly affected. This was the biggest crisis for the Rice Cooker Division since its establishment in 1958.

Yūki Ogasawara, who was in charge of overseas sales of rice cookers, flew to Hong Kong with Sakamoto's successor, for price negotiations. He pleaded with Mong to raise the price by forty percent. Ogasawara fully expected a sharp drop in sales as a consequence of the rise, but there was no way National could maintain its current price. Mong, however, was not easily persuaded, as Shun Hing was also facing a tough situation. The crisis had shaved three-quarters off the value of Hong Kong stocks in less than ten months. One-half of Shun Hing's staff cafeteria had been turned into an emergency warehouse for surplus stock. Over the next three days, Mong, Ogasawara, and his boss scrutinized the cost of every part, down to the cardboard used in the packing boxes. Eventually, they agreed on a significant price increase.

As expected, sales of rice cookers plummeted by more than fifty percent, from approximately 156,000 units sold in 1974, to 78,000 in 1975. The factory desperately needed a hit item that would get its production targets back on track.

Mong's inspiration for the congee-making rice cooker came from an appliance that was already a bestseller in the United States, especially with working-class families: the slow cooker, better known under the trademarked name of Crock-Pot. Earlier slow cooker models consisted of a ceramic pot surrounded by a metal casing containing a heating element, while the more advanced, 1974 Crock-Pot featured a removable stoneware liner fitted inside an enamel cooker. These pots were designed to cook pot roasts, stews, or beans, unattended, at a low heat over several hours. Mong thought something like the Crock-Pot would be perfect for cooking Chinese congee or herbal medicine, as they required similar cooking times and temperatures. He therefore asked the National Rice Cooker Division to produce a rice cooker model based on the slow cooker that could cook congee and did not consume much electricity. The rice cooker team was willing to go along with Mong's demands, partly because they looked up to him and partly because they saw Hong Kong as the gateway to Asia and Asian communities around the world. If they could come up with a product that was successful in Hong Kong, they were convinced it would also do well elsewhere.[37]

Mong basically asked them to clone the Crock-Pot, but the Matsushita engineers were determined to create their own, more advanced product. Yoshiaki Sano, a 45-year-old engineer, was Sakamoto's right-hand man. He recounts:

> "I thought it was a shame to just copy [the Crock-Pot]. I wanted to make a rice cooker that would cook congee exactly the way Hong Kong people like it."[38]

Hong Kong people traditionally used clay pots to cook rice and soup, both staples of any Chinese meal. Unlike the Japanese, who were used to cooking rice in metal pots before the rice cooker came along, Hong Kong people preferred ceramic pots and thought that food cooked in them somehow tasted better. But ceramic pots cracked easily and were difficult to keep clean. Sano insisted to his staff that they had to find a way around this:

> "If [Chinese people] believe that congee is best cooked in a ceramic pot, our job is
> to use our technology to recreate that same taste in our metal pot."[39]

Sano, although his manner was humble, had already accomplished much as an engineer. He was the one who, at the age of thirty-two, had invented the rice cooker switch that jumps up to signal the rice is ready. His words were quietly convincing and Mong agreed that, instead of ceramic pots, they should go with metal pots coated with porcelain enamel.

Enamel coating was commonly used in kitchen appliances. But in this case, the enamel pot was to be placed directly on top of the heating element for as long as eight hours. Whenever there was a sudden change in temperature, the enamel cracked. Maintaining a low heat over several hours also turned out to be a challenge; the micro computerized temperature control was still several years away. But Sano's team finally finished the first prototype, and when Mong paid a visit to their factory in Himejima, Sano cooked Chinese congee and offered it up for him to taste.

Mong, however, did not like it. It was more like Japanese *okayu* and did not taste like the Cantonese *juk* he loved. *Juk* was thicker in consistency and richer in flavor, as it was common to coat the rice with a little peanut oil before cooking it and to use chicken stock instead of plain water. In Japan, congee is sometimes described using blossoms as a metaphor for the grains of rice: a bowl of congee becomes "white blossoms in full bloom." The "blossoms" in Japanese *okayu* are fuller, whereas the "blossoms" in Cantonese *juk* are smaller; they have dissolved and thickened the soup. Unless the rice cooker could cook authentic *juk*, it would not appeal to Chinese consumers.

Sano was fully prepared for Mong's high expectations and was not even surprised by his reaction. So he and his team went back to work and improved the technology, hoping to master the subtle difference in consistency. When the next prototype was ready, they invited Mong for another taste test. Sano recounts, "We knew we had to respect Chinese tastes. We had to ask [what they thought of the congee our rice cooker produced]; otherwise, we would never know. We wouldn't know until we asked, and until they taught us."

In the summer of 1976, Mong and his family were planning a vacation at his villa in Ito (伊東) on the Izu Peninsula (伊豆半島), south of Tokyo. So instead of his going to Osaka, Mong asked Sano to meet him in Ito. Sano cancelled his own vacation plans and headed for the "congee camp" with one of his colleagues from Matsushita Electric Trading. They boarded a *shinkansen* bullet train with four rice cooker prototypes packed in cardboard boxes and a set of tools. Mong had brought with him to Ito the Thai jasmine rice that is commonly used for congee in Hong Kong. Local preferences and conditions had to be replicated, for the tests with the prototypes to be of any value. Mong had to be satisfied with the results himself, as a consumer, before he could agree to the rice cooker going on sale in Hong Kong.

The morning after their arrival in Ito, Sano and his colleague took a taxi to Mong's villa, which overlooked the Pacific Ocean. "Now, let's start the experiment."[40] At Mong's urging, Sano set up the four units and began the tests. Sano and Mong were not the only ones giving up their holidays to do this. Mong's wife, Serena Yang, also took part in the experiment, while Sano's colleague accompanied Mong's young children to a nearby exotic plant and animal park. The three of them spent the whole day following the same traditional Cantonese congee recipe, cooking batch after batch of jasmine rice, making small adjustments each time, and tasting the results. Finally, after their sixth attempt, Mong nodded and smiled, "Yes, this is it." Sano remains impressed by Mong's dedication, "You know, most people wouldn't go that far."[41]

Mong immediately made a further design request: "Make the body look stunning." Shortly before Christmas 1976, National's slow cooker export model made its debut in Hong Kong. National called it the Multi Rice Cooker SR-40S and gave it a completely transparent glass lid. The enamel body was a shimmering orange, which the Japanese engineers felt was too bright but Mong thought was eye-catching. The sales pitch emphasized that the rice cooker was versatile, a strong selling point with Hong Kong consumers:

> 3-in-1 appliance—rice cooker, slow cooker and steamer. Heat-resistant glass lid closes in flavour and nutrients. Removable enamel pot.[42]

Finally, the National overseas sales team created a free recipe book to be handed out along with the cooker. They believed that the "3-in-1" rice cookers would not sell in large quantities unless consumers knew how and what to cook in them. The team consulted a native Cantonese chef at the Royal Hotel's Dragon and Phoenix Restaurant (龍鳳) in Osaka, whom Mong had introduced to them, and asked him to develop recipes for the multifunction rice cooker. They realized that only authentic Cantonese food, rather than the "Japanized" version eaten in Osaka, would appeal to the Hong Kong palate. They eventually developed twenty recipes together. Takekazu Nishiwaki, a member of the overseas sales team responsible for the cookbook, shares his take on the project:

> The best way [to launch a new product] is to make it a collaborative effort and to incorporate the ideas of the local market representatives. That way, Mong-san and his people felt they were responsible for the product. They knew they had to sell it; they made sure it would sell.[43]

Whenever a new rice cooker was launched in the market, Shun Hing would collect customer feedback and report to Osaka. Matsushita executives valued Shun Hing's market intelligence and, because of it, considered Hong Kong the ideal test market for their products. In addition, whenever representatives from National's production unit visited Hong Kong, Mong would have his Japanese-speaking employees take them not only to their various retail outlets but also to Shun Hing's appliance repair shops, or "service stations." He wanted the Japanese engineers to better appreciate the needs of their consumers and to see for themselves how and why their products broke down, so that they could eliminate these defects from future models. Mong once told a young Matsushita employee, completely in awe of Mong's dedication, "The rice cooker is like my own son. If your child was to become a delinquent, would it make you happy?"[44]

"Eating Rice from the Same Pot"

There is a Japanese saying, "*onajikama no meshi wo kuu*," which literally translates as "eating rice from the same pot" but metaphorically signifies "working together on a challenge." Anthropologist Emiko Ohnuki-Tierney explains how the act of eating rice bonds people together in Japan: "If you eat together, you are members of the same social group; *you* become we as opposed to *they*."[45] Unfortunately, the relationship between Japanese manufacturers and their Asian distributors has typically been asymmetrical. In the 1960s, most Japanese manufacturers dreamed of making it in the glamorous and lucrative American market, and few were willing to listen to the suggestions of Asian agents or consumers, let alone involve them as equals in the process of product development. But the National rice cooker team and Mong developed a more symmetrical partnership: they defined their roles, had frequent interactions, and dealt with cultural differences without either party forcing a single "right" interpretation on the other. Local concepts of taste, color, and shape were respected: jasmine and japonica rice had distinctive tastes, which both Mong and the National team sought to preserve. The localization of rice cookers could be dismissed simply as a successful market strategy driven by profit. But what matters here is not *why* but *how* rice cookers were localized. In the long term, this partnership approach generated enthusiasm and ideas for the localization process from Hong Kong, and as a result, National rice cookers became competitive in other parts of Asia and among Asian diasporas.

"Mong-san taught us," says the now 79-year-old Yoshiaki Sano, "that we have to understand the market, we have to understand the people, and we have to understand how they cook rice to produce [rice cookers for the overseas market]."[46] This is the same Sano who invented the automated rice cooker switch, helped develop a model that cooked congee, and was later appointed director of the Rice Cooker Division. He explains what it takes to adapt a kitchen appliance to suit culturally specific tastes:

> We have to know how people use our product in their everyday lives. [Our overseas customers] evaluate our product based on their own traditional way of doing things. First we learned how [Hong Kong people] cook rice, then we installed a glass window in the lid, and then we made the glass convex.
>
> If we want people [from different cultures] to use our rice cookers, we have to understand how they use them, and then create a model that meets their local

Sakamoto's grave in Osaka where Mong paid his last respects in 1986.

needs. We learned that we could not simply take our [Japanese] product and expect it to sell in other markets.

Thanks to this lesson, our rice cookers have become popular all over the world.[47]

In 1979, the year over 6 million National rice cookers were exported worldwide, the man who had made it his mission to take Japanese rice cookers to the world, Tatsunosuke Sakamoto, passed away. Seven years later, in 1986, on a visit to Japan, Mong asked to pay his respects to Sakamoto's grave, in the foothills of the mountains that lie between Osaka and Kyoto. Sakamoto's successor, Sano, accompanied him. Recalling their visit to Sakamoto's grave, Sano says quietly: "Mong-san was the only one who asked to visit the grave. This is something no Japanese business partner would have done."[48]

It was a cold, rainy Sunday in February. Mong brought flowers to put on the tomb, and putting his palms together, stood, uncharacteristically solemn, in front of it. Perhaps he was remembering the times he and Sakamoto had spent together, united in their determination to adapt the Japanese rice cooker for the Chinese market.

2

---•---

You Have to Diversify to Survive
The Anxiety that Fuels the Hong Kong Entrepreneur

Queen Elizabeth II unveils a plaque at the official opening of the William
M. W. Mong Building at Cambridge University, March 8, 1996.
Courtesy of William Mong

Encased in one of the walls of William Mong's office is a huge aquarium in which beautiful iridescent carp swim to and fro. Framed memorabilia include pictures of Mong: receiving the Japanese Order of the Sacred Treasure Gold Rays with Rosette, having lunch with Queen Elizabeth II, shaking hands with Chinese Premier Zhu Rongji (朱镕基), and being awarded an honorary doctorate by Chris Patten, the last Governor of Hong Kong and then-Chancellor of the University of Hong Kong. Mong is a consummate businessman who, in addition to his native Cantonese, speaks fluent Japanese, English, and Mandarin, and moves effortlessly in many different circles, including among some of the most influential people in the region. Making the best of his versatile linguistic skills, cultural awareness, and ability to capitalize on transnational networks, Mong established himself as a successful intermediary between the business cultures of Japan and Hong Kong and became known as the "King of Electrical Appliances" in the Chinese-speaking world. Noting the confident smile on his face, one cannot help but wonder whether anything ever scares this man. Mong, however, maintains that behind this self-assured façade lurks deep-rooted anxiety:

> "You see, being Chinese, there is no peace. You are always thinking ahead. You have to diversify to survive."[1]

The Mong family has been involved in trading goods with Japan ever since Mong's grandfather moved from Guangdong (廣東 also known as Canton) to Nagasaki (長崎) at the end of the Qing Dynasty, over a century ago. In those days, Chinese merchants who, like the Mongs, left their home and moved to another country to do business, despite contributing to the transnational flow between the two countries, usually did so without enjoying the support or acceptance of either. They were often treated as outsiders and found themselves living in a kind of limbo, disconnected from their country of origin yet unable to integrate fully into the society of their adopted one. This was also a particularly unstable period in China's history, a time when the country was weakened by invasion, revolution, and incessant conflict.

It was, however, not just "being Chinese" that fueled Mong but also "being Hong Kong Chinese." His generation grew up as the subjects of two empires, Britain and Japan. They also experienced the treatment accorded to former Chinese citizens by China's ruling Communist Party. There was a constant feeling of anxiety because there was no way of knowing what tomorrow might bring. Hong Kong entrepreneurs of his generation, however, did not let it get them down; rather, this insecurity only made them more versatile and adaptable in the face of adversity. As historian Steve Tsang puts it, they "reacted to a desperate need to succeed in order to survive."[2] They were attuned to the times and so were able to capitalize on business opportunities. It is this attitude that lies at the root of Mong's entrepreneurial spirit, of his desire to go after the National business, of his drive to localize its products, including the rice cooker, for the Hong Kong market: he saw an opening and he went for it.

Nagasaki: A New World

Let us first turn our attention to Nagasaki, the city that was once Japan's gateway to the world. The Tokugawa Shogunate (德川幕府), as part of its "national seclusion" policy enacted in the early seventeenth century, had officially designated Nagasaki as the only Japanese port in which Chinese and Dutch commercial vessels were allowed to enter and trade.[3] This was part of the Tokugawa Shogunate's grand strategy to solidify its power by monopolizing foreign trade and preventing Christian missionary interference. Of the Chinese traders, merchants from Xiamen (Amoy, 廈門) in Fujian (福建) Province were the most powerful, while many of their crew came from Fujian's poorer northern region. There were also a number of silk merchants from Nanjing (南京) and Ningbo (寧波),

in the Yangtze River Delta area. Few, however, came from areas farther south, such as Guangdong Province.[4]

In order to prove they were not Christians, before landing, the merchants were made to tread on a tablet bearing the image of Jesus Christ. In the 1620s, some Chinese merchants took it upon themselves to construct three temples on the hills overlooking the city.[5] Chinese traders usually kept a statue of the sea goddess *Tin Hau* (天后) (or *Matsu* 媽祖) onboard, and, upon arrival in Nagasaki, they would carry it to one of the three temples, where it would remain until their departure. The procession from the port to the temple was a festive one, made to the accompaniment of Chinese trumpets and gongs, and lit by Chinese lanterns. This was also a way of demonstrating to the Japanese authorities that they were not Christians.[6] The merchants were then taken into town and crammed into a walled Chinese quarter. The wide variety of Chinese dialects spoken within its walls testified to the diverse regional backgrounds of its occupants.[7]

The Qing Dynasty historically forbade emigration. Official Qing government documents stated that people who left the country were "deserters, traitors, rebels and conspirators," and a series of imperial edicts issued between 1656 and 1712 declared overseas travel and residence to be "a capital crime punishable by beheading."[8] Public opinion also frowned on young people wanting to emigrate, because it meant leaving behind parents with no one to care for them, and ancestral graves with no one to tend them. However, by the late nineteenth century, this ban on emigration was in name only. Under pressure from the British and the French, who were in need of cheap labor for their colonies, the Qing government decided to allow its subjects to travel overseas and emigrate.

The Western powers also opened a new channel for emigrants from southern China via Hong Kong to Nagasaki. Following the arrival of the American Commodore Matthew Perry's Black Ships in 1853, the Tokugawa Shogunate reluctantly opened its door to foreign trade.[9] When Nagasaki eventually became an open port in 1859, British merchants started sailing there via Hong Kong, and many Chinese from what is now known as the Pearl River Delta in Guangdong Province came with them.[10] The British Empire was at the height of its power, and the number of territories under its control was so vast that it was often said that "the sun never sets on the British Empire." It was already heavily involved in the trade of luxury items, such as tea and silk from China, and later balanced the trade deficit by exporting Indian opium to China. The British refusal to comply with Qing government laws regulating the flow of opium led to the First Opium War in 1839 and the subsequent annexation of Hong Kong Island. Lying as it does at the tip of Guangdong Province, it provided a strategic base for British troops in East Asia. In the late 1860s, towards the end of the Tokugawa Shogunate, British merchants started bringing guns, vessels, and machinery to Nagasaki, and they built houses in the foreign settlement district located at the top of Minami Yamate Hill.[11]

In 1896, in the wake of the Sino-Japanese War (1894–95), the Hongkong and Shanghai Banking Corporation opened its first Nagasaki branch. The bank, a potent symbol of British colonial rule, was popular with Chinese merchants because of its

The façade of the Hongkong and Shanghai Bank's Nagasaki branch,
which opened in 1896.

emphasis on trade finance and foreign exchange. When the branch was relocated to
the Nagasaki Bund and reopened in a fine colonial-style building, to commemorate the
occasion, Chinese merchants living in the city sent the bank a pair of silver vases bearing
the following inscription in English and Chinese:

> To the Hongkong and Shanghai Banking Corporation,
>
> The prosperity of commerce depends greatly upon the circulation of money. Prior
> to the establishment of your Bank at this port in 1896 the merchants of Nagasaki
> had difficulty in securing advances of money through the security of banks. Since
> then the credit of your Bank has been shown to us as well as to foreigners. We, the
> undernamed merchants, have been greatly profited through securing advances of
> money from your Bank.
>
> (Reported in an English-language daily, *The Nagasaki Press*, January 15, 1904)

Thus, British capital and investment made doing business a much easier proposition
for those who often received unfavorable treatment at the hands of the Japanese. With
the advent of British colonial rule in Hong Kong, people living in nearby Guangdong
Province seized this opportunity to start migrating overseas.

The Sino-Japanese War was also a turning point in the central government's attitude
to Chinese emigration.[12] Those who had been referred to by the Qing government as
"deserters, traitors, rebels and conspirators" were now referred to as "overseas Chinese
(華僑)." It was in the aftermath of their crushing defeat by a much smaller nation that,
according to historian Wang Gungwu, the Qing Dynasty first became aware of the
immense untapped financial resources that lay in the hands of these overseas Chinese
they had originally so despised. This led to a complete reversal in the Qing government's
thinking, and its officials set about trying to raise funds among overseas Chinese groups

by appealing to their sense of community and patriotic feelings for the motherland.[13] This approach was later adopted by the revolutionary Sun Yat-sen and his followers, who also looked to overseas Chinese businessmen for the funds needed to finance their struggle to overthrow the Qing Dynasty and establish their own government. After the war, the desperation felt by those trying to rebuild the country was shared by the merchants who had decided to leave and migrate. Thus, the term "overseas Chinese" became more widespread. It upheld the idea that this migration was only temporary and that those who had left would eventually return to the motherland.

It was around this time that both Mong's paternal and maternal grandfathers moved from Guangdong Province to Nagasaki. His father's father, Mong Fai-tong, was from Panyu (番禺), a town to the south of Guangzhou (廣州). His mother's father came from Jiangmen (江門), a small town situated on the Pearl River. Mong says he does not know why they ultimately chose to leave for Japan. In July 1894, when the Sino-Japanese War was about to break out in the north of the country, a plague swept through Guangdong Province, adding to the misery of the peasant population. This may be the reason why they headed for a new land. In 1896, Nagasaki City had a population of around 72,000; of these, 706 were Chinese, the vast majority of them male migrant workers seeking their fortune.[14]

Some time after arriving in Nagasaki, Mong Fai-tong got a job selling vegetables in a market and traded dried food and household goods on the side. His account of how bean sprouts got their Japanese name is one of Mong's favorite stories.

> My father's father was running a grocery stall in a Nagasaki market. He grew his own bean sprouts and then sold them on the stall. But back then, the Japanese had never seen or even heard of bean sprouts, so they didn't sell well.
>
> One day, a Japanese housewife came to his stall, looked at the bean sprouts with curiosity and asked what they were. My grandfather, who spoke only a few words of Japanese, responded very quickly [in Cantonese], "*Ngar choi. Mou yan sik.* 芽菜，冇人食。 (Bean sprouts. No one eats them.)". But the housewife misinterpreted "*mou yan sik*" as "*moyashi.*"[15]

Mong maintains that the origin of *moyashi*, the name given to bean sprouts in Japanese, actually comes from the Cantonese *mou yan sik* (no one eats). But since a reference to bean sprouts has been found in a seventeenth-century Japanese-Portuguese dictionary, one has to assume that Mong's version, charming though it is, is just family lore.

In 1898, during the cherry blossom season, the Mong Fai-tong household witnessed the arrival of its first son and William Mong's father, Mong Wing-shun, or Kwok-ping as he was later called. This was also the year that the United States made Nagasaki a supply base for its war against the Spanish in the Philippines. Over 726 foreign ships arrived in the port of Nagasaki that year, and the town, which had fallen behind Kobe (神戶) and Yokohama (橫濱), regained its credentials as a bustling trading center for a short while.[16] Until the arrival of the Americans, goods exported from Nagasaki had consisted mainly of coal and seafood: the dried abalone, sea cucumber, and shark's fin so prized during the Qing Dynasty. Sugar from the south largely made up the rest of its imports.

Mong Kwok-ping grew into a healthy young boy and was sent to Kaisei Junior High School in East Yamate, around 1910. Kaisei was a Catholic boys' school located at the top of the Dutch Slope, a pleasant hillside residential area. In those days, junior high school lasted five years and therefore students were seventeen years old by the time they graduated. In 1911, the number of junior high school graduates for the whole of Japan was only 17,561.[17] Kwok-ping's parents must therefore have regarded education as extremely important and had sufficient funds to allow him to stay in school until he was seventeen. At Kaisei Junior High School, Kwok-ping worked on his language skills. In addition to the Cantonese that he spoke with his father, he became highly proficient in Japanese, and received extensive tutoring in English.

Mong's mother, Wong Fa-yuk, was born in Nagasaki in 1902. By then, the number of overseas Chinese living in the city had greatly increased, to 1,064.[18] Fa-yuk attended the Kwassui Girls' School. The school, founded by an American Methodist missionary, was located in East Yamate, the same district as Kwok-ping's school. When she turned 18, Fa-yuk's father suggested an arranged marriage. The chosen fiancé was Kwok-ping, four years her senior.

Soon after World War I, the engaged couple left Japan along with Kwok-ping's family. The vibrancy that had characterized Nagasaki when it was the country's only port open to the West and China had long since evaporated. In 1921, the total number of foreign ships entering Nagasaki was only 142, one-fifth of what it been the year of Kwok-ping's birth.[19]

Anti-Japanese sentiment had been simmering since the establishment of the Republic of China in 1912. But it was during World War I, when the Japanese seized control of the city of Qingdao (青島) on the Shandong peninsula (山東半島) from the Germans, that this resentment came to a head. Anti-Japanese demonstrations initiated in 1919 by students in Beijing, known as the May Fourth Movement, spread to the rest of the country.[20] A drive to purchase Chinese domestic products and boycott all things Japanese gained significant support among Chinese people. Chinese merchants in Nagasaki, as purveyors of Japanese goods and currency, were hard hit. Between 1922 and 1923, they were forced out of business, one after the other.[21]

The new world that Kwok-ping gave up Nagasaki for was Hong Kong. At that time, Hong Kong was still a slow transit trade port that suffered in comparison to Shanghai and its cosmopolitan Bund district. But, after a long and uncomfortable sea voyage from Nagasaki, entering Victoria Harbour, lined with three- or four-storey-high colonial buildings on each side, must have been an amazing sight. Since the days of opium trading, much of the colony's economic power had been in the hands of taipans, or influential Western businessmen, chief among whom were those belonging to the British firm of Jardine Matheson & Co.[22] Japan, in contrast, had little influence in the British colony. In 1924, imports from Japan into Hong Kong, including those from Korea and

Taiwan (both under Japanese rule), amounted to only 10.8 percent of total imports into the territory.[23]

Singing Japanese Lullabies in a British Colony

After arriving in Hong Kong, Kwok-ping and Fa-yuk headed to Kwok-ping's "hometown" of Panyu, to the south of Guangzhou, which they were visiting for the first time. They sought their ancestors' blessing for the marriage and took wedding photos at the Sincere Department Store in Guangzhou. In a departure from tradition, they chose to wear Western clothes for the pictures: a wedding dress for her, a silk hat and tails for him. They then settled down in Hong Kong. Kwok-ping, having decided that he wanted to run his own business one day, signed up to work at the Hong Kong branch of Mitsubishi Corporation, with the purpose of gaining some trading experience. Mitsubishi Corporation was the trading arm of the powerful conglomerate. By the time Kwok-ping joined the company, the Mitsubishi group's empire extended to shipbuilding, paper milling, mining, banking, brewing, and machine building, providing a young man with ample opportunities to broaden his understanding of the business world. Mitsubishi Corporation's Hong Kong branch office was officially opened in 1906 and was located at 14 Pedder Street in Central.[24] At the time of Kwok-ping's employment, the items exported by Mitsubishi to Hong Kong included coal, glass, and metal. In view of the international nature of the corporation's business, Kwok-ping's multilingual skills were considered a definite asset.

William Mong Man-wai was born on November 7, 1927, in the company housing provided by Mitsubishi Corporation. He was the middle child of five, and Kwok-ping and Fa-yuk's second son. He had one older sister, Stella, an older brother, Jeffery, and two younger sisters, Lillian and Esther. The Mitsubishi company apartments were located in a three-storey block on Cameron Road, a few streets up from the legendary Peninsula Hotel. The building was also home to several Japanese expatriate families.

At home, as Mong and his siblings knew little Japanese, most conversations were conducted in Cantonese. Mong's parents were native Japanese speakers and both spoke with a Kyushu (九州) accent. Fa-yuk had sung Japanese rhymes to the children as babies, and Kwok-ping could sometimes be overheard humming the melancholy Japanese lullaby "*Itsuki no Komoriuta*," which tells the story of a live-in nanny from a village in Kyushu lamenting having to work away from home. Moreover, in the days when Kwok-ping was still working at Mitsubishi, he had often invited Japanese customers back to the house.

When he turned one and a half, Mong came down with a mysterious illness that baffled every doctor his parents took him to. His stomach swelled up to such an extent that his face seemed shrunken and totally out of proportion with the rest of his body. He was sent to different hospitals; however, doctors there were unable to find the cause of his affliction and gave up on his case. Mong heard about what happened next from his mother:

Mong's parents, Mong Kwok-ping and Wong Fa-yuk, pose in Western
wedding clothes inside Guangzhou's Sincere Department
Store, early 1920s.
Courtesy of William Mong

My father and mother were very worried about me. In those days, my father used
to take the Star Ferry from our home in Kowloon to his office on Hong Kong
Island.

One day, on the ferry ride home, my father somehow got talking to a Japanese
doctor whom he then invited back to the house. The Japanese doctor took one look
at me and said, "This isn't that serious." My father does not remember exactly
what it was, but he recalls the doctor telling him that I would make a complete
recovery if I took vitamin something or other.[25]

They rushed to a pharmacy and gave me the medicine they had purchased there;
within a month I had totally recovered.[26]

William Mong (left) pictured with his brother
Jeffery in Hong Kong in the late 1920s.
Courtesy of William Mong

Mong's parents later told him:

> "You might have died and gone straight to heaven from such a disease. God must have somehow brought this upon you as a sign that you should work hard and take good care of your business."[27]

Mong laughs, saying, "Should I ever make it to heaven, I certainly won't find any of my friends there." Mong is not particularly religious; however, in the midst of explaining his views on religion, he suddenly utters the word *kamisama* (神様) or "god" in Japanese. Mong also believes in luck and likes to ensure that it is on his side. In the aquarium in his office, there are nine carp. The number nine is of special significance to the Chinese. In Chinese, *nine* (九, *jiu*) has the same pronunciation as *eternity* (久, *jiu*), and *fish* (魚, *yu*) has the same pronunciation as *abundance* (餘, *yu*). In other words, the nine carp, or *jiu yu*, represent the hope of infinite wealth. Mong faithfully observes traditional Chinese customs that are believed to bring good luck, as do many Hong Kong tycoons who have followed a similar path to fortune.

Japanese Occupation

Kwok-ping remained at Mitsubishi Corporation for twelve years before resigning to set up his own company, as he had always intended to do, and going into business with his two younger brothers, Wing-fat and Wing-cheung. As mentioned, Kwok-ping's childhood name was Wing-shun. He took the second part of each of their names and christened the new company Shun Fat Cheung Brothers Company (信發祥兄弟公司).[28] It specialized in trade with Japan, importing plugs, sockets, electrical wires, mosquito repellent, fertilizer, clothes, and paper, in addition to the traditional dried seafood.[29]

Although Kwok-ping had grown up in Japan and was therefore familiar with the country, it would have been a bold move for a Chinese merchant to deal exclusively with Japan in pre-World War II Hong Kong. One of the philosophies of Hong Kong entrepreneurs comes from an ancient Chinese saying from the Warring States Period. It goes, "Better to be the beak of a rooster than the rump of a bull (寧為雞口，無為牛後)." In other words, it is better to be the leader of a small group than a subordinate in a large organization.[30] By establishing a working relationship with Japan early on, Kwok-ping opened the way for his son to become the "King of Electrical Appliances," as he eventually became known. In later years, whenever he was asked about the secrets of his success in business, Kwok-ping would answer "always be ahead of the competition."[31]

Kwok-ping and his family moved out of the Mitsubishi Corporation's company accommodation and moved into their newly built house on Ashley Road, behind the Peninsula Hotel and only five minutes down the road from their previous flat. Their new home was a Western-style two-storey residence with a small garden. They also employed two live-in maids. Fa-yuk spent most of her days at home, taking care of the household. Mong recalls:

My mother was very sweet. She was always gentle with us and I never saw her get angry. I think it was her Japanese upbringing and mission school education that made her such a patient and kind mother.[32]

My father, however, had a quick temper (laughs). Whenever my mother informed him that we had been naughty, my father would frighten us by saying "I'll burn moxa on your skin!" It was terrifying.

My father had a hot temper and my mother was gentle. He was stubborn and she was accommodating. But my father never laid a hand on us, so it was really just a scare tactic.[33]

In the days before World War II, the family vacationed in the city's lush green suburbs, at a bungalow that Kwok-ping leased from the colonial government. William Mong recounts the days spent with his father:

We would take a taxi to get there from our home in Ashley Road; back then, it only cost two dollars from Kowloon to the New Territories, a distance of about twenty kilometers (12.4 miles). We would go there almost every weekend though my father couldn't always make it. We would swim and go fishing. My father enjoyed fishing and so do I. Occasionally, we would drop our lines in nearby Victoria Harbour.[34]

As the political situation between China and Japan deteriorated in the run-up to World War II, the Mongs had to adjust their behavior: both Fa-yuk and Kwok-ping gradually had to stop speaking Japanese outside the home.

After Japan invaded China in 1937, all Hong Kong people loathed the Japanese. My parents never dared to speak Japanese outside the house for fear of being mistaken for Japanese.[35]

Mong's paternal grandfather and grandmother seated.
Standing: Mong's father, Kwok-ping (center),
with his brothers, Wing-cheung (left)
and Wing-fat (right), Hong Kong, late 1940s.
Courtesy of William Mong.

The Japanese army occupied Hong Kong on Christmas Day 1941, and ruled the territory for the following three years and eight months. Mong witnessed firsthand the brutality of the Japanese occupation.

> I witnessed Japanese soldiers cutting off the heads of Chinese people down at the Victoria Harbour pier; they made them all line up and then cut off their heads one by one.[36]

The war put an end to their peaceful family life. The Mongs moved to Guangzhou on the Chinese mainland. After spending a year at a school in Guangzhou, William left his family and started moving from one place to another, deep inside the Chinese heartland, so as to be able to continue with his studies.

> Teachers told us that children were not being allowed to attend school once the Japanese army arrived. So, Chinese schools had all relocated inland, out of reach of the invaders. My classmates and I followed, moving to Shaoguan (韶關), Guilin (桂林), Kunming (昆明), and then Chongqing (重慶), because we really wanted to study.

> I continued to receive money from my father, even during wartime. There was an underground route, you see. We could also exchange letters.[37]

In May 1943, while Hong Kong was still under Japanese occupation, Kwok-ping purchased a house in Kowloon Tong (九龍塘), one of the city's quieter suburbs. It cost him 22,000 Japanese military yen, the currency issued by the Japanese Imperial Army administration that had replaced the Hong Kong dollar. The application form to register the sale of the house was addressed to the "Governor of the Occupied Territory of Hong Kong: Mr Rensuke Isogai" and was written entirely in Japanese, an indication of the extent to which the occupying Japanese army had taken control of the territory's administration. The house was in fact a good bargain. The following year, when Japan's defeat at the hands of the Allies appeared inevitable, the value of the Japanese military yen dropped overnight.

The war with Japan ended in August 1945, and Mong was reunited with his family in Guangzhou, where his father was doing business, before returning to Hong Kong by ferry. In those days, Guangzhou was a chaotic and lawless town, with no clear authority in place and an untrustworthy military and police force. Mong recalls,

> "It was a dangerous place. There were many crooks in Guangzhou, some of them in the army."[38]

One story goes that Kwok-ping used to exchange household goods for bars of gold, which he would then strap to his body before crossing the Hong Kong border.

Civil War in China

At the end of 1945, Mong decided that he wanted to study at a university on the Chinese mainland. He recounts how he took the entrance examination for National Southwestern Associated University (西南聯合大學), a wartime consortium of three prestigious northern Chinese universities—Peking, Tsinghua, and Nankai—that had by necessity relocated to Kunming in the southernmost province of Yunnan (雲南). But by the summer of 1946, the three universities had returned to their original locations, and the students who had been admitted were able to choose which of the three they wanted to attend. Mong says he chose Tsinghua University and registered himself under a false name, fearing that his father's well-known business association with the Japanese might hurt his chances. Mong booked his passage on a ferry to Shanghai. Once there, he found the majority of students drawn to the ideals and precepts of Communism and witnessed the strength of the anti-Kuomintang movement. At university, Mong's major was aeronautical engineering. He said that, from a very young age, he had dreamed of servicing airplanes. "My mother said, 'Remember? When you were a child, you always used to say you wanted to be an engineer who repairs cars or airplanes'."[39]

Mong's dream, however, was crushed by the advent of civil war. In 1948, as the People's Liberation Army was about to enter Beijing, he received an urgent letter from his father, requesting his immediate return to Hong Kong.

> I wanted to remain in China until I graduated. But my father said, "Stay if you wish, but I will not be sending you any more money!"
>
> You see, my father, like most people of his generation, didn't like the Communists.[40]

Mong acceded to his father's request and returned to Hong Kong without protest.

> "In the old days, unlike today, sons listened to their parents; it was natural for them to do so."[41]

By then, Mong had already made up his mind that he did not want a job working as an engineer for a large corporation for the rest of his life. Instead, he aspired to start and run his own business, as his father had done before him.

> In Hong Kong, there were many people who had majored in engineering or medicine at an overseas university but who chose not to become engineers or doctors upon their return to the city. What they really wanted was to run their own business.[42]

The idea of making one's fortune by running one's own business indeed lies at the heart of Hong Kong's entrepreneurial spirit but is something that would not have been allowed at that time in communist China.

As a result of his firsthand experience of the chaos that preceded the revolution, he also had a deep-seated desire to do something for his country. Mong, however, never mentioned his Chinese educational background after his return to Hong Kong. The colonial government's police department had started keeping an eye out for suspected communist sympathizers, whom they would summon to their headquarters on the Central waterfront for questioning.[43] Therefore, Mong did not want to attract attention to himself. He worked for a while for a company his uncle had established after the war. Then, following in the footsteps of his older brother, Jeffery, he joined the crew of a passenger liner and went to sea.

After finishing high school, Jeffery had become purser on one of the ships that plied the Asia to South America route for Royal InterOcean Lines. As a crew member on a Dutch passenger liner, Jeffrey was increasing his cultural awareness and developing his own transnational networks. His travels took him to the then-British protectorates of Singapore and Malaya, as well as to South America via South Africa.

> The ship had made a stop in Durban, South Africa, when my brother suddenly came down with appendicitis. This was a time of strict racial segregation in South Africa, and so Asians were not allowed to be treated in hospitals reserved for White South Africans. Instead, he was sent to a hospital for Blacks. Upon his discharge, a fellow crew member arranged for my brother to spend a few days with a Chinese couple he knew, a Mr and Mrs Wong, who ran a general store in town. Jeffery stayed at their home for several days, during which he also had a chance to get to know the Wong's daughter, Hilda.

> Sometime later, Mr and Mrs Wong traveled to Hong Kong to look for a prospective marriage partner for their daughter. My brother and Hilda liked each other, and so this story had a very happy ending.[44]

And that's how it came about that Jeffery married Hilda, an overseas Chinese from South Africa.

Mong too was eager to see the outside world, but he was not at all interested in becoming a sailor, even though, at the recommendation of his father and brother, he did try it once. But for the length of the six-month voyage, out of his own salary he paid another crew member a part-time fee to cover his onboard duties.

> Wherever the ship docked, I went sightseeing. I didn't have anything else to do. There was a nurse's office onboard, and I was allowed to sleep there.

> So it was all quite easy. I didn't have to work at all. Haha![45]

This is indeed thinking outside the box. It also leaves one wondering whether an ordinary employee at a giant corporation would be able to get away with paying another staff member to do his duties. But Mong's unconventional—and sometimes outrageous—ideas would eventually lead to the localization of Japanese products for the Chinese market, and this innovative way of seeing and doing things came about precisely because he did not work *for* a Japanese corporation but rather worked *with* a Japanese corporation.

School of Little Sparrows

In the autumn of 1949, at the suggestion of his father, Mong traveled to Japan, at the time still under US occupation. The plan was for him to attend a Japanese university. When Mong's own children were old enough, however, he made them all go to the United States to study, as he himself had dreamed of in his youth. He remembers,

> "At that time, it was quite difficult to go to America, and my father couldn't really afford to send me there. Unlike today, when people can just jump on a plane, it was a long and expensive journey."[46]

Only four years had passed since the end of the war, but Mong decided to put his feelings aside, and made his way to Japan. He was also keen to put some distance between himself and the watchful eyes of the British colonial government.

It was his second visit to the country. In the spring of 1934, when Mong had just turned six, his mother had taken him and his sister Lillian to Japan. During the trip, Mong had suffered from a heat rash that had worsened into a running sore. His mother, thinking that a dip in the hot springs would cure him, had taken him to Nagasaki and Amakusa. At the time, Nagasaki, which was in the throes of a recession, had been playing host to an International Industrial and Tourism Exposition. The event had been an enormous success and had seen an attendance record of 628,784 visitors, nearly 2.5 times the city's population, in just two months.[47] Mong, his mother, and sister had spent six months in the city, staying at the house of one of Fa-yuk's aunts.

Over fifteen years had passed since then. This time, he was visiting Japan alone. His ship sailed to Yokohama via Kobe. Kiyoshi Hara was there to welcome him at the pier. Hara was a friend of Kwok-ping who had worked at Mitsubishi Corporation's Hong Kong branch during the war. Because Mitsubishi was alleged to have acted as a Japanese government agent in the regulation of international trade under the Japanese occupation of the city, after Allied forces regained control of Hong Kong, Hara was made a prisoner of war. He was later released and returned safely to Japan. He had since retired and was leading a comfortable life.

The two of them took a train from Yokohama and headed to Hara's home in Higashi Ginza (東銀座). It was a cozy little two-storey house, with a beautiful bathtub made from Japanese cypress. The Haras, who had no child of their own, treated Mong like a son. Mong, however, found it difficult to communicate with them, as he could only speak broken Japanese. He explained,

> "I really couldn't speak much. So, I decided I had to do something about it. When I set myself a task, I always succeed in accomplishing it."[48]

The first step was to learn the language, so he enrolled in a primary school in Kanda (神田), one of Tokyo's oldest districts. The president of Chiyoda Chemical Industries, another business associate of Kwok-ping, took him under his wing and secured special permission for him to attend the school. This was truly an extraordinary arrangement and shows how powerful Kwok-ping's networks were in Tokyo. The 22-year-old Mong spent six months there studying Japanese with classmates less than half his own age.

However, even with the help of a textbook, he struggled with basic Japanese *hiragana* characters. Therefore, he would wake up early, board a streetcar from Ginza, and arrive at the school around 7:15 a.m. Then, before the official start of the school day, a teacher would give him an extra class in reading and writing.

> It was Mr Murakami who gave me a lot of help. He asked me to arrive early in the morning so that he could give me extra coaching. We would go over the contents of that day's lesson in the primary school textbooks so that I would have a better grasp of what was going on in class.[49]

The children adored him and called him *onii-chan,* our big brother. Mong took Japanese reading and music classes with them and played with them during school breaks. "It was fun. I will never forget it. Children are amazing, really," Mong recounted with a big smile on his face.

School finished at noon, and Mong would head back to the Haras' home. After lunch, Hara would check through Mong's homework and teach him to read Japanese-language newspapers. Occasionally, Mong went out on errands. He would stand in a long line waiting for rations like bread, rice, oil, and butter for Mrs Hara.

The first children's song he learned at primary school was called "School of Sparrows (*Suzume no Gakkō*)," whose lyrics consisted of a simple repetition of sounds like "chi chi pappapapa." But over the next six months he made remarkable progress, and he soon knew by heart the nursery rhymes his mother had sung to him as a child.

After Mong had completed his studies at the school, he decided to stay on at the Haras for a while. He would wander around Yurakucho (有樂町), near Ginza, occasionally catching a movie with Mr and Mrs Hara or enjoying an evening drink at one of the yakitori stands under the railway overpass. A glass of beer cost ¥5, and for just ¥100 several people could enjoy drinks and snacks. For Mong, it was also a good introduction to Japanese society.

American GIs could often be seen having a good time at a side-street bar, oblivious to the Japanese military songs playing in the background.

> When walking through Ginza at night, I could hear Japanese military songs playing. Wartime songs. But the American GIs and other Allied Forces' soldiers had no idea what they were and would dance along to them in bars or cabarets. I thought them really naive. Japanese military songs had anti-American lyrics. To me, it was all wrong.[50]

Mong's tone sharpens when the conversation turns to war. Memories of World War II were still fresh in 1950. The *Overseas Chinese Daily* (華僑日報), Hong Kong's leading Chinese-language newspaper of the time, had applied the term "Japanese enemy (日敵)" to the Japanese military during the war and continued to use it, even though the Japanese occupation had ended.[51] Movie theaters in Hong Kong were playing *Fort Santiago*, a film about the violence of the Japanese military assault on the Philippines.

Advertisements for the film in the local papers screamed, "Rape! Slaughter! Torture! Plunder! If the Japanese were ever allowed to rise again, what kind of world would we live in? Look at the past, and take from it lessons for the future." The ad underscored the film's popularity by stating, "Full house everyday. Still showing."[52]

Being Chinese, Mong was not sure how he would be treated in Tokyo. Rather surprisingly, Mong says he had no negative experiences during his stay at the Haras. Whenever he went shopping or took a train, kind-hearted people would offer him assistance. No one ever attempted to deceive him either. He recalls, "They don't cheat others, and I am most appreciative of that. I hate both cheating and being cheated."[53]

All in all, Mong spent over a year at the Haras. He gave up on the idea of entering university, as there was no way he could afford a private institution's tuition fees. He did, however, become fairly fluent in the Japanese language, which was indispensable for his future role as an intermediary. And eventually he returned home to Hong Kong.

Hong Kong advertisement for the Filipino movie *Fort Santiago*. The film, which depicts Japanese wartime atrocities, was a box office hit in the city.
(*Overseas Chinese Daily*, February 13, 1950)

Safeguarding the Family's Fortune

In Hong Kong, Mong's father had set up with some friends a new company called Yue Shun Cheung Co. Limited (裕信祥有限公司) and had become known for his successful business dealings with Japanese corporations. The Shun Fat Cheung Brothers Corporation, which he had established before World War II, had been dissolved. Each brother had gone his own separate way during the war: Wing-Shun and Wing-fat had stayed in Hong Kong, but Wing-cheung was doing business in Shanghai.

Mong's brother, Jeffery, quit his ship's purser job and joined his father's new company. The range of imported goods was expanded and the company started to import cement, building materials, and manganese, used in the manufacture of batteries. It also became an agent for Kao soap and Asahi Aji, a chemical flavor enhancer (MSG).

> In fact, initially both my brother and I were planning to join our father's company. But it's dangerous for two brothers to both be working for the same company. If there is a major problem, the whole family risks becoming penniless.[54]

As a means of minimizing the risk of family bankruptcy, one should not put all one's eggs into the same basket. Kwok-ping's sons followed him into the trading business; however, so as to avoid the pressure of having the entire family's fortune tied up in a single venture, each set up his own independent trading company. It is still common practice in Hong Kong to diversify the family business so as to guarantee economic survival into the next generation—yet another example of how anxiety fuels Hong Kong entrepreneurs.

As a consequence, it was quite acceptable for the second or third son, rather than the eldest son, to end up supporting the family financially. As long as someone in the family was successful and "brought honor to the ancestors," that was what mattered. The concept of safeguarding the family's fortune and glory from one generation to the next, and thereby paying homage to one's ancestors, is fundamental to traditional Chinese society. The successful son takes care of his parents and siblings. In Mong's case, he observed this tradition, and his parents lived with him, the second son.

Eventually, Mong's brother and two of his sisters moved to North America. Mong's youngest sister, Esther, moved to Vancouver and, prior to the Hong Kong handover, his sister Stella followed her children to the San Francisco Bay area. Only Mong and his younger sister, Lillian, remained in Hong Kong. His brother Jeffery kept his company in Hong Kong but lived in Vancouver and traveled back and forth between the two, a state of affairs best summarized by the Cantonese expression *tai hung yan* (太空人), or "astronaut," used to describe a man who leaves his family in their adopted country and comes back to Hong Kong alone for extended periods to work. Nevertheless, even when there are family members living far away from home, the Mongs come together and help each other whenever needed.

Ethnic Chinese merchants involved in international trade in many cases did not enjoy much state support and therefore had to find ways of measuring up to fierce competition on their own. Inevitably, they would turn to those they could trust: their close relatives and extended family. The family network provided a safe means of sending money, among other things, back and forth across national borders. This practice of relying on family members for the circulation of goods and currency also served as the model for the establishment of a transnational Chinese business network. Liao Chi-yang, a historian who specializes in ethnic Chinese businesses in Nagasaki from the late nineteenth to the early twentieth centuries, describes the situation faced by these Chinese merchants as follows:

> Chinese merchants always operated in an extremely challenging business environment. In order to survive, they had to involve themselves in multiple areas of the business while building up strong trade networks, especially through blood relatives and regional associations, and, at the same time, continuously expanding their product lines or sales area.[55]

In 1952, the Mongs took a further step in the diversification of their business. William established a small trading company called Shun Wo Company (信和公司) and started importing a small number of goods from Japan.

> It was a small business. I didn't have a lot of money at the time. I think it was a good thing that I set up my own company. Had I joined my father's company, I might have quarreled with my brother after my father passed away. It would not have been good for the family.[56]

Mong (seated front, second from left) with his parents, Kwok-ping
and Fa-yuk, brother Jeffery and sisters, Esther, Lillian,
and Stella. Hong Kong, mid-1950s.
Courtesy of William Mong

When Mong started his own business, his father told him there were a couple of inviolable business rules that he should follow:

> My father? My father taught me and my brother well. He told us not to speculate or gamble. So I don't even know how to play mahjong.
>
> And he told us to avoid borrowing money from the bank to finance our businesses. Banks will lend you an umbrella on a sunny day, but take it back on a rainy day. He said we should always keep that in mind. So I seldom borrow money from the bank. I always use my own money to do business.[57]

Ironically for such a bold and innovative entrepreneur, the Mong family's business principle is rather old-fashioned: "Develop a business slowly but surely on a strong foundation of trust." In later years, Mong's Japanese associates have come to characterize his attitude to business as extremely cautious. Mong never hesitates to take steps to ensure he stays ahead of the game. But after making that bold initial step, he follows his father's advice of not taking too many risks, not making any unnecessary moves, and not changing business partners. Some of his business associates at Matsushita found these concepts to be rather at odds with such an enterprising personality; they certainly seem conservative in a Hong Kong business environment where speculators have become billionaires overnight through the buying and reselling of property. But the Mongs are not just entrepreneurs; they are intermediaries whose position is highly vulnerable, who have to balance foreign and local demands, and whose survival depends on trust.

With his father's principles in mind, Mong took up his role of intermediary between Hong Kong and Japan and began importing chinaware, gramophones, and 78rpm records. Imported records included melancholic tunes that he had become familiar

Mong's parents in Hong Kong in the 1970s.
Courtesy of William Mong

with during his days in Tokyo, such as "Suzhou Serenade (*Soshū Yakyoku*)" from the soundtrack to the Japanese film *China Night (Shina no Yoru)*. This was in fact a Japanese propaganda film set in China during the Sino-Japanese war that featured a love affair between a Japanese sailor and a Chinese woman. There was also a recording of the American country favorite "Tennessee Waltz" performed in Japanese by the 14-year-old Chiemi Eri. Mong imported these items in small numbers only:

> "It wasn't that long after the war, so it was still very difficult to sell Japanese records."[58]

Mong also imported elegant artificial flowers from Japan, which he supplied to Sincere and Wing On, two of Hong Kong's oldest department stores. These were different from the Hong Kong-made plastic flowers that later became a big hit in Europe and the United States.

The turning point in Mong's career came a year later, by way of his father's contacts in Japan. In March 1953, in the month that sees the red-purple flowers of the bauhinia bloom, the managing director of Matsushita Electric subsidiary, Matsushita Electric Trading, Tsuneo Jinnai, met with Mong's father, Kwok-ping. Kwok-ping was already doing business with Matsushita Electric Trading, importing carbon sticks, one of the core components for batteries. Jinnai said that Matsushita was looking to sell their National brand electric household products in Hong Kong and asked whether Kwok-ping would be interested in handling this business. Kwok-ping did not answer yes; instead, he told Jinnai that his son had studied engineering at university.

This conversation marked the beginning of what was to become Matsushita Electric's long association with William Mong.

3

You Salarymen Can't Think Outside the Box!
A Hong Kong Entrepreneur Takes
on a Japanese Manufacturing Giant

Konosuke Matsushita (left) and Mong shake hands
at a company event in 1963.
Courtesy of Shun Hing Group

William Mong officially started business with Matsushita Electric Trading on August 15, 1953. In a move that foreshadowed the synergy that would come to characterize the relationship between his trading firm and Matsushita, Mong changed its name from Shun Wo Company to Shun Hing Hong (信興行), meaning "to develop a business on a strong foundation of trust." From the beginning, Matsushita Trading adopted a hands-off approach and gave its Hong Kong agent free rein to manage the sales of its products in the city. This provided Mong with the confidence and motivation to put forward his own ideas about which models to introduce and how best to adapt them for the local market.

A self-employed entrepreneur, William Mong was the antithesis of the Japanese salaryman, a term generally used to describe male white-collar employees working for large corporations. The stereotypical Japanese salaryman followed set routines from which he rarely, if ever, deviated, followed his superiors' orders to the letter, and accepted his given place in the complex corporate hierarchy without questioning. In exchange, the company guaranteed his middle-class lifestyle even after retirement. Secure in the knowledge that he was set for life, there was little motivation to step outside his comfort zone and take chances.

The fact that Mong had his own company, even though a small one, and was not a salaryman working for Matsushita, clearly gave him the incentive to explore new sales opportunities. As his own boss, Mong could say what he wanted to Matsushita. However, when he spoke out, it was not only with his own interests in mind, but he made sure that his initiatives also benefited Matsushita. As a result, Matsushita factories in Japan began manufacturing products that appealed to Hong Kong consumers and catered to their household needs.

Mong was not a conventional Chinese trader either. Traditionally, Chinese traders' main imports from Japan had been non-processed goods, such as dried seafood and raw materials, because they were in high demand. Moreover, items such as Japanese shark fins and carbon sticks for batteries did not carry a "Made in Japan" label, which meant that, once they were in the stores, no one could tell where they came from—an important consideration in the aftermath of World War II.

By going into business with Matsushita and gaining exclusive rights to promote and sell the company's products, Mong was responsible for creating brand awareness of a Japanese manufacturer who was virtually unknown in Hong Kong. In other words, Mong was importing consumer durables that might or might not sell, and having to carve out a new market for them. This was well beyond the scope of what conventional Chinese merchants were prepared to do. In addition, he was promoting "Made in Japan" goods just eight years after the end of the war, when anti-Japanese sentiments were still high.

According to Mong, "In this world, there are no eternal enemies and no eternal allies (沒有永遠的敵人，沒有永遠的朋友)."[1] It is good to be flexible and able to adapt to any situation. The phrase is so ingrained in Cantonese that, in Hong Kong, it is widely believed to have originated locally. But, in fact, they are the words of the British politician Henry John Temple, Third Viscount Palmerston, who was Foreign Secretary at the time Britain annexed Hong Kong.[2] When the phrase found its way into Britain's colony in China, what had started life as a foreign policy statement quickly turned into a business mantra. Mong, for one, believes that "there are no eternal enemies and no eternal allies" is the Cantonese businessman's creed, and that this approach is what makes it possible for him to conduct business all over the world. It is a reminder that businesspeople have to use their own judgment: they cannot blindly trust common sense or follow the recommendations of those around them. Despite the overwhelming anti-Japanese sentiment that prevailed in Hong Kong, Mong saw business potential in Japanese home appliances:

An early Shun Hing billboard at the Star Ferry Terminal.
Hong Kong, 1956.
Photo by Kiyoshi Nakane

In Hong Kong, you could buy products manufactured in the West. But they were limited to things like radios and amplifiers. Home appliances, like washing machines, were rare. Now that the war was behind us, I was confident that the standard of living in Hong Kong would improve. And if it did, I knew there would certainly be a demand for quality home appliances.[3]

Mong looked to the future with confidence and, firm in the belief that the company's products would soon become an indispensable feature of any Hong Kong home, decided to do business with the Japanese manufacturing giant.

In order to officially start trading with Matsushita, Mong had to first put up a bank-issued letter of credit stating that he had the capital necessary to sustain his side of the partnership. For this, Mong needed to secure the sum of HK$10,000. Some time later, a good friend of his at Matsushita Electric Trading, having heard a rumor that it was Mong's father who had loaned him the money, teased him: "So your old man did give you a leg up after all!" Mong, however, insisted "It was money that I had sweated blood and tears for."[4]

The company operated from a single room in an office building at 81 Des Voeux Road, occupied by numerous other small firms. This is where the Hang Seng Bank Headquarters stand today. It faced the bustling commercial artery, its trams shuttling back and forth. The office was reached by climbing the stairs to the third floor, past a restaurant sign that, translated into English, read "Fragrant Garden – Tea, Noodles, Vegetables and Alcoholic Beverages." The cramped room with its veneered partitions was shared by Mong, his two employees, and a treasured telephone. In 1953, despite a population of 2.25 million, Hong Kong boasted a mere 30,000 telephone numbers.[5]

Looking back to 1953, the year he first established his company, Mong recalls it as a time when Hong Kong was finally starting to recover from the deprivations it had suffered during the war. It was also four years after the founding of the People's Republic of China by Mao Zedong, and refugees from mainland China were continuing to flock across the border into Hong Kong. The city had already experienced a dramatic surge in population, and the availability of low-income housing had become a pressing issue. Squatter areas had sprung up overnight and were flooded with people living hand to mouth and scraping out a living from whatever employment they could find. On the night of December 25, 1953, a fatal fire occurred in the Shek Kip Mei (石硤尾) squatter area in Kowloon: 2,580 wooden huts went up in flames, and 57,151 residents were made homeless. In direct response to this tragedy, the colonial government launched a public housing program and started construction on Hong Kong's first public housing estate.[6]

In early 1953, Japan's presence in Hong Kong was, at best, marginal. Although Japan was the third largest source of imports into Hong Kong, after China and Britain, of the 14,500 expatriates living in the colony, the general recollection seems to be that there were no more than ten Japanese nationals among them.[7] The Bank of Tokyo, which specialized in the provision of trade finance and foreign exchange services to Japanese businesses, did not open a Hong Kong branch until October 1953, and it was another year before any of the major Japanese conglomerates would resume their operations in the colony. It was therefore the versatile Chinese traders who, thanks to their abilities to operate effectively in both a Chinese and Japanese business environment, initiated the transnational flow of "Made in Japan" products.

An Appliance Trader without Appliances

Mong was enthusiastic about selling modern appliances. But the range of National brand products that were suitable for export to Hong Kong was extremely limited.

> The goods Shun Hing Hong imported from Matsushita Electric Trading into Hong Kong initially were umbrellas, sports shoes, plastic-coated electric wire and pearl handbags—imitation glass pearls, that is. There were very few National brand home appliances at the time I established the company.[8]

While, in 1953, Mong's Shun Hing Hong was a small venture with only three staff members, Matsushita Electric Trading itself employed only fifty-five, having just barely managed to stay in business during the American occupation of Japan.

Matsushita Electric Trading was incorporated in 1935, when the founder of Matsushita Electric Industrial, Konosuke Matsushita, decided to set up the company's trading division as a separate entity, dedicated to the sale and export of National appliances abroad. Matsushita Industrial would manufacture the goods, and Matsushita Trading would sell them and ship them overseas.

In 1946, however, by order of General MacArthur's occupation headquarters, Matsushita Electric Trading was made to sever all links with the Matsushita group and forced to operate on its own, without the support of its parent company. Arataro

Takahashi, the chairman of Matsushita Electric Trading from 1955 to 1983, was the Konosuke Matsushita right-hand man who concluded a landmark technology transfer agreement with Dutch manufacturer Philips in 1952. Takahashi recounted his firm's postwar challenges in a 1970 corporate newsletter:

> Matsushita Electric Trading had to suspend operations for a while by order of the occupation authorities. Moreover, because Matsushita Electric Industrial had mistakenly been categorized as a *zaibatsu* and therefore targeted for dissolution, we were made to become an independent firm, entirely separate from our parent company.
>
> Eventually, and under strict economic guidelines, the occupation authorities allowed the private sector to resume overseas trading activities. Since we no longer had any connection to our parent company, we had no choice but to stop dealing in the electrical appliances which we, as a trading company, had specialized in, and, instead, had to try our hand at selling products we knew nothing about.[9]

According to historian John Dower, *zaibatsu* (財閥) were "gigantic financial and industrial oligopolies that dominated the presurrender economy."[10] Allied occupation authorities attempted to dissolve *zaibatsu* such as Mitsubishi, Mitsui, and Sumitomo as part of an anti-trust drive to increase competition within the economy. The campaign was also an attempt to weaken big businesses that were perceived to have colluded with militarism. As a result, Matsushita was listed as a *zaibatsu*, and Matsushita Electric Trading was made to leave the group for nearly five years, starting in December 1946.[11]

Matsushita Electric Trading had by necessity started dealing in commodities such as rubber, leather, and oil, the market value of which tended to fluctuate wildly. Inevitably, as prices crashed and business partners went bankrupt, the trading firm's bottom line suffered. The occupation authorities eventually reversed their decision on Matsushita, and by May 1949, Matsushita Electric Trading was free to rejoin the Matsushita group. And yet, the poor financial standing of the group initially prevented it from doing so. By the spring of 1951, at a time when Matsushita Trading was at its lowest ebb, the Korean Peninsula was at war. And while the provisioning of Allied forces during the Korean War jump-started the postwar Japanese economy, during the first year of the war, Matsushita Trading was on the brink of bankruptcy.[12]

In August 1951, Konosuke Matsushita, the founder of the recovering manufacturing giant, stepped in. He agreed to take care of the enormous debt that Matsushita Electric Trading had accumulated. Thus, it was able to renew its ties with its parent company, Matsushita Electric Industrial, and set about rebuilding its business.[13] The National product line for export, however, was fairly limited at the time, and Japanese staff did not possess the know-how to effectively promote National's products overseas. Therefore, the company relied on the local market knowledge of its agents in Hong Kong, Singapore, and Thailand to sell its products.[14] In Hong Kong, Matsushita Electric's business transactions with Mong initially consisted of shipments of umbrellas, sports shoes, and imitation pearl handbags.

Thirty Vacuum Tube Radios

The first National branded and manufactured items that Mong imported into the territory were vacuum tube- or valve-type radios. This was well before the age of the mass-produced transistor radio that elevated the status of goods made in Japan. It is hard to imagine going anywhere in the world today and not, at some point, coming into contact with a famous Japanese brand: Sony, Canon, or Toyota, to name a few. But, in the wake of the Allied occupation, not a single passenger car was being manufactured in Japan, and Japanese radios, the country's most popular electrical devices, were neither sophisticated nor affordable. Radios were considered a luxury item in Japan, one that, for example, a Japanese university graduate on a starting salary of ¥7,000 to ¥8,000 a month could not afford. Making radios that people could afford became the first priority of National's headquarters in Osaka.

Most Japanese households typically owned one radio, whose wooden frame was so bulky that it could actually be considered a piece of furniture. National's plan was therefore to produce a reasonably priced radio that families would buy as a second set for their homes. The Japanese government had in 1951 issued broadcasting licenses to sixteen new commercial radio stations in fourteen cities; these were in addition to Japan's existing public broadcaster, NHK.[15] Now that most urban households had two or three stations to choose from, National launched its 1952 advertising campaign promoting the purchase of a second set:

> A Second Radio for Your Home!
>
> Commercial broadcasters are now in operation. You may want to try more than one program. How about a second radio for your home? In the United States, most households already own a second set.
>
> HS- 700 model. 12,300 yen.
>
> National Radio[16]

In Japan's electric appliance stores, a new manufacturer, Sanyo, was at the time causing a sensation with its radio, sporting plastic, as opposed to wooden, casing and priced at ¥8,950, over twenty-five percent lower than the price of National's conventional model.

Sanyo was founded in 1947 by Konosuke Matsushita's brother-in-law, Toshio Iue. Iue was a former National executive whom the Allied occupation headquarters had forced to resign from Matsushita in 1946. The Matsushita managers, who had always looked down on Sanyo as second-rate, were caught off guard when it came up with its popular plastic radio, Japan's first, and realized that they could no longer rest on their laurels.[17] National started manufacturing plastic radios that were affordable, portable, and fashionable. As a result, National's 1952 ad copy "A Second Radio for Your Home!" became "A Radio for Each Room" just two years later.

As the domestic market continued to expand, National took the initiative to start exploring the export business. In September 1954, Matsushita Electric Trading's

Managing Director, Takayoshi Yamamoto, set off on a market research exercise around Southeast Asia, taking with him a single white portable radio as a sample. The PL-420, a vacuum tube-type radio, was National's star product. It was battery operated, making it possible for the copy of a Japanese print advertisement featuring the rising film star Ayako Wakao to proudly boast: "Wherever you go for fun, your portable radio can go with you."[18] A plastic radio that could be carried around like a handbag, versus one that resembled a piece of furniture plugged into the wall, was truly groundbreaking.

Yamamoto made Hong Kong the first stop of his Southeast Asian tour. As soon as Mong saw the PL-420, he grabbed it and rushed off to show it to potential retailers so that he could start taking orders for it. Yamamoto never got it back. Overseas business trips were rare in 1954, so rare that Yamamoto's trip later got a mention in Matsushita's corporate history. Foreign currency was in short supply, and travel allowances were purposely kept at a minimum. The National brand was virtually unknown outside Japan, and yet Yamamoto had to continue his travels through the region without even a sample to assist him in his negotiations.[19] As a result of this market research exercise, however, Yamamoto discovered that battery-powered radios were in great demand in Southeast Asia, and that, despite protectionist trade policies, it was relatively easy to obtain permission from Southeast Asian governments to import radios and batteries from Japan.[20]

Mong immediately ordered thirty of the PL-420 model for sale in Hong Kong. For Matsushita Electric Trading this was not only a large order but also something of an adventure. The newly appointed director of the factory that manufactured the PL-420 radio was 37-year-old Keiichi Takeoka, a highflyer who went on to become president of Matsushita's subsidiary in the United States. He desperately wanted the export of National products to be a success. With regard to Mong's order for thirty radios, however, Matsushita Trading executives proceeded to pour cold water on Takeoka's aspirations:

> "These exports are an experiment," they told us. Well, that was another way of saying they had no idea if they would sell. Of course, we were trying to export to the United States as well at that time. And we had sold some radios in Southeast Asia too. But we were passionate about exploring the export business, so it was discouraging to hear that they considered this a mere experiment.[21]

Mong recalls that the import cost of the PL-420 was HK$78, while the wholesale price was HK$95, "so the profit margin was very small."[22] The HK$17 profit on a single radio represented two or three days' wages for a skilled artisan, or not quite half a month's wages for an inexperienced factory line-worker.[23]

Nevertheless, Mong was made to work hard for that "very small profit." In 1954, audio products were usually referred to as "wireless (無線)" and often sold by specialist retailers, much as computers are today. Mong did the rounds of the wireless and electrical appliance shops located in Central on Hong Kong Island, and on Nathan Road in Kowloon. But their shelves were crammed with top-quality radios imported from the West. A Matsushita Electric Trading Fiftieth Anniversary commemorative book describes the market position occupied by National brand radios at that time, relative to those of its main competitors, as follows:

> In 1954 the market for radios was dominated by the leading European and American electrical goods manufacturers — Philips, Grundig, Telefunken, GE and Emerson. This was the case not only in the advanced industrialized nations of Europe and North America, but even in developing countries. Just by looking at the various companies' product catalogues, one could tell that Japanese manufactured goods were not competitive.
>
> Design too needed to be completely revamped… Matsushita therefore purchased radios from the leading European and American manufacturers of the time, pulled them apart and studied them. We then went about developing new models, adding our own design touches.[24]

The free port of Hong Kong was a showcase for these top-quality Western radios, to the detriment of Japanese models. Selling National brand radios, a company whose name recognition was close to zero in the territory, was therefore no easy task. Japanese manufacturers in general had yet to shake off their prewar image of producing only low-quality gadgets that would break down after just half a day's use. It was another three years before the debut of the transistor radio, an event that would elevate the "Made in Japan" label to a mark of quality.

Moreover, anti-Japanese sentiment in Hong Kong was still strong. A store owner to whom Mong showed a vacuum tube-type radio responded to his sales pitch with: "Jap goods? Can't you even wait until the blood's dry?!"[25] Unflattering comments, such as "What the hell is this?" or "Can I really get a sound out of a Jap radio?" were steadily being relayed to the Matsushita Trading office in Osaka.[26] Time and again, Mong emphasized that the National radio was value for money and managed to persuade a retailer to take on one or two sets.

Mong and his associates considered at length the means by which they could get National radios to crack the Hong Kong market. A Chinese character equivalent of the National brand name was essential. Coca-Cola (可口可樂) had come up with a clever one, a four-character version meaning "tastes delicious." What should the characters for National be? Mong and his staff racked their brains. Finally, they came up with "Lok Seng Pai (樂聲牌)." "Lok Seng" means "enjoyable sound."

> We chose the characters partly because the only National product I was selling at the time was a radio. We chose "Lok Seng" to emphasize the clarity of the sound, and how pleasurable it is to listen to. It also sounded a bit like "National."[27]

Thanks to the Cantonese tendency to pronounce the letter *n* as *l*, the English "National" became "Loshonal," from which Mong then got "Lok Seng" and to which he added the "Pai," meaning *brand* in Chinese.

No one imagined then that, over the course of the next fifty years, Lok Seng Pai would grow into a major brand, recognized not just in Hong Kong but also in southern China and in Chinese diasporas all over the world.

A National delivery van parked outside a store
in Shanghai Street, Kowloon, 1956.
Photo by Kiyoshi Nakane

The Handshake with Matsushita's Founder

In late 1955, having successfully disposed of the thirty plastic radios, William Mong was given the rare opportunity of an audience with Konosuke Matsushita, the founder and then-president of Matsushita Electric Industrial.[28] According to Mong's recollections, the purpose of this meeting was to discuss the possibility of Shun Hing Hong becoming the sole agent for National products in Hong Kong, something that had been discussed repeatedly with Matsushita Electric Industrial's subsidiary, Matsushita Trading. For Mong, this meeting was to decide the fate of his company.

> Matsushita Electric Trading had already said they'd like to hand things over to me. I said to them, "If Matsushita deals with other [import companies] in Hong Kong, I have no incentive to stay with you." But though they wanted to make me sole agent, they couldn't give me the final yes, because it was Matsushita Electric Industrial that produced the goods.[29]

In other words, Konosuke Matsushita's seal of approval was necessary.

A 1962 *Time* magazine article called the Matsushita president, "the Henry Ford of Japan's appliance industry."[30] In Japan, he was the highest income earner, thus the "No. 1 taxpayer" and revered as a virtual "god of corporate management (*keiei no kami-sama*)." He had started as an apprentice bicycle repairman and made his way to the top, founding Matsushita Electric in 1918.

By 1949, he was overseeing an electrical appliance empire that employed 1,500 people. When Matsushita was listed as a *zaibatsu* during the Allied occupation, however, the number of staff fell to a quarter of the group's original personnel. This dark period in the company's history was described, not without some humor, by Matsushita in his memoirs, as a time when "the firm's debts were a billion yen, and I became for a while Japan's No.1 tax defaulter."[31] The news of the tycoon's tax woes was reported on the radio and in newspapers nationwide. This was indeed a time of hardship for Konosuke Matsushita: despite being the master of a mansion so fine that it had its own tea ceremony room, he had to go without many basic daily necessities during the occupation.[32]

The day Matsushita Trading's Managing Director, Tsuneo Jinnai, accompanied Mong to the Matsushita Head Office in Kadoma, a peaceful suburb of Osaka, for his meeting with Konosuke came just three years after the end of the American occupation. Mong recalls,

> "Konosuke-san's office at the time was in a two-storey building, a really old building."[33]

The office was unexpectedly small, and when Mong sat down on the sofa in the reception room, a small cloud of dust arose from the cushions. Jinnai first explained to the president what Mong had accomplished in Hong Kong, selling thirty National radios, and then it was Mong's turn to speak. He spoke in Japanese, without an interpreter:

> I said I would do everything in my power to sell his company's products.
>
> At the end of my little speech, Konosuke-san said to me, "Fine Japanese you speak." And so I told him how I'd taken six months to complete the six-year Japanese primary school curriculum in Japan, and spent two years living with a friend of my father in Tokyo.
>
> Konosuke-san said, "I admire you." He had left school after primary two or three himself. Then he said, "We've both been through a lot, haven't we?"[34]

At the end of this exchange, Mong appealed to Matsushita, who, at almost sixty, was older than Mong's own father, by saying: "I really want to handle National products."

By the time this meeting took place, managers in Matsushita's Radio Division had already been involved in numerous business discussions with Mong, who was several years their junior. Their recollections of him are telling:

> Mong-san can speak Japanese, right? That made me feel very close to him, especially since I don't speak English at all. It made me feel we have to do something for this guy.
>
> Wow, he was young. Yet I felt he really knew his business, and worked so hard at it. He really knew the market, how it would respond to new products.
>
> He was truly a tough negotiator, because he'd come along having checked out all the facts. He was simply amazing. I thought: I'd better be certain of any move I make and be fully prepared when I meet with him.
>
> In a nutshell, it's all down to the blood in his veins, the blood of those overseas Chinese traders. He doesn't miss a trick when he's counting the pennies. And he can twist people around his little finger. He was always willing to welcome and

entertain guests with fabulous food and wine. We Japanese are no match for him in this area.[35]

Mong made his determination to handle the Japanese company's products clear. To which Matsushita, speaking in the Osaka dialect, responded, "Got any cash?"

> I told him, "I have no money."
>
> Then he said, "Neither do we. I suppose you know that? When Japan lost the war, the occupation army gave us a hard time. So, well, I'll give you exclusive sales rights, and you must work very hard to deserve them."
>
> I said, "If you don't give me the exclusive sales rights for good, I'll have problems later on."
>
> So then he said, "Fine. We don't need a contract. Mong-san, I trust you. Do you trust me?"
>
> "Of course, and I will go on doing so," I replied.
>
> With that, we shook hands. "We don't need a contract." And based on this one mark of trust, we've been doing business for fifty years.[36]

As far as Mong remembers, this is the sequence of events that led to Konosuke Matsushita making the 27-year-old sole agent for National products in Hong Kong and Macau.

Over half a century has passed since Mong and Matsushita's handshake in Osaka, and as yet there have been no documents exchanged between the two companies setting out the terms of their business relationship. In this absence of a formal written contract, Shun Hing is unique among Matsushita's agents worldwide.

Maybe it was a case of Mong being in the right place at the right time; it was definitely a case of Matsushita Electric not having the know-how to effectively market its goods overseas. This may well be why they put their entire Hong Kong business in the hands of a Chinese entrepreneur. Whatever the reason, this handshake inspired Shun Hing Hong's employees with exceptional loyalty, and they energetically set about promoting the National brand in the city and beyond.

Of course, Shun Hing's dedicated and highly creative sales efforts meant that, from the beginning, National's Japanese salarymen were facing an uphill battle to satisfy their Hong Kong agent's demands. For them the handshake turned out to be a preamble to "mission impossible."

Words into Action

Once Shun Hing Hong had become Matsushita's sole agent, Mong's friends began suggesting it might be time for him to marry and settle down. But Mong recalls,

> "I didn't have anyone in particular in mind. And, well, I really had no experience of romance either."[37]

One day, in 1954, Mong's older brother, Jeffery, came to him and announced that he had found the perfect girl for him in Kobe, Japan. She was the daughter of a successful Chinese businessman who had long been involved in the import and export business. A friend of Mong's father agreed to make the introductions.

Serena Yang Hsueh-chi lived in a Victorian mansion located at the top of the hill, where most of Kobe's wealthiest Western expatriates had their residences. At a time when the majority of the country was struggling to rebuild itself after the devastation wrought by World War II, Serena was living the high life, spending her days horseback riding and courted by her admirers. Her friends talked her into dating Mong and, while still a student at Kwansei Gakuin University, she eventually became engaged to him.

After graduation, at the behest of Mong and his father, Serena went to work for Matsushita Electric Trading in Osaka. They both encouraged her to learn as much as she could about the way Japanese business works and to build up her network of contacts before going to Hong Kong. It was extremely rare in those days for a major Japanese corporation to hire an ethnic Chinese employee.

One day, during their engagement, Mong told Serena, "As soon as I have sold ten thousand radios, I'll marry you." The director of Matsushita's radio factory, Keiichi Takeoka, was left to ponder how on earth Mong had come up with such a figure:

> "That was an enormous figure—impossible to achieve if you were just thinking of the Hong Kong market."[38]

The total number of National radios exported from Japan to the rest of the world in 1956 amounted to no more than 42,000. In addition, in the mid-fifties, National was still considered a second-class brand in Hong Kong. Undeterred, Mong rented a giant advertising billboard in Mongkok (旺角), Kowloon's busiest shopping district. The ad featured a Japanese actress, sporting the cropped, tight pants made popular by Audrey Hepburn in the film *Sabrina* and carrying a portable radio on her arm as if it were a handbag. The advertising slogan made it clear that the National radio was value for money:

NOW YOU CAN AFFORD A SUPER RADIO
NATIONAL RADIO[39]

There was absolutely no guarantee that an item that had become a hit in Japan would perform well in Hong Kong, no matter how affordable it was. Mong wanted to import products that would appeal to Hong Kong people and cater to their domestic needs. He wasted no time in starting to gather his own market intelligence. Following the delivery of his products to his business partners, he never failed to visit them and to take note of their comments and reactions.

Whenever he visited Japan, the first thing he did after his plane had landed at Tokyo's Haneda Airport was to walk through the streets of the Akihabara (秋葉原) electrical appliance district, checking out the latest offerings of National's main competitors. Only then would he make his way down to the company's Radio Division in Osaka. "I was

"Now you can afford a super radio." Shun Hing promotes the
handheld National radio in Mongkok, Kowloon, 1956.
Photo by Kiyoshi Nakane

really impressed by his zeal; at the same time, it scared you," recalled the Division's
Product Planning Department head at the time, Kiyoshi Nakane.[40]

Although the Radio Division's managers were now looking at exporting their
products to various overseas markets, the export volume was initially not large enough
for Matsushita to cast a new metal pattern mold and open a new production line. The
Asian model was therefore produced using the same mold as the domestic model but
with the addition of a voltage converter and some add-ons to enhance its look. For
example, if a dial on a Japanese radio was plain black, Mong would suggest adding gold
trim around it to give it a little Chinese flair.

National's DX-350 radio was a big hit in Japan at the time. It was sleek, with a
brown plastic latticework pattern over the speaker, and no National radio had ever had
a better sound quality. It had even won a special award for industrial design from one
of Japan's largest newspapers, *Mainichi Shimbun* (每日新聞). Mong was fully aware of
these facts before going into one of his regular meetings with the National radio factory
executives. He insisted that he needed a spin-off of the model for Hong Kong so as to be
able to promote the radio as an award-winning product from Japan.

There was another issue on which Mong refused to budge, and it had to do with
a radio tuning device that was quite popular in Asia in the 1950s called the "magic
eye." The magic eye was a small, round tube that was fitted to the front panel of large
radios. Traditionally, tuning had been an audio process: one searched for the best signal
by adjusting the dial while listening to the radio. The magic eye, however, turned this
process into a visual as well as an audio one. It contained two needles that aligned
whenever a listener had tuned into a radio station at the point of its greatest signal
strength, thus serving as a visual confirmation that the listener should be getting the
clearest sound. Mong was quick to notice the potential value of this device.

Mong asked the Radio Division to affix this magic eye to the relatively small DX-350, because he was convinced that Hong Kong consumers would be more inclined to purchase a deluxe appliance with lots of accessories. Unfortunately, attaching a magic eye to the DX-350 proved to be a real challenge. A large section of the radio's front panel was covered in latticework, making it extremely difficult to carve out a round hole, even using a sharp knife. In addition, the voltage in Hong Kong was twice as high as that in Japan, thereby necessitating the mounting of a voltage converter close to sensitive parts inside the radio's body. The chunky converter could easily damage the sleek plastic body. The National engineers seriously doubted whether the radio would make it to Hong Kong in one piece:

> "We had a hard time, but we were made to go through with it."[41]

In these situations, the Hong Kong entrepreneur rarely relented until he got complete agreement from the Japanese side, and even then he would return to make sure that his requests were being acted upon. Technical engineer Hisashi Kusugami manufactured several radios for the Hong Kong market and can attest to Mong's zeal, and sometimes obsessiveness, in dealing with these details:

> Any number of times he'd double and triple check. I said, "Okay, got it; we'll do it."
>
> Next day there'd be another meeting. "What we discussed yesterday, it's okay, right?" he would say. "You'll do it, right? Delivery date's so-and-so. You've got that?" "Got it. We'll do it." That's how all our conversations with him would go.
>
> Then before he flew back to Hong Kong, I'd go and give him an update. "Those changes—I'm counting on you, you understand, right?" he would say.
>
> Well, I could understand that he really cared about his business. Still, I sometimes wondered: Doesn't he trust us even a little? (Laugh)[42]

The weeks leading up to the Chinese Lunar New Year, which traditionally falls between mid-January and mid-February, were a peak season for sales in Hong Kong, and, if goods were to be ready on time, made for an extremely busy August at the Matsushita factories. Instead of looking forward to the week-long *Obon* holiday when Japanese people traditionally travel back to their hometown to honor their ancestors, Hisashi Kusugami and his colleagues had to contend with a flood of orders from Hong Kong.

Some at Matsushita complained that Mong was arrogant, stubborn, and out of control. But once the goods he had ordered were delivered to him, Mong never failed to sell every one of them, and never returned a single unsold item to Japan. Whether they liked it or not, the Matsushita men were learning to adapt their products for the Hong Kong market.

The year 1957 saw the dawning of a new era for National, with the shipment of their first transistor radios. Two years previously, a small business venture, Tokyo Tsushin Kogyo K.K., now better known as Sony, had launched Japan's first commercially produced transistor radio. Matsushita, however, still lacked the technology needed to manufacture the transistor at the heart of the device. The director of Matsushita's radio factory, Keiichi Takeoka, was faced with a dilemma:

> "We had no choice, so we went and bought the technology from Sony."[43]

In Takeoka's view, acquiring the transistor from a major competitor was the only way Matsushita would be able to start manufacturing a transistor radio model. He went so far as to consult Konosuke Matsushita on the issue. Surprisingly, Matsushita strongly encouraged Takeoka to "go for it," saying that, as far as he was concerned, National could purchase parts from anywhere in the world—provided the quality was good and the price low.

Armed with the borrowed technology, National set about manufacturing its own "super radios." Matsushita Electric was known for its ability to not only develop user-friendly products but also replicate its competitors' latest hits. Playing on the company's name, some joked it should be changed to "Maneshita," or copycat. As the following exchange, related by one of Sony's two founders, Akio Morita, goes to show, Konosuke Matsushita was rather open about the practice:

> Once I had a conversation with Mr Matsushita, and he joked, "Yes, we have this laboratory in Tokyo. It's called Sony, ha ha ha! Any time we come across an interesting new item made by Sony, we use their good idea as a starting point for our own."[44]

Matsushita's founder was greatly admired for his entrepreneurial spirit. And, unlike many Japanese conglomerates, the company did train and encourage some of its senior staff to think like entrepreneurs. Yet even they have had cause to marvel at the business acumen shown by William Mong.

On to Southeast Asia

National radios began turning up in the most unexpected places. Since they were battery-powered, they could be used in even the most remote corners of Hong Kong. They were considered priceless possessions by residents living in districts not yet connected to the city's electricity grid, as well as by Hong Kong's sizeable boat-dwelling population. Since voltage was not a problem, they made good souvenirs for foreign tourists visiting the colony. And since the radios were portable, they were a popular item for re-export, making their way through unofficial channels from Hong Kong to retail stores in neighboring Asian countries, such as the Philippines and Indonesia.

Mong takes members of Matsushita's first "radio fact-finding
expedition" to meet shop owners in Kowloon, 1956.
Photo by Kiyoshi Nakane

In 1956, a full year prior to the launch of National's own transistor radio model,
the then-executive in charge of new product development, Kiyoshi Nakane, took
part in Matsushita's first ever "radio fact-finding expedition" and spent almost three
months traveling through Asia, stopping over in Hong Kong, Saigon, Phnom Penh,
Bangkok, Calcutta, Bombay, Madras, Colombo, Singapore, Kuala Lumpur, and Manila.
Everywhere they went, the National team would make a record of the number of local
radio stations, specific voltage requirements, and design preferences. Their ambition was
to manufacture radio sets that would appeal to each country's local market.

One day, while busy taking notes in one of Manila's many electrical appliance
shops, Nakane suddenly found himself staring across the counter at a National radio.

> There were National products for sale in Manila. "That's strange," I thought.[45]

Matsushita was unable to export National radios to the Philippines at the time, as its
government kept a tight control on international trade, in order to avoid the outflow of
foreign currency. So what was a National brand radio doing in Manila? Nakane started
making inquiries and soon found out that the radio had originally been imported into
Hong Kong. It was "knocked down" in Hong Kong, entered the Philippines in pieces,
and re-emerged as a National radio after factory reassembly.

> We had no idea this was going on. We had always wondered why we were
> receiving so many orders for radios from Hong Kong, when it was such a small
> market, but that was the explanation.
>
> Then we thought: Well, we should make good use of this route.[46]

Back then, in the late 1950s, market leader Sony was busy concentrating its sales efforts
on the United States and not paying much attention to what was going on in Hong Kong

or other Southeast Asian markets. Mong, however, had been taking advantage of the vast Chinese transnational networks that extended throughout Southeast Asia to expand his sales reach and increase National's market presence. It was thanks to this strategy that, in 1958, four years after announcing his engagement to Serena Yang, Mong reached his self-imposed sales target of 10,000 radio sets.

Keiichi Takeoka, who went on to become president of Matsushita Electric Corporation of America, recalled that doing business with Mong was a brisk affair. Whenever a new product was launched, Mong would provide quick feedback and immediately start developing a market for it. Through Mong's efforts in Hong Kong, Matsushita was able to gain a strong sense of whether or not its new products would work in its overseas markets; the city was therefore an ideal test market for Matsushita.

> When we first exported our radios to Hong Kong, we felt absolutely confident of
> our success, before anywhere else. Mong-san appreciated our confidence in him,
> and expanded the business further and further for us.[47]

As soon as Mong had fulfilled his pledge of selling 10,000 radios, he asked Serena Yang to come to Hong Kong so that they could be married. On a cold winter's day, Serena's family, friends, and colleagues, including Keiichi Takeoka, went down to the Kobe docks to see her off. The bride boarded a Dutch passenger ship and left Mount Rokko behind her. As the boat left its moorings, she stood on deck, waving goodbye and clutching in her hand one end of a brightly colored streamer that she had flung over the side of the departing ship. Her mother, draped in a long fur coat, clasped the other end tightly against her breast, as if she never wanted to let it go.

"You're in for it Now"

In 1959, radios made up sixty-seven percent of Matsushita Electric's total exports, and National was looking to diversify the range of its products for overseas export.[48] It was around this time that Mong began importing National brand automatic rice cookers and electric fans. This product diversification meant that Mong and his company now had to deal with a number of separate factories, all located in different sectors of the Osaka suburbs. For the first time, Matsushita Electric Trading assigned a specific employee to coordinate negotiations between Mong and the various product divisions.

The original Matsushita staff member assigned to look after the Hong Kong account was 27-year-old Junichi Ukita, whose unruly hairstyle would prompt Mong to jokingly state that he looked "like Beethoven" and cart him off to one of the barbers involved in his rice cooker demonstrations (Chapter 1). According to Ukita, he received a lot of sympathy from his colleagues for being assigned to look after Mong who, despite being one of the most important customers for Matsushita Trading, was already well-known for his propensity to micro-manage every aspect of his dealings with the Osaka factories:

> I was suddenly called in by Mr Mamoru Matsumoto, the head of the Export
> Division. I was wondering what the problem was, and then he says to me, "you're
> in charge of Hong Kong, starting tomorrow. Mong-san's coming."
>
> Well, I've really been landed in it now, I thought.
>
> Of course, since my colleagues were off the hook, they came out with all sorts of
> stuff, "You're in for it now!" and so on, trying to scare me.[49]

Prior to his appointment, Ukita had been in charge of the export of "dynamo lamps"
for bicycles. He knew nothing about transistor radios, yet they were the main purpose
of Mong's visit to Osaka, and he was arriving the very next day. Ukita had no choice
but to get hold of a copy of the National radio catalogue and start cramming model
specifications and item numbers on the Hankyu commuter train home.

> I had no choice but to memorize the whole catalogue, and I managed to do that to
> some extent on the train. But you can't memorize model after model all at once,
> right? As it turned out, Mong-san seemed to understand the situation, resigned
> himself to my total ignorance, and taught me every little thing I needed to know.
>
> Mind you, I really couldn't even begin to aspire to Mong-san's incredible level
> of product knowledge. I mean, he made it his job to know everything about
> everything, since even a small detail could affect his own bottom line.
>
> After all, I was just the new guy in charge, right?[50]

Mong's head was already full of National product information, and he made sure he kept
abreast of any new developments, since ultimately it was the future of his own company
that was at stake. His firm's profits were in direct proportion to the amount of effort he
put into conducting his business. And since he was self-employed, there was no chance
that he might be transferred to another division. Therefore, his understanding of National
products and their market potential for Hong Kong was unparalleled.

Mong's knowledge is so extensive that, even fifty years later, he can still recall
hundreds of National product model numbers and specifications. As Ukita's former
colleague Shoichiro Koyama observed:

> "He knows the National product range better than any Matsushita Trading staff
> member who has been assigned to look after the Hong Kong market in the last
> fifty years, I'm sorry to say."[51]

Mong was also extraordinarily good with figures. Anecdotes of how "Mong-san would
haggle over a single yen" during price negotiations were recounted by several Matsushita
sources. In the days before pocket calculators, the Matsushita representatives would
have to prepare extremely carefully to avoid being cut to pieces during their financial
dealings with the Hong Kong entrepreneur.

Shuzo Imamura, the head of the Radio Division's Technical Department, would go
into negotiations with Mong, armed with formulae and charts that took into consideration
the gross margin and exchange rate. With the assistance of these formidable tools,

Imamura could ask what the retail price for a specific item would be in Hong Kong dollars and then immediately work out the wholesale price.

> We would ask, "How much will this sell for?" and then he would say, "Well, about this much." Then we would reverse the calculation. Because we had our formulae, we could work out at once roughly what the margin would be.

> The negotiations went on until sunset. Yes, he certainly was persistent; there's no doubt about it.[52]

Mong visits the Matsushita radio factory in Osaka to source
new products for the Hong Kong market, 1959.
Courtesy of Junichi Ukita

If the Matsushita men tried suggesting that he should be able to ask for a higher retail price in Hong Kong, Mong would switch tack:

> "Tell me, gentlemen, where do your watches come from?"

The Matsushita senior executives looked down at their wrists, each and every one of them sporting either an Omega or a Rolex.

> "Where did you buy them? In Hong Kong, right? Why did you buy them there? Shall I tell you why, gentlemen? It's because in Hong Kong, you can buy the world's best brands at low prices, isn't that right? National products may be among the world's best, but when they are offered for sale in Hong Kong, people expect to be able to buy them at a lower price than anywhere else."[53]

Junichi Ukita, Matsushita Electric Trading's staff member in charge of Hong Kong exports, accompanied Mong to his price negotiation sessions with the different factories. He often had cause to sigh at Mong's unrelenting negotiating style:

> Well, Mong-san was so dedicated. For those of us who are salarymen, when we felt we had done our part, we tended to take it easy. But for him, it's his own

business that's at stake, and what's more, he's just incredibly passionate about his work.

For example, on price. When he was pressing for the price of an item to be reduced from 100 yen to 95 yen, as an intermediary between the Matsushita factories and Shun Hing, I would think that 100 yen was already a good bargain and that he should accept it. But for Mong-san, since he's factoring in costs and prices in Hong Kong, only he knows what he can and can't accept.

He's like that when he calls you, he's like that when he meets you, he's always thinking about the bottom line.[54]

Woe betide anyone who made a business trip to Hong Kong, enjoyed the Mongs' warm hospitality, and rashly promised an order. Hisashi Kusugami was one of many Matsushita employees to be overcome by Mong and his wife's attentiveness as hosts. Kusugami spent a sweltering summer day with Mong, making the rounds of Hong Kong's many radio retailers. Every time that, drenched in sweat, he would enter a shop, the shopkeeper would offer him an ice-cold Coca Cola, which he could not refuse.[55] Then it would be back into the scorching heat, and on to another store and another ice-cold Coca Cola. By the end of the day, Kusugami's stomach felt like it was going to explode. Back at his hotel, he spent a painful, uncomfortable night, only to be awoken the next morning by the delivery to his room of a bowl of *okayu*, the rice congee that is the perfect palliative to an upset stomach. Recalls Kusugami,

"Mrs Mong had made me some rice congee for breakfast, and she sent *umeboshi* pickled plums too. It was such a treat, I was so grateful."[56]

The Mongs made sure that the congee was cooked in the Japanese- rather than Cantonese-style, and sent it over with it the perfect accompanying condiments from Japan.

In those days, Hong Kong did not have any Japanese restaurants, so Matsushita executives who found Chinese food too exotic for their taste would be treated to homemade lunchboxes with Japanese-style fish cooked in broth.

Even visitors arriving at Kai Tak Airport at 11:00 at night would be greeted in the arrivals hall and whisked off to a banquet prepared in their honor. Mong would immediately make a mental note of any dish pronounced "delicious" by a Matsushita executive and, be it abalone, snake soup, or thousand-year-old eggs, that same dish would be brought to the table on the next visit. This was fine hospitality indeed.

Overcome by gratitude, the Matsushita man would return to Osaka having agreed to an impossible order, only to see the production manager turn pale at the news. Sheepish retractions would result in vigorous complaints from Mong: "You were happy to okay it then. What's the problem now?"[57]

Thinking Outside the Box

Mong liked to speak his mind. Even the Japanese wording of a telegram could become a point of contention. Mong traveled to Osaka every other month to purchase products. During his stay, he would often need to send telegrams to his wife, who ran Shun Hing Hong in his absence. Matsushita's staff would draft them in Japanese, and the text then had to be typed up using the Roman alphabet, just like Chinese *pinyin*; each telegram could contain no more than twenty-one letters. Whenever Ukita assisted with the drafting of the telegrams, he had the unpleasant experience of having to listen to the Chinese-born Mong criticize his Japanese composition:

> He'd say things like, "This Japanese wording of yours is wrong! This is the right phrase," and we would argue bitterly on the street.

> I got upset so I told him: "Stop telling me what to do. I'm a Matsushita employee and I don't work for your Shun Hing!"

> Then he would lecture me: "You salarymen can't think outside the box!"[58]

"You salarymen can't think outside the box!" was a reproach Mong often directed at the Matsushita Electric Trading employees assigned to look after the Hong Kong market. Why do you blindly trust in common sense? Why can't you use your own judgment? Why don't you improve this product? Why can't it be cheaper? Why do you make compromises? "Thinking outside the box" was the cornerstone of Mong's entrepreneurial spirit. And according to many of the Matsushita men who worked closely with Mong, of all the things he would say to them, this was the criticism that got to them the most.

> "Yes, I am a salaryman, right?"[59]

Ukita would respond angrily to Mong's accusations. However, fifty years on, Ukita maintains that he learned a lot from working with Mong. After his stint looking after Hong Kong, he was put in charge of Matsushita's subsidiary in Thailand before eventually taking over a 400-employee Matsushita affiliate in Australia. Faced with unfamiliar situations, he would often find himself thinking: If Mong-san were in my shoes, what would he do?

> Don't impose the Japanese headquarters' way of doing things in overseas markets; find out what the local way of doing things is. After all, local people know what is right for their market. This is the lesson I learned from him.[60]

Salarymen often made the mistake of blindly implementing strategies devised by a group of executives at their headquarters in Japan, and failed to secure the confidence and commitment of the local agent or affiliates. The Japanese "box," however, was not necessarily the best fit for international markets. Ukita learned that ideas that would have never occurred or would have seemed impractical to Japanese executives mattered greatly if one wanted to break into overseas markets. Mong's browbeating of the Matsushita factories into manufacturing specific models for export was the perfect illustration of this: many of the products he helped develop turned out to be huge hits in Asia and big money-spinners for the company.

> What it amounted to was more or less new product development. After all, different countries had different voltages. And even if the factories complained about it, once they finally agreed to go along with Mong-san's stringent specifications, the end product was more competitive, and good not just for Hong Kong but for other markets like Thailand and Singapore too.
>
> So once, convinced by Mong-san's passionate demands, we had struggled to fulfill his various requirements, we found our competitive edge sharpened. Sales in other markets also benefited. If sales were up, profits went up too. When all was said and done, we were grateful to Mong-san.[61]

Ukita spent four intense years working with Mong before being transferred to another post within Matsushita Electric Trading.

> "When it was time to move on, I felt relieved, but sad too—truly mixed feelings."[62]

4

Water Flows Downward
Hong Kong as a Gateway to Asia

National fans and refrigerators displayed in a Waterloo Road
shop window. Hong Kong, circa 1960.
Courtesy of Junichi Ukita

During the 1960s, just as William Mong's business was showing signs of rapid growth, Hong Kong's versatility began to play an increasingly important role in Matsushita's plans for market expansion. The city was a showcase for National appliances, providing the company with the exposure needed to attract the attention of international buyers and consumers. It was the test market for new export items such as refrigerators and washing machines, and a gateway to Southeast Asian markets that remained off-limits for political or economic reasons. A free port, whose favorable customs regulations enabled the easy flow of goods into and out of the city, Hong Kong became the Japanese manufacturer's strategic base at a time when protectionist trade policies were the norm in many other parts of the world.

Sometime in 1960, an unexpected call came through to the office of Matsushita Electric Trading in Tenjin-bashi (天神橋), Osaka. It was made by a European buyer who specialized in importing goods from Asia, and the reason for his call was to get more information about Matsushita's National line of products. Matsushita did not have an authorized dealer or any plans to promote its products in Europe at the time. European countries had their own excellent brands of radio, as well as protectionist trade policies, and Matsushita's executives were fully preoccupied with their efforts to break into the lucrative US market. Nevertheless, European buyers had spotted National products in Hong Kong's electrical appliance stores and wanted to know more.

Hong Kong was the gateway to Asia, and most of the flights and ships originating in Europe stopped over in the city on their way to Japan. Being a free port, the tiny colony had become a showcase for products from all over the world, and international buyers were always on the lookout for the next big thing. Among the familiar European and American brand appliances, the National radios, irons, electric fans, vacuum cleaners, and rice cookers caught the eye of the European dealers. They took a closer look at this Japanese "newcomer" to the market's products and were impressed with what they saw; besides, they were more affordable than their European counterparts. After arriving in Japan, they looked up National's phone number in the Yellow Pages. Among the buyers who contacted Matsushita Electric Trading were European agents of some of National's Japanese competitors, Hitachi and Sanyo.

Calls from European buyers interested in representing the firm kept coming into the Matsushita Electric Trading office in Osaka. Finally, in October 1960, Matsushita Electric Trading assigned two people to start up the company's European and African Section. National radios gradually started to gain in popularity in Switzerland, France, Italy, and Denmark, before "unofficially" making it over the border from West Germany into Poland and other countries in the Eastern Bloc. And this unpredicted global flow of the National brand was all due to its appliances being given exposure in Hong Kong's shop windows.

As its export business started to take off, Matsushita began publicizing its products in Japanese newspapers with the slogan "We Proudly Present Made in Japan."[1] The confidence levels at Matsushita Electric Trading improved dramatically after this transistor radio success, and the company was convinced that its latest products would sell well in the West.

In July 1962, Hong Kong became an even more prominent international showcase for National products. Shun Hing opened a National showroom—the first outside Japan—on the ground floor of Chungking Mansions (重慶大廈), a commercial building in the heart of Kowloon's Tsim Sha Tsui (尖沙咀) tourist and shopping district. Today, Chungking Mansions is a labyrinth of low-budget backpacker hostels, Indian and African eateries, money changers claiming to offer the best rates in town, and just outside the building, hawkers tempt gullible tourists with offers of "fake Rolex, fake Rolex" in the language of whichever country they believe them to be from. But in 1961, the year Chungking Mansions was built, it was a five-block, seventeen-storey, luxury apartment complex with ten elevators. National's showroom occupied the best location, facing Nathan Road. Over 1,000 guests, including Hong Kong's rich and famous, attended the opening ceremony.[2]

Sponsored feature commemorating the opening of
the National Showroom in Hong Kong's
Chungking Mansions.
(*Overseas Chinese Daily*, July 3, 1962)

Just a few blocks up the road, a sky-blue neon sign, Hong Kong's biggest, displaying the English "National" and Chinese "樂聲牌 (Lok Seng Pai)," lit up the nighttime sky, dazzling passers-by. Neon signs in Hong Kong have always been huge, but this one, at a height of twenty-nine meters (over ninety-five feet), was exceptionally so. Mong wanted to improve recognition of the National brand in Hong Kong, and the sign was so imposing that it could not be missed.

The reputation of Lok Seng Pai was on the rise in the city, to the extent that other Japanese brands striving to make an impact in Hong Kong attempted to make their Chinese name sound like National. The Japanese audio equipment manufacturer, Fujiya, for example, chose to market itself under the Chinese name, "Fu Seng Pai (富聲牌)." Shun Hing, the company Mong had started with three employees, now employed over eighty.

National's giant neon sign in Nathan Road in the 1960s.
Courtesy of Shun Hing Group

Konosuke Matsushita's "Three Sacred Treasures"

The creators of the National brand, Matsushita Electric, had become Japan's number one household appliance manufacturer. This was a time when the three most desirable home appliances—the washing machine, the black-and-white television, and the refrigerator—were referred to as the "Three Sacred Treasures," so named after the three items that constitute the Imperial Regalia of Japan: a copper mirror, a sword, and a jewel. Just as the Japanese crown prince has to be presented with these three sacred treasures to ascend to the Chrysanthemum throne, so a Japanese family had to own the expensive trio of washing machine, TV set, and refrigerator to join the middle classes or, at least, to feel like they had.[3] Theses appliances were in such great demand that a popular phrase in the industry was "Whatever we make, we sell! (*tsukureba ureru*)."

The royal wedding of the then-Crown Prince Akihito, now Emperor of Japan, and a non-royal, Michiko Shoda, on April 10, 1959, was the first media event of the Japanese TV age. Although her grandfather was a business tycoon and founder of the Nisshin Seifun Flour Milling Company, she was not of aristocratic birth and was the first commoner in modern history to marry into the Japanese imperial family. There was therefore a touch of the fairy tale about her story, and the public, especially women, could not get enough of it. More than half a million people lined the streets of Tokyo to cheer the royal couple, who rode first in a Victorian horse-drawn carriage, and then later in a Rolls Royce. The event dramatically boosted ownership of a television set, from just 10.4 percent of urban households in 1958 to 44.7 percent in 1960.[4] National was the sole sponsor of the nationwide live broadcast of the wedding, which ran for twelve hours, from 6:00 a.m. to 6:00 p.m., on the KRT network (today's TBS)[5]

National's founder, Konosuke Matsushita, was held up as the model of the successful Japanese industrialist, both in Japan and abroad; in 1961, he topped the list

of Japanese billionaires for the fifth time. In 1962, *Time* magazine featured an article entitled "Japan: Asia's First Consumer Market," and put Matsushita's portrait on the cover. The magazine praised him as the man who had brought electrical appliances to the masses, while at the same time slightly deriding him as having "the self-effacing look of an elderly, underpaid school teacher."

The article also asserted that Matsushita's exports were "helping to erase the old image of Japan as the producer of cheap junk." To illustrate this point, *Time* reported that National televisions, sold under the Panasonic brand in the United States, were available to buy at Macy's Department Store.

> In dramatic evidence of the changing international reputation of Japanese goods, New York's Macy's last week took full page newspaper ads to tout Matsushita's "world-wide reputation for finest quality, finest performance," and to boast that it had the U.S.'s first stock of his Panasonic portable television sets.
>
> (*Time*, February 23, 1962)[6]

This was a dream come true for the Japanese company's senior management.

In November 1963, Matsushita visited Hong Kong to attend Shun Hing's tenth anniversary celebrations. In honor of his visit, William Mong paid for the entire front page of the colony's best-selling Chinese-language newspaper, the *Overseas Chinese Daily*. The advertisement carried a photograph of Matsushita and the words: "Welcome to Hong Kong, Mr Konosuke Matsushita."

Shun Hing's official anniversary date was actually August 15, but Mong decided to postpone celebration of the company's tenth anniversary for three months, to November.

> Why did we postpone it for three months? Matsushita Konosuke-san was planning to come to Hong Kong to attend the celebration as were many other guests. Summer in Hong Kong is just too hot, so we decided to move the date of the anniversary to November 15.[7]

Mong did not hesitate to change his own company's anniversary date. He made the decision out of consideration for Matsushita, who was turning 69 that year.

Unfortunately, in 1963, southern China was hit by a serious drought, and this caused severe water shortages in Hong Kong, whose own water resources were limited. In order to deal with the crisis, the Hong Kong government introduced stringent rationing, and tap water was available for only four hours every four days.[8] As soon as the water came on, people would start storing it, using every household container they could get their hands on. Everywhere in the territory, people desperate for water waited in line with eighteen-liter (five gallon) cans.

Mong and his associates had a frantic time trying to ensure Matsushita would have enough water to meet his needs during his stay at the Miramar Hotel in Tsim Sha Tsui. But surprisingly, on the day Matsushita arrived in Hong Kong, the heavens opened and rain started pouring down on the city. As Japan Airlines flight 453 made its approach into Kai Tak Airport, already world-renowned as one of the most challenging in which

Mong greets Konosuke Matsushita and his wife at Kai Tak Airport.
November 14, 1963.
Courtesy of Shun Hing Group

From left to right: Mong's father, Kwok-ping; Arataro Takahashi
(Chairman of Matsushita Electric Trading); Konosuke Matsushita
and his wife, Mumeno; William Mong and his wife, Serena Yang.
Attending Shun Hing's 10th Anniversary celebrations.
Hong Kong, November 15, 1963.
Courtesy of Shun Hing Group

to land a plane, rain was falling so violently on the runway that many wondered if the plane would make it safely to the ground. It did, and press photographers greeted the "international billionaire" with a storm of flashbulbs.[9]

As National's business gained momentum in Hong Kong, Mong's business sense did not go unnoticed: other Japanese electrical goods manufacturers tried to tempt him away with offers to act as their agent in the territory. Among them was Sony's founder, Akio Morita. Matsushita's rival, Sony, had initially seen Hong Kong as a manufacturing

base rather than as a market for its products, and, in 1959, in the midst of the Cold War, the company had set up a transistor radio assembly factory in the city.

Factories that Manufacture Freedom

As a consequence of the United States' policies to contain the spread of communism in Asia, Hong Kong had begun to move away from its role as a transit port that shipped Chinese goods, to set itself up as a manufacturing base that produced its own goods for export. During the Korean War (1950–53), the United Nations had banned all trade with China and imposed severe economic sanctions against the country. China had shut itself off from the rest of the world and restricted its international trade. This was highly damaging to Hong Kong's position as a transit port. Chinese entrepreneurs, however, were adaptable when the situation called for it, and Hong Kong was soon on the way to becoming the "factory of the world." If there were no products to re-export, then why not make their own? Textile manufacturers, especially spinners from the Shanghai area, began setting up factories in Hong Kong and spinning cotton thread using the latest technology from the West.[10] Garment makers and light industrial manufacturers from the United States, Europe, and Japan, whose profits had been suffering from a sharp increase in the cost of domestic labor, also found Hong Kong attractive as a production base.[11]

Since the establishment of the communist government in China in 1949, Hong Kong's population had risen dramatically, effectively doubling between 1947 and 1963, from 1.8 million to 3.6 million. Desperately poor villagers unable to make a living in China climbed mountains and waded through rivers to reach Hong Kong and give themselves a better chance in life.[12] Most of these people came with nothing and owned nothing. They sought help from their relatives in Hong Kong who, if they were lucky, gave them a place to stay. Those without connections collected whatever materials they could lay their hands on and constructed temporary shelters referred to as "wooden huts (木屋)." It was, of course, illegal to build these wooden huts on land they did not own. Squatter settlements, therefore, tended to spring up on the lower slopes of hills, sites generally undeveloped at that time. During the summer typhoon season, they had to contend with the risk of landslides, and during the dry winter season, they had to worry about fires. In the late 1950s, according to one estimate, there were over 250,000 people living in these hillside squatter areas.[13]

Under colonial rule, the welfare of this low-income Chinese refugee population was of secondary importance to the government, if that Eventually, however, the British colonial government could no longer ignore the surge of immigrants from across the border and was left with no choice but to come up with a public housing policy that led to the construction of "settlement blocks," and the moving of squatters from their wooden huts to seven-storey apartment buildings. Seen from above, these buildings resembled the letter *H*: two parallel residential wings with communal facilities located in a middle section linking the two. Each unit consisted of a 120-square-foot room. Residents had to share the limited number of communal toilets, shower cubicles, and kitchen stoves that were available on every floor. Quarrels broke out constantly in the long lines of people waiting for their turn to use these facilities.[14] The conditions in these settlement blocks were harsh and the patience of their residents was tested daily.

This surge of immigrants provided Hong Kong with an abundant source of cheap labor, but this was not the only reason why the city appealed to foreign investors. As a British colony it had law and order, and a laissez-faire economy. Its long-held position as a transit port had ensured the establishment of an efficient transportation infrastructure and excellent communication facilities. In addition, its status as a free port, with no levies on freight, made it an ideal place for investment.

Once factories started manufacturing "Made in Hong Kong" products, they were exported to the West in accordance with international trade agreements, like the General Agreement on Tariffs and Trade (GATT) that the United States had taken the lead in establishing. The US government also took steps to open its market to foreign products. These initiatives were all part of the US government's grand strategy to contain communism in Asia, through the promotion of trade activities among "free" capitalist nations, encouraging Asian economies to grow, and raising the standard of living of Asian citizens.[15]

A Meeting with Sony's Founder

As mentioned, Sony had selected Hong Kong as the site for its radio factory in 1959. But it was not until 1962 that the company officially launched its Asian retail operations, lagging well behind Matsushita in this area. Sony had largely been concentrating its export efforts on the American market and that same year had gained the world's attention by opening a Sony Shop on New York's Fifth Avenue, joining the ranks of Tiffany, Gucci, and Cartier. A few months after the inauguration of the New York store, Sony launched its Hong Kong retail business.

The following year, in the summer of 1963, a Consumer Electronics Show was organized in Chicago, at which both Sony and National were to be exhibitors. Mong accompanied the Matsushita delegation to Chicago. Sony's display was located in the same exhibition hall as National/Panasonic's. One of Sony's founders, Akio Morita, stood at the booth and greeted visitors, giving out product information in English to potential customers. Sony's Hong Kong agent had previously introduced Mong to him, and when Mong walked into the Sony booth, he recognized him immediately.

> Morita-san greeted me by name, "Mong-san, you are here too!" And he asked when I would next be in Japan. …He then gave me his business card with his direct line.[16]

Several weeks later, Mong traveled to Tokyo on business and checked into the city's brand-new Palace Hotel in Marunouchi, directly across from the Imperial Palace. He called Morita from his hotel room. As it happened, Morita was in Tokyo, and he asked Mong if he was free for dinner the following evening.[17]

> The next morning, Mong received a phone call from Morita's secretary.
>
> The secretary told me that Vice-President Morita wished to entertain me with dinner. I asked the location, and was told, "Yanagibashi." It was a high-class geisha district. I had never been there before.[18]

Yanagibashi (柳橋) is a small canal bridge in Tokyo's old town. High-class teahouses offering food, drink, and geisha entertainment were dotted throughout the district, which at the time was considered more prestigious than either of the other two geisha districts of Shinbashi (新橋) or Akasaka (赤坂). Its patrons included leading politicians and businessmen. As privacy was paramount, it provided the ideal location for a confidential meeting. Mong recalls:

> When I got there, it was just the two of us. Food and wine were served, and then he asked me how my business was doing. I said, "It's doing very well, better than I could ever have hoped." Then, Morita-san asked whether I would be willing to look after Sony's products.
>
> "Well, that is very kind of you," I replied, "but at the moment I'm entrusted with all of Matsushita's business."
>
> So he said: "Why don't you just set up another company? That would take care of it. Isn't that what people in Hong Kong do?"
>
> Apparently he knew a lot about business in Hong Kong![19]

Certainly, it was fairly common in Hong Kong for a businessman to run two companies, which could then act as agents for rival manufacturers.

> I told him: "No, Morita-san, I can't do that. If I were to do so, what would prevent Matsushita from doing the same thing to me? They could authorize somebody else to set up a new company to sell products manufactured under a different brand name from National. Or Matsushita might give additional rights to some other company to be its agent in Hong Kong too… I might just get myself into a lot of trouble."
>
> Morita-san continued: "Mong-san, you are a brilliant businessman. It'd be Okay."
>
> I replied: "I gave my word to Konosuke Matsushita."
>
> The discussion came to an end, and he did not pursue the matter further. Morita-san said to me: "I understand now. I appreciate your time today; let's talk about this again in the future if the chance arises."
>
> So I thanked him for dinner and we parted company.[20]

Although Mong was ready to do almost anything to diversify his business, he had not broken his word to Matsushita, and Morita had not attempted to coerce him into representing Sony's products. When Mong recounted this incident he smiled: "I would say both of us were remarkable!" In fact, whether consciously or not, Mong was acting in accordance with the principles passed on to him by his father; being in the vulnerable position of intermediary, he had to be extremely careful not to do anything that would undermine the trust put in him by Matsushita.

Over twenty years passed before the two men had the opportunity to meet again in the mid-1980s. Then one day, during a visit to Hong Kong, Morita gave a lunchtime talk to some of the city's leading businesspeople in a banquet room at the Furama Hotel (富麗華酒店), which Mong attended. Morita's speech, delivered in English, was an account of the process by which Sony had come up with its Walkman.

> After the speech, Mong made his way over to Morita's table.
>
> At first, Morita-san didn't really recognize me, so I explained to him who I was. Then he grabbed his wife, who was sitting next to him, and said to her, "This is Mong-san. He's the only man in the world who's ever refused an offer to become a Sony agent."

Doesn't Mong have any regrets about saying no to Sony?

> Well, if you ask me whether it was better to handle Sony products or Matsushita products, it would have to be Matsushita. After all, Matsushita had a greater range of products for me to sell.[21]

In those days, Sony specialized in and excelled at producing wireless products such as radios, whereas Matsushita Electric manufactured just about any appliance that operated on electricity. Taken in the context of the retail industry, Sony was a "boutique"

1963 ad highlighting the wide range of National
products available in Hong Kong.
(*Overseas Chinese Daily*, November 12, 1963)

to Matsushita's "department store." After sales of the National wireless radio took off, Mong was ready to start developing the market for a broader variety of products. National produced a wide range of home appliances that included not only smaller items such as rice cookers and irons but also large items such as refrigerators and washing machines, two of the "Three Sacred Treasures" most sought after by Japanese households. Refrigerators and washing machines were considered major purchases, not least because of their price tag. When it came to exporting them overseas, their size was a logistical nightmare for Matsushita. And the destination of Matsushita's first commercial shipment of National refrigerators in 1958 was to be none other than Hong Kong.

Refrigerators with Extra Ventilation

Hong Kong was the ideal test market for National, from both a sales and a logistical perspective. When the company came up with new products for export, most of the first shipments were destined for Hong Kong. Mong and his associates quickly gathered market intelligence and provided feedback to the factories in Japan. Hong Kong was the testing ground for National "white goods (*shiromono* 白物)," a label used in Japan to refer to a variety of household appliances, including refrigerators, washing machines, and cookers. The name came about because these appliances were given a white enamel finish by their manufacturers.

When household refrigerators first became available in Hong Kong, the most popular models were Italian. In 1960, one in three refrigerators imported into Hong Kong was made in Italy, and by 1963, the number had risen to one in two. After Italian came American, British, and finally Japanese; in fact, the Japanese models accounted for just ten percent of the total Hong Kong market. In a 1960 newspaper advertisement stating "Refrigerators—All Brands Available" by one of Hong Kong's major refrigerator retailers on King's Road, near Victoria Park, of the twelve brands listed, only two were Japanese: Mitsubishi and Hitachi. National was not even included in the list.[22] The success of their transistor radios had made Japanese manufacturers leaders in the wireless market, but this was hardly the case when it came to refrigerators. Mong did some market analysis, and concluded that National's full-size refrigerators would not be able to compete with Western alternatives in Hong Kong. Therefore, he decided to aim for the niche market and import thirty of National's smaller refrigerators.

Refrigerators were luxury items, both in Hong Kong and Japan. In 1960, only one in ten Japanese urban households owned a refrigerator.[23] The fairly small, ninety-five-liter National refrigerator advertised in a Japanese newspaper during the summer of 1960 cost as much as ¥60,000, more than 1.5 times the average Japanese monthly salary of the time. The color ad showed a slice of chilled bright red watermelon, and the caption illustrated just how much of an investment buying a refrigerator had to be:

> We made this refrigerator with the hope that it will last you well into your grandchildren's generation.[24]

A 1960 billboard showcasing National's appliances,
known collectively as "white goods" in Japan.
Star Ferry Terminal, Hong Kong.
Courtesy of Junichi Ukita

In those days, importing larger appliances was a challenge, as cargo containers were not yet an option. Because refrigerators were such an investment, when Mong's order for thirty refrigerators was shipped from Kobe to Hong Kong, each one of them had to be individually sealed into a wooden crate. After the shipment arrived in Victoria Harbour and the crates were opened, however, Mong was dumbfounded.

> The refrigerators had dents all over them, the doors were broken, and the motors were not working properly. There were all kinds of problems.[25]

Mong's company immediately filed a claim for compensation to the office of Shoichiro Koyama, the Matsushita manager in charge of exports to Hong Kong. The claim was not made by telegram but via an expensive international telephone call. Mong believed that the blame lay with the Japanese dockers who must have been rough in their handling of the crates. Koyama still remembers the incident:

> We were both trying to put the blame on each other. He was blaming the Japanese dockers while I was sure it was the Hong Kong dockers' fault. But in the end, whoever was to blame, for Mong-san, the real question was, "How could this be allowed to happen when I've paid good money for them?"[26]

Koyama, a former rugby player at Waseda University (早稻田大學), was not one to take these things lightly. He carefully looked into the matter and was determined that the same mistake not be made twice. His team at Matsushita Trading concluded that the problem lay with the wooden crates: they looked too sturdy and did not allow for any view of their contents, which was probably why the dockers had not handled them with proper care.

For the next shipment, he therefore decided to use wooden frames instead of crates; the frames would provide good protection while at the same time enabling part of their contents to be visible to the naked eye. When Mong's new order for eighty refrigerators

arrived, Koyama instructed his subordinates to personally go to the warehouse and ensure the appliances were packed according to his instructions. Furthermore, when the refrigerators were ready to be loaded onto the ship that would carry them to Hong Kong, Koyama himself went down to the Kobe docks:

> "I brought a big bottle of sake for the dockworkers and said to them, 'I'm counting on you. Please, please be careful when handling our fridges'."[27]

The shipment arrived in Hong Kong. Looking at the refrigerators through the wooden frames encasing them, there appeared to be no dents. But once the frames were removed, in Mong's presence, he saw that the refrigerators that emerged were studded with holes.

A plywood plate had been nailed to each wooden frame listing the refrigerator's serial number. To prevent damage to the goods inside, the nails used to fix the plate onto the frame had to be of an exact length; however, because workers had run out of the ones normally used, Koyama's subordinates had unthinkingly hammered in different, much longer, nails. These nails were so long that their points had pierced right through the wooden frame and penetrated into the refrigerator's outer shell. No one was aware of the mistake until the shipment was delivered to Hong Kong.

Mong was overcome by frustration. He saw no point in storing the damaged goods in a warehouse, instead shipping them directly to his house in Kowloon Tong and stacking them up in a line in his garden. "That night, I slept on top of them, in the garden. Really!"[28]

About the same time, he ran into a problem with a shipment of electric fans. The electric fan was one of Matsushita's most popular non-wireless home appliances. Initially, however, the Matsushita fan factory had been reluctant to export them overseas, because they were satisfied with domestic sales. But the factory had finally relented in 1958 and, worn down by Mong's relentless persuading, had started exporting fans to the Hong Kong market.

Up until 1960, Matsushita Trading, which also looked after international logistics, had always shipped the fans in individual boxes almost fully assembled, but on this occasion they tried packing their constituent parts together, all the blades in one box, and all the guards in another, so that the shipment would be more compact. When the different boxes were opened in Hong Kong, however, Mong's staff found that the number of blades did not match the number of guards.

Immediately after these unfortunate incidents, Mong made a business trip to Osaka. He had scheduled a high-level appointment with the then-chairman of Matsushita Electric Trading, Arataro Takahashi, and the president, Shozo Iimura, neither of whom had any knowledge of Mong's recent shipping woes. The Matsushita Electric Trading office had moved to a prime location on Midosuji, Osaka's main thoroughfare. As soon as he walked into the office, Mong reeled off a long list of complaints to Misao Naka, a novice who had joined Matsushita in 1962, and had been put in charge of both refrigerators and electric fans. Unfortunately, Naka's boss, Koyama, was out of the office that day. The mild-mannered Naka stood by stoically as Mong made absolutely clear his feelings over

Getting the packing right. A National refrigerator arrives intact from
the factory in Japan. Hong Kong, 1960.
Courtesy of Sadayoshi Sakamoto

the fan and refrigerator shipping fiascos. When Mong had finished, Naka begged him
not to bring up the issue during his meeting with Takahashi and Iimura. "Fine," Mong
agreed, and off he went.[29]

Mong's departure was soon followed by an angry call from the chairman's office,
ordering whoever was in charge of refrigerators to join the meeting. Unfortunately, since
all his bosses were out of the office, young Naka had no choice but to go himself. He
was once again made to bear the brunt of the angry criticism aimed at his section. What
had happened to Mong's promise not to say anything? Mong later explained to this
business novice that he had not intended to complain, but as soon as he had entered
the conference room, the two executives had begun to make stringent demands. They
had received complaints from their Southeast Asian agents that National products were
being re-exported from Hong Kong and were hurting their business. Mong parried their
assault with his own charges. According to Naka, this is what Mong said to them in order
to regain the upper hand:

> I thank you for all your support, but actually there's something else I want talk
> to you about: the losses I have suffered as a consequence of the poorly packed
> shipments I've received.
>
> The refrigerator packing was sturdy enough this time, that's true. But the fridges
> were full of nail holes. It doesn't matter how strong the packing is, if you've
> already made holes in the doors.
>
> And then there were the electric fans. I thought I'd paid for both blades and
> guards.[30]

Mong did not stop there; he took his complaint over the hole-ridden refrigerators all the
way to the top, to the most senior executives at Matsushita Trading's parent company
and the manufacturer of the products he sold, Matsushita Industrial.

This incident was made public during a banquet held in honor of Mong's mother, Fa-yuk. In 1966, Fa-yuk, who had been born in Nagasaki, visited Japan for the first time in four decades. In a show of filial piety, Mong organized a sumptuous banquet in the basement of Osaka's Royal Hotel. The hotel had been built by business leaders from the Kansai area to provide VIPs visiting from abroad with first-class accommodation. In the marbled lobby hung countless paintings by the Japanese artists favored by the rich and powerful at the time, such as Ryohei Koiso and Ikuo Hirayama. In the lounge, kimono-clad waitresses poured English tea into delicately warmed china cups. Mong's banquet was to be held in the hotel's Chinese restaurant. Invitation letters, written in formal Japanese, were sent to thirty of Matsushita Electric Industrial's top executives.

Dear Sirs,

In this fine season of overflowing vitality, when the trees are covered with deep green, I wish you increasing joy in the success of your daily endeavors.

I would like to offer my deepest gratitude for the understanding and warm support that you have bestowed upon Shun Hing Electronic Trading, thanks to which the company's business has been steadily growing.

The occasion on which I write is the visit to Japan of my father, Kwok-ping, and my mother, Fa-yuk. My father has frequently been coming to Japan on business, but my mother has been staying quietly at home, taking care of the household.

Born in Japan, and having lived there until her marriage to my father at 18 years of age, my mother is overflowing with joy and nostalgia at visiting her birthplace, and we would like to take this opportunity to express our sincere gratitude to all of you who have extended exceptional support to us, and renew acquaintance with those of you whom we have been privileged to meet on the occasion of your visits to Hong Kong, by holding a dinner in the Dragon and Phoenix Chinese Restaurant of the Osaka Royal Hotel, at which we earnestly hope to gain the favor of your presence.

In the menu to be offered, we intend to have specially prepared some unusual dishes not to be found at Chinese restaurants in Japan.

A good fine day in June

William Mong Man-wai
Managing Director
Shun Hing Electronic Trading Company Limited

Matsushita Electric's founder and chairman, Konosuke Matsushita, attended the reception with his son-in-law, Masaharu Matsushita, who was also the company's president. During the banquet, Mong addressed the assembly with the following words of welcome:

Matsushita is truly an amazing firm. It sent me refrigerators that were pierced with holes, and threw in expensive metal nails at no extra charge!

When I saw the holes, I thought for a minute that Matsushita had invented a new refrigerator that facilitates the internal circulation of fresh air, in what was no doubt an attempt to gain the competitive edge in overseas markets.[31]

The company founder was, understandably, furious.[32] Details of this episode also made it back to the ears of Matsushita staff involved in the international side of the business. Mong did not hesitate to speak up when he felt both Matsushita and Shun Hing could benefit from his comments, and he often got his point across by means of cheeky jokes.

Incidents such as these, however, led to Matsushita making dramatic improvements to its logistical operations. A working group was formed to look into refrigerator packing, and Mong's father, Kwok-ping, was invited to join it as a consultant. He was well-respected, and Matsushita Trading often turned to him for advice. When the refrigerator packing working group met in Osaka, Kwok-ping explained that goods cannot be distributed from behind an office desk; you have to check up on every detail yourself.[33] To illustrate his point, he quoted one of his strongly held trading principles:

> "You must ship the products as if they were your daughter that you were giving away in marriage."[34]

As a consequence of Kwok-ping's recommendations, Matsushita Trading adopted the policy of always having its own staff present, regardless of the weather, which could be bitterly cold in winter and scorchingly hot in summer, for both warehouse packing and port shipment. In the words of Koyama, the man ultimately responsible for the hole-ridden refrigerator debacle: "Exporting to Mong-san, we even learned about packing."[35]

Around this time, Matsushita began expanding the range of its products for export, which had previously been limited to predominantly wireless products such as transistor

Mong cheekily refers to the refrigerator packing incident during a dinner attended by Konosuke Matsushita and 30 company executives. Osaka Royal Hotel, June 15, 1966.
Courtesy of Shun Hing Group

radios. In markets across the world, wireless products had always been the biggest foreign currency earners; they accounted for over two-thirds of Matsushita's overseas sales revenue, whereas non-wireless products, which were collectively referred to as "home appliances," accounted for less than one-third. In 1959, radios made up almost sixty-seven percent of Matsushita Trading's total exports; and ten years later, televisions, radios and tape recorders were still accounting for approximately sixty-five percent of the company's exports.[36]

In Hong Kong, however, the sale of Japanese white goods really started to take off in the late 1960s. As discussed, in the earlier part of the decade, the most popular refrigerator models were Italian; Japanese were only a distant second. In 1964, the year of the Tokyo Olympic Games, forty-eight percent of the 29,401 refrigerators imported into Hong Kong were Italian, twenty-three percent Japanese, and the remainder, American, British, French, or West German. William Mong decided to try and boost the market share of National refrigerators by importing its more compact, space-saving models that were better suited to Hong Kong's cramped living spaces than were the larger Italian ones.

Another factor that played a crucial part in reversing the fortunes of the Japanese refrigerator was Hong Kong's humid climate. Since Italian refrigerators were designed for dry weather, as the air temperature around the refrigerator rose, condensation ran down the external walls, causing large puddles of water to form on the floor. Japanese refrigerators, in contrast, were far more resistant to humidity.[37] By the time Munich hosted the 1972 Olympic Games, sales of Japanese refrigerators in the territory had overtaken those of their Italian competitors.

Try a Washing Machine Free for Five Days

The washing machine, another so-called white good, was the last of the "Three Sacred Treasures" to be introduced to Hong Kong homes. In 1967, the year of the Kowloon riots, the number of washing machines imported into Hong Kong stood at about 14,000, less than one-third the number of both black-and-white televisions and refrigerators imported into the city. Most people in Hong Kong had never used a washing machine, let alone a spin dryer. To promote sales, Mong's Shun Hing set up a "demonstration team." The team would visit apartment blocks and give residents the chance to experience the convenience of having a washing machine.

House calls were a proven tactic for Mong. In 1959, when he first introduced Japanese rice cookers to the Hong Kong market, he and his associates would frequently visit a Hong Kong Island public housing estate to demonstrate their use. Without appointments, he would go from door to door and, when welcomed, would set up a rice cooker in the living room. This door-to-door approach generated good word of mouth, and effectively jump-started the rice cooker business in Hong Kong (Chapter 1). This time around, Shun Hing allowed interested residents to keep a washing machine in their homes for a five-day free trial period.

Shun Hing set up its five-person washing machine demonstration team in the summer of 1968. The model they promoted was a twin tub machine: one tub was for washing clothes, the other to spin dry them. It had been advertised in the Japanese press under the name of "Ultra High Speed—*Uzushio* (whirlpool)." The first thing Shun Hing did was to place an advertisement in local newspapers and magazines:

> Please Try it for Free.
>
> National's Brand-new Washing Machine.
>
> Realizing there are customers who are interested in purchasing a washing machine, but are unsure of how to use it, or have questions as to its effectiveness, and are therefore delaying their decision to buy one, for the next six months, from 1 July to 31 December this year, our company will happily dispatch experienced staff members to your home to demonstrate National's new washing machines.
>
> After the demonstration, you are welcome to keep the demonstration model for a five-day free trial period, so that you can witness for yourself its outstanding performance.
>
> (*Overseas Chinese Daily*, July 11, 1968)

The ad invited prospective buyers to contact them by filling in an application slip, giving their name, address, the size of their household, telephone number, and preferred washing machine model. The sales team believed that Hong Kong people's fondness for free services would make them think that there was nothing to lose and make the offer irresistible. As soon as they received an application, the five-member team would load a washing machine onto a seven-seat van and head for the potential customer's home. Once there, they would install the washing machine, demonstrate to the interested party how efficient the machine was, and show how no housewife should be without one.[38]

Shun Hing employee Tommy Ho was part of this washing machine demonstration team. In those days, the washing machine was not fully automatic, and clothes had to be moved back and forth between the two tubs three times. Ho and his team would wash the clothes in one tub, move them to the spin dryer to get rid of the soapy water, and then put them back in the original tub for a rinse before giving them a final spin. Ho recalls that the powerful spin dryer was what impressed his potential customers most.

> At that time, washing machines were "twin top," one side for washing, and one side for spinning. We were confident that, if people used this washing machine for some time, they would become interested in buying it, because after just one spin cycle, the laundry dried very quickly. So, we wanted to demonstrate the effects of spinning.
>
> People also assumed that a washing machine used a lot of water. But actually, it didn't. If they followed the procedures correctly, spinning would remove most of the soapy water so that clothes didn't have to be rinsed again and again [as they did when you washed them by hand.]

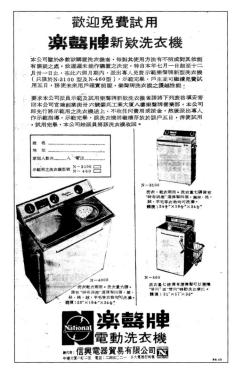

Shun Hing ad offering customers a five-day free
trial of the latest National washing machine.
(*Overseas Chinese Daily*, July 11, 1968)

> So we explained that a washing machine didn't need a lot of water. Actually, it
> would save time and save a lot of water. [39]

After the demonstration they would leave the machine behind for a five-day free trial period and no obligation of purchase.

Five days later, if customers who were ready to purchase the washing machine, Shun Hing would replace the trial machine with a brand-new one. If customers were not ready to purchase, Shun Hing would send a van to pick up the machine at no charge. In fact, the majority of people who tried the machine did not buy it, but this was not an issue; what mattered was that they would share their, in most cases positive, experiences with their mothers, sisters, and neighbors. The initiative ran for six months.

In 1971, the US manufacturer Westinghouse Electric set up a similar all-female washing machine demonstration team and, in 1973, the Italian firm of Zoppas Electric offered a free one-week trial service.[40] Judging from the newspaper ads in Hong Kong, however, Shun Hing was breaking new ground in 1968 with its National washing machine sales strategy. Within seven years of setting up its demonstration team, washing machines had become standard items in many middle-class households.

Even as sales of so-called white goods increased thanks to his strategy of importing smaller, more compact models, Mong made more money from sales of wireless goods. However, because he had played such a fundamental role in their successful localization and the logistical arrangements necessary to their safe delivery to Hong Kong, he held a special place in his heart for non-wireless appliances. Misao Naka, the man who had been summoned for a dressing-down by the chairman and president of Matsushita Trading, subsequently spent eighteen years in charge of the Hong Kong export market. According to Naka, William Mong's contribution to the successful export of National's white goods was considerable:

> He would come to Osaka, and at the planning meeting for the design of the following year's fridge model, he'd argue over all sorts of things, right down to the minutest of details. For example, the refrigerator handle: he had definite views on which side of the door it should be. All the same to me, I used to think.
>
> Still, we discovered that when we did go along with his suggestions, the sales proved him right. …He was a significant factor in the success that National's white goods enjoyed in overseas markets.[41]

In 1967, the development of the modern container ship revolutionized marine transportation. The first container ship to carry Matsushita cargo left Japan for the west coast of the United States. It was not until after 1970 that container freight became standard on the Hong Kong route, its introduction leading to a rapid decrease in the number of damaged shipments, and therefore fewer disputes.

Making Sense the Mong Way

While Mong was contributing to Matsushita's logistics know-how in packing the merchandise for export, he was also looking to squeeze additional profits from the actual shipping of the goods. In 1972, Misao Naka took over as manager of Matsushita Trading's Hong Kong Section. Shortly after Naka's promotion, Mong approached him with a request to switch from their current shipping company to a cheaper, Hong Kong one. At that time, the shipping of orders from Matsushita's factories in Japan to Mong's warehouses in Hong Kong was carried out under the international commercial terms of C&F (today's CFR, or Cost and Freight), which meant that the seller was responsible for all transportation costs from the time the merchandise left Japan to the time it arrived in the port of Hong Kong. In other words, it was Matsushita's right and responsibility to choose a reputable shipping firm that would ensure safe delivery of its goods to Hong Kong, and Naka wanted to stay with a company he trusted. He therefore turned down Mong's request:

> I told him bluntly, "This doesn't make sense. With a C&F contract, we as shippers have the right to choose the shipping company we want to use. Mong-san, all you need to do is claim your goods when the shipment arrives."

Then I said: "You have no right to tell us which shipping company we have to use." (Laugh) And then he got into a terrible rage.[42]

Naka had often been overpowered by Mong in their arguments, but this time he was quite confident. He had majored in business and economics at university and studied trading theory and operations. The workings of C&F had been thoroughly drummed into him.[43]

The question remained as to why Mong was so keen on this particular shipping company. The truth was finally revealed when someone from the firm that Mong wanted to use actually called Naka's office to complain. The caller stated that Mong had offered the Hong Kong shipping company the business with Matsushita on the understanding that in return they pay Shun Hing a five percent commission on every shipment, and now he wanted to hear from Naka why they needed to comply with Mong's demands.

This was unthinkable, and Naka remonstrated strongly with Mong. Both Mong and Naka refused to back down, so the final round of this protracted dispute was played out in front of the president of Matsushita Trading, Shozo Iimura. According to Naka, this is how Mong appealed to Iimura:

> Yes, I asked for a five percent commission from that shipping company. But my intention was to lower the goods' retail price.
>
> What's wrong with selling things cheaper? Come on, Iimura-san. Who is in the right here?
>
> C&F may well stand for Cost and Freight, but in practice, aren't I the one who's actually paying for all this? I'm trying to rationalize the freight I'm paying, that's all! I'm the one making efforts to rationalize and make the freight cheaper, not you! And thanks to this new deal, I'll be able to sell the goods cheaper, and I'll sell more of them![44]

This came at a time when Matsushita Trading was striving for the "rationalization" of its own operations, following the Nixon administration's discontinuation of the fixed dollar–yen exchange rate in 1971 and the currency fluctuations that ensued. Then the 1973 oil crisis hit, dramatically increasing the price of oil in many countries, including Japan. Under these difficult circumstances, Matsushita Trading was keen to cut costs and rationalize expenditure. Mong's rationalization argument therefore struck a chord with Iimura, who had not previously thought of questioning pre-existing logistical arrangements, and he decided to go along with the Hong Kong agent's request: "When you put it like that, it's difficult for us not to agree with you. What Mong-san is saying is right, isn't it?"[45]

Mong therefore got to keep his five percent commission. And there is no evidence that the retail price of National products in Hong Kong was reduced as a consequence of the lower shipping costs. The defeated Naka was absolutely flabbergasted: "Well, the way he explained it, he might have a point. But whatever happened to the *C* in C&F? It had ceased to count for anything. It didn't make sense, did it? But for that guy, it made sense."[46]

Shozo Iimura, President of Matsushita Electric Trading (third from
left) in discussion with Mong (second from left). Hong Kong, 1964.

And Mong was not the only one to think this approach to business made economic
sense. It went without saying that any owner of a self-financing business enterprise
would seek to rationalize operating costs by selecting the shipping company with the
lowest rates. Even though it undeniably provided both sides with a certain peace of
mind, it would have been considered odd to continue dealing with a more expensive
shipping company merely on the grounds of maintaining a long-standing business
relationship. Security and peace of mind do not necessarily count for much when it
comes to economic pragmatism. Mong had his own views of what constituted good
business sense, and forced the salarymen at Matsushita to question their practices.

Hong Kong was a testing ground for Matsushita, for its latest products, its logistics,
and even occasionally, the patience of its employees. But the free port also offered the
Japanese manufacturer an opportunity to expand its export market and adopt a more
global outlook.

Taking Advantage of Chinese Networks across Asia

As mentioned at the beginning of this chapter, in addition to being a showcase for
National appliances and the test market for the company's new export items, Hong Kong
served as a gateway to Southeast Asian markets that remained off-limits for political or
economic reasons. To gain a historical perspective on Hong Kong's position as a major
Asian maritime hub, however, it is necessary to go back in time to the end of World War
I (1914–18).

In 1918, the Nagasaki Chamber of Commerce issued a report on the trade of dried
seafood products, such as squid, abalone, and shark's fin. According to this report,
ninety percent of all dried seafood imports into Hong Kong were handled by Chinese
merchants. Japan was the biggest supplier of dried seafood to Hong Kong, accounting

for half of the total volume, followed by the "South Seas" including Southeast Asia, and the United States. The majority of these seafood imports, however, did not stay long in Hong Kong. Only ten percent was consumed in the territory; the rest was re-exported to cities across southern China and Southeast Asia: fifty percent to Guangdong (廣東) and Guangxi (廣西), twenty percent to Shantou (汕頭) and Xiamen (Amoy, 廈門), fifteen percent to Southeast Asia, and five percent to Shanghai and neighboring areas.[47] The dried seafood example is just one of many that illustrate how Hong Kong functioned as a hub for Chinese maritime networks, most of which had developed organically as the product of personal relationships built up along ethnic Chinese merchant lines rather than as a result of official trade agreements between nations or large corporations.[48]

Half a century later, and the range of Japanese products imported into Hong Kong was no longer limited to dried abalone and shark's fin; it extended to transistor radios and rice cookers. In addition, Hong Kong people's spending power had increased, and more imported products were staying in the territory. Nevertheless, Hong Kong remained a transnational network hub. Imported products sold in Hong Kong were often priced lower than they were in the rest of Asia, by virtue of Hong Kong's position as a free port with no customs duties or taxes. In fact, the market was so competitive that it was sometimes cheaper to buy National rice cookers in Hong Kong than it was in Japan in the 1960s and 1970s.

Once National products arrived in Hong Kong, no one knew for sure where they might be headed next. They would occasionally show up in the shop windows of Asian countries that Matsushita had no formal business dealings with and would catch Matsushita's fact-finding missions by surprise. As long as Hong Kong was a free port, there was nothing anyone could do to prevent the informal flow of its products. As Mong explained to the Matsushita employees in charge of the export side of the business, "Water flows downward." This expression forms the second part of the Chinese proverb "People aim high, and water flows downward (人望高處，水向低流)." For Mong, the transnational movement of Japanese products from Japan to other countries in the region via Hong Kong was as natural as water flowing downward, and this was all part of the art of doing business.

> This flow of [electrical] products from Hong Kong to the Near and Middle East occurred because they were more affordable in Hong Kong. Merchants bought the goods in Hong Kong and then carried them back to their own countries, because even after [paying for the transportation], the price worked out cheaper than importing them directly. This was one option.

> Another option was re-export, and there was a lot of it going on. Some Hong Kong retail shops that carried [National] appliances in Hong Kong would place orders for additional products and sell them on to trading companies that would then re-export them to other countries.[49]

From the 1960s to the late 1970s, before China opened its doors to the outside world, National products flowed along this maritime route through Hong Kong mainly into

Southeast Asia. For example, between 1967 and 1976, there was no direct export of National rice cookers from Japan to the Philippines. Instead they were shipped from Osaka to Manila via Hong Kong. They went on to become a big hit.

National single-band radios re-exported from Hong Kong enjoyed similar success in Jakarta. Battery-operated radios were particularly prized, as they were not powered by electricity and therefore voltage was not a problem. This was extremely pertinent in Southeast Asia where, in 1970, only the privileged had access to a steady supply of electricity. Battery-operated radios were also prized by Chinese traders throughout the region, as they could be used as a form of currency when making international payments. Whereas the exchange rates for local currencies had a tendency to fluctuate wildly, the value of the radios remained constant. According to one estimate, there were over 20 million Chinese immigrants living in Southeast Asia.[50] Through this vast transnational network, National products began spreading across Asia and beyond.

Following the end of the Allied occupation of Japan in 1952, Matsushita had set about appointing agents to sell its products in three Asian cities: Bangkok, Hong Kong, and Singapore. There were many Asian countries, however, that remained completely off-limits to Matsushita, some because of internal political turmoil, some because of their adoption of staunch protectionist policies to avoid the outflow of precious foreign currency. According to the accounts of several former Matsushita employees, re-export from Hong Kong to these countries was often the only option to break into these potentially lucrative new markets. Sometimes, however, re-exported goods from Hong Kong turned up in countries where Matsushita had signed formal dealership agreements with a local agent.

Singapore was one such example. Matsushita's sole agent in Singapore was a Dutch trading company called Hagemeyer. Singapore was a highly structured market, and it had been stipulated in the contract that Hagemeyer was to be the only channel by which National radios were to reach Singaporean consumers. Nevertheless, identical radios to the ones imported by Matsushita's designated Singaporean agent started arriving in Singapore via the Hong Kong re-export route; they were what we refer to today as parallel imports or gray products. In addition, these re-exported radios were being sold at a lower price than the ones imported directly from Japan. There were two reasons for this. First, Mong, thanks to his bargaining powers, had purchased the radios at a lower price from Matsushita than Hagemeyer had, and second there were no customs duties in Hong Kong. Even accounting for the transportation costs between Hong Kong and Singapore, the re-exported radios were more affordable than goods directly imported into the city-state. As a result, the Singapore radio market was in turmoil and the local agent found itself in the difficult position of having to launch a claim against Matsushita Trading in Osaka.

Because Hong Kong was a free port, however, there was nothing anyone could do to stem this transnational flow of re-exported goods. As Mong put it, "Water flows downward": lower-priced modern appliances will flow along established, well-informed networks to markets where there is a demand for them.

As a consequence of the political turmoil faced by the country in the late 1960s, Indonesia was temporarily off-limits to Matsushita. Prior to the turmoil, the world's fourth most populous nation, spread over an archipelago that includes more than 1,000 inhabited islands, had been a sizable market for National radios. Under a licensing agreement with Matsushita, an Indonesian firm, GOBEL, had produced single-waveband transistor radios using National parts, and sold them under the "TJAWANG" brand.[51]

In 1965, a group of junior military officers attempted a coup, kidnapping and murdering six anti-communist army generals. These events led to the downfall of the Sukarno regime, and Matsushita was forced to suspend its business operations in the country, a suspension that lasted five years.[52] During this time, however, National radios kept making their way into Indonesia via Hong Kong. Mong recalls that the R-210 transistor radio was the most popular model imported into the country.[53]

Once Indonesia regained political stability, Matsushita set up a joint venture with GOBEL and in 1973 opened a manufacturing plant in Jakarta. It was only logical that the first item off the production line should be the popular, single-waveband National radio that had already proved such a hit. Yet the radios they produced did not sell, or at least did not sell well. The problem lay in GOBEL's distribution network. As the company was owned by an indigenous Indonesian entrepreneur, it struggled to make any inroads into a sector largely dominated by ethnic Chinese businessmen and was therefore unable to capitalize on the Chinese networks through which the radios had previously been imported into Indonesia via Hong Kong.

It was at this juncture that Mong came to the rescue. He bought up the Indonesian-made National radios, shipped them to Hong Kong, and then loaded them back onto container ships headed for Indonesia. Once they were there, he used his previously established ethnic Chinese distribution networks to make them available to Indonesian consumers. It was indeed a strange business. The result? "They sold!" Mong smiles: "Because I had established connections with [distribution] networks in Indonesia, sales of the radios were assured. I managed it by making good use of these networks."[54]

For a while, therefore, until National was able to establish an effective sales and distribution network in the country, Mong handled the export of Indonesian-made National radios and imported them back into Indonesia. He was also skilful in making use of these Chinese transnational networks to develop his business in other Southeast Asian countries such as Singapore and Malaysia.

Hong Kong itself may have been only a small market, but Asia was its vast hinterland and presented ample opportunities to the Hong Kong entrepreneur looking to increase his sales.

5

Pay in Hong Kong; Pick up in China
Bringing Modern Convenience across the Border [1]

Pay in Hong Kong; Pick up your National TV and
cassette player in Guangzhou, China.
(*Wen Wei Po*, June 3, 1979)

"What on earth is going on?" Kyoichi Yoshioka, looking at an order sheet that had just
come in from Hong Kong, could not believe his eyes. It was the beginning of 1979, and,
seven years after joining Matsushita Electric Trading, he had recently been assigned to
the company's Hong Kong Section. Radio-cassette recorders were a hit item at the time.
Returning to the office after the New Year holidays, he was stunned to discover that the
number on the order sheet was double that of the previous month.

> When I took up the post, my predecessor gave me an overview of the Hong Kong business. He told me that orders for radio-cassette recorder models had amounted to about 20,000 units per month. But when I looked at the order sheet from Shun Hing the following month, it wasn't 20,000 but 40,000.
>
> That's just impossible. I thought, what on earth is going on?
>
> Anyway, we had to make the tape recorders, so I rushed to the factory. Inevitably, they asked, "How is this possible?"[2]

The Tape Recorder Division manager asked him why the order had doubled; Yoshioka had no idea. On the Hong Kong order sheet, there was just the number 40,000, with no further explanation. In those days, international calls were still expensive and only for extreme emergencies. So, Yoshioka sent a Telex instead, asking why the order had doubled. A reply Telex came back immediately, and the mystery was solved: "They are for China."

Mao's China had staunchly rejected the trappings of wealth, and kept tight control on anything considered foreign. But on a more practical level, the country could not afford to let goods manufactured overseas flow in, because it was short of foreign currency. Therefore, the majority of people in China lived without the convenience of modern appliances. But when Deng Xiaoping launched his Open Door Policy in December 1978 and reopened the country to those who had left for more affluent societies, many Guangdong natives returned to China to visit their families, bringing with them Japanese electrical appliances from Hong Kong.

Modern Appliances for Cousins in China

Hundreds of Hong Kongers were crowding into the Kowloon terminal waiting for trains to China in 1979. Secondary school student Henry Chan had his hands full of gifts for his cousins in Guangzhou. With his right hand, he pulled a cart to which was strapped a color television in a big cardboard box, and a large travel bag was slung over his left shoulder. The bag was full of clothing for his uncle's family, some of it new, some of it old. He also carried imported goodies: fruit candies, five cans of Coca Cola, and the malted drink mix Horlicks. The bag was heavy for his small frame, but Henry thought his cousins would be happy to see what they had brought. He knew that, in China, even basic necessities were hard to come by.

Henry traveled with his parents and an uncle, each of them loaded with as much luggage as they could carry. Henry's younger brother and sister had also come along for the ride, so he had been charged with taking care of them. Henry kept reminding himself to be careful not to lose sight of them and to make sure he kept hold of his luggage. Were he not attentive, he would be an easy target for pickpockets, and there were many of them along the way. It was a sweaty summer day, and he had to grasp the handle of the cart firmly. Every now and then, his parents would give him a break by carrying the bag of clothing and Coke cans for him, but he was told that the television set was his responsibility.

At the Chinese Customs checkpoints in Shenzhen (深圳), a sleepy town immediately across the border from Hong Kong that had been newly designated a Special Economic Zone by the Chinese government, they were going to declare the television set as a gift from Henry to his uncle in Guangzhou. That summer of 1979, secondary school students across Japan were flocking to games arcades to play the video game Space Invaders, a predecessor of Pac-Man. In Hong Kong, however, many secondary students like Henry were accompanying their parents on trips to visit their cousins across the border.

Before the implementation of Deng Xiaoping's Open Door Policy, the long journey that Hong Kongers had to undertake in order to visit their hometown in China was even more grueling. For every trip a "Letter of Introduction" was required. This document could be obtained prior to departure from the state-run travel agency, China Travel Service (中國旅行社); the alternative was a long wait in line at Customs checkpoints. The most common method for Hong Kongers to enter China was to take the Kowloon-Canton Railway (KCR) train to Lo Wu (羅湖), near the Chinese border, and then cross into Shenzhen on foot.[3]

When Hong Kongers visited their generally less well-off family members in China, it was expected they would come bearing plenty of gifts. The nature of these gifts, however, changed over the years. In the immediate wake of the Cultural Revolution, the visitors brought with them basic necessities such as clothing, towels, peanut oil, powdered milk, and Chinese herbal oil, often wrapped in bags that they slung over a carrying pole. In their efforts to give their relatives as many items of clothing as possible, Hong Kongers would often make the journey wearing several pairs of underpants, or several layers of cloth temporarily sewn into the shape of long pants. If discovered, these extra items were confiscated by the Customs officers. Some Hong Kongers also brought in cash for their families and relatives.

In the mid-1970s, the first home appliance Mrs Chiu purchased as a gift to take to her relatives in China was a rice cooker. The Chius lived with their four young children in a public housing estate in Sau Mau Ping (秀茂坪), East Kowloon. Mrs Chiu was a native Hong Konger, born in 1948. After working in a garment factory, she had married her husband, a native of Foshan (佛山) in Guangdong Province, where most of his family members were still living. She recalls her family's expeditions to China, prior to the implementation of the country's economic reforms in 1979, as frantic, and likens them to "fleeing from war." She describes what her family had to go through to get on a train at the Kowloon-Canton Railway's terminal in Hung Hom (紅磡):

> Every time we went to Foshan, we had to line up overnight in the underground passage, the one that leads to the Hong Kong Coliseum. We had to arrive early the night before, around 10 p.m., because no buses would run after 11 p.m. We had to line up in the passage with our luggage and children until 7:00 the next morning when the train station opened.

> All we could do was wait, because you only got to know the train's schedule on the day of departure when you bought the tickets, and there were always lots of people.
>
> It was exhausting to wait overnight with your children and luggage. It was like fleeing from war. Well, that's what every trip to China felt like to me anyways. And it was even worse with children.[4]

Still, Mrs Chiu wanted her husband's family to have a better life and to enjoy the convenience of modern appliances from Hong Kong. So, she continued to visit Foshan twice a year, each time bringing with her one new appliance. With her on the train, in addition to these gifts, she had her baby, diapers, powdered milk, and even clean water in which to dissolve the milk, as she did not want the infant to get sick from drinking untreated water in China.

The rice cooker Mrs Chiu chose to take with her to China was one of National's Hong Kong models, with a glass viewing pane molded into the center of the aluminum lid. She bought the largest model available, one that could cook enough rice for sixteen people at a time. She says, "our family in Foshan never told us what they wanted. But I would think about what they might find useful and that's what I would bring. I bought a rice cooker because I thought it would make life easier for them and because everyone was using one in Hong Kong. And the National rice cooker was durable."[5]

The frequent trips across the border carrying appliances were a financial burden for the working-class family. But Mrs Chiu desperately wanted to help her husband's family:

> "Of course it was hard for us financially. Electrical appliances were very expensive at the time. But well, they were our family, so it wouldn't have been right to be counting the cost. These appliances were still affordable to us in Hong Kong. We just needed to save money on other things in our daily lives. So that was just fine."[6]

After their arrival in China, it was compulsory for Hong Kongers to register with the local police station. In those days, food provisions were rationed. Visitors, therefore, had to get their pass stamped and obtain meal coupons from the police to ensure they had rice and other staples to eat during their stay with their relatives. The "Letter of Introduction" could be used for one trip only. Every time Hong Kongers wanted to travel to China, they had to apply for a new letter in order to get a permit.

As China began to lift its bamboo curtain, however, regulations for entering the country were gradually relaxed. By the summer of 1979, Chinese residents in Hong Kong and Macau were able to visit China without a "Letter of Introduction." In its place, China Travel Service and designated Chinese banks started issuing a special travel pass called a "Home Return Permit (回鄉證)." This pass was valid for three years and functioned like a passport, in that it allowed Hong Kong and Macau residents of Chinese descent to travel to their ancestral hometowns in China. As a result, many middle-aged and older Hong Kongers who had emigrated from Guangdong Province took trips to visit the relatives they had left behind. These trips often involved younger members of the family, such as Henry Chan. Because so many people decided to make the journey, the train to the border was often so packed that only passengers waiting in a long line at the terminal station in Hung Hom could board it; there was no chance of getting on at any of the intervening stations.

The number of visitors to China jumped from 1.56 million people in 1978 to 3.82 million in 1979, and reached 11.67 million in 1984.[7] Approximately ninety percent of these visitors were people of Chinese descent, who were referred to as *tongbao* (同 胞), or compatriots, by the Chinese Communist Party. *Tongbao* was a political term used to designate former Chinese citizens who had left the country but shared the same motherland as their Chinese "brothers and sisters." As the number of Hong Kongers visiting relatives on the Mainland increased, so expectations grew with regard to the size of the appliances brought as gifts. What had started with relatively small items, such as rice cookers and radio-cassette recorders, was scaled up to include television sets.

One "Gift Appliance" per Person per Year

With effect from January 1, 1979, Hong Kong and Macau visitors over sixteen years of age were authorized to bring in one taxable consumer product per person as a gift, on the condition that the recipient not be allowed to sell it. This, of course, implied that such resale was rampant. The Chinese Customs' list of permitted "valuable goods" included wristwatches, radios, cassette recorders, television sets, cameras, electric fans, and calculators.[8] By June 1979, bicycles and sewing machines had been added to the list.[9]

Of the appliances brought in as gifts, the television set was by far the most popular item. By then, more than ninety percent of households in Hong Kong owned a television set, and among them a further forty-eight percent owned a color television. Across the border in mainland China, however, the television set was an object of desire. Although the tax on a television set brought in as a gift from Hong Kong was a whopping fifty percent of the standard price paid for one at that time, the new regulations were still considered a groundbreaking development, in that a Hong Konger could now legally bring a television set into the country without fear of it being confiscated or of being fined.

To control the quantity of items carried in, the Chinese Customs issued a short handwritten notice on December 29, 1978, and set a quota for such gifts: one large appliance, including television sets, per person per year. In addition to this, visitors could each bring in one calculator per trip.[10] Six months later, on July 1, 1979, the list was expanded to include one small home appliance per trip: a rice cooker, an electric kettle, a shaver, or an iron.[11] Once the rule was in place, large quantities of these gift appliances began finding their way from Hong Kong to China's Guangdong Province by train.

Henry Chan's mother had six siblings, five of whom had moved to Hong Kong. Their eldest brother, however, had stayed behind in Guangzhou to care for their parents and tend the ancestral graves. He worked as a waiter in a Chinese restaurant. Whenever the five younger siblings living in Hong Kong visited him in Guangzhou, they asked him what they could bring to make his and his family's life easier. Henry recalls that a television set was the next item on his wish list in 1979:

> "One of my uncles in Hong Kong visited China a lot and so had used up his quota of gift appliances. My mother had also used up her quota. But I was now eligible to bring a TV into China, so my family told me to carry a TV set."[12]

It was Henry's uncle in Hong Kong who had actually paid for the television set. On his way to the China Travel Service offices, he had spotted a National Quintrix model color television sitting in the middle of a shopwindow. The uncle splashed out on a color, rather than black-and-white, model. Their relatives in Guangzhou believed that those who had left for Hong Kong led affluent lifestyles. Henry's uncle, therefore, had to live up to their expectations or he would lose face, an important consideration for the Chinese when it comes to gifts. And now, his nephew Henry was carrying the television across the border in compliance with the regulation of "one appliance per person per year."

It was not by accident that Henry's family had chosen a National color television set as a gift to their Mainland relatives. In 1978, a year before China had officially started allowing electric appliances to be brought into China, Mong's Shun Hing had already recognized this market's huge potential. It had responded quickly by establishing a China Section and entered into negotiations with the Mainland officials overseeing international trade affairs. Within the same year, Shun Hing had completed its first business transaction with the Guangzhou Friendship Store (友誼商店), a government-operated department store open exclusively to foreign residents and visitors to the city. The first re-export order received from the store was for none other than black-and-white television sets, which Shun Hing duly sent across the border. Tommy Ho, who was responsible for television sales in China at the time, recalls:

> Our first shipment consisted of 7,000 seventeen-inch black-and-white TVs, which were sold to the Friendship Store in Guangzhou, payment to be made after delivery. In those days, the Chinese government would not authorize anyone in China to import foreign goods, except for the Friendship Stores, which were permitted to import small quantities of goods for foreign residents in Guangzhou, including overseas Chinese and citizens of Hong Kong and Macau.

> At that time, Friendship Stores only accepted coupons (Foreign Exchange Certificates, 代用券) issued by the Chinese government, which had to be purchased with foreign currency. This was to prevent any local Chinese from shopping at the Friendship Stores, as local residents were not entitled to purchase the coupons.

> The 7,000 TVs sold out very quickly, which showed us that demand for the product was high. We were astonished. We also got a sense of the huge potential of the China market.

> From then on, Shun Hing established a business relationship with the Friendship Stores. We went on to sell them rice cookers, electric shavers, color TV sets, and other items.[13]

In the years following the end of the Cultural Revolution, the National brand was virtually unknown in China. And there was still a long time to go before Japanese manufacturers were given the option of exporting their products directly into China. In the meantime, Hong Kong began to serve as China's gateway for Japanese appliances.

Adapting a Hong Kong Model for China

When China opened its doors in 1979, the world was still in the midst of the Cold War. The differences in ideology between the East and the West even extended to the color encoding systems used for their television sets. Although both China and Hong Kong used the PAL color encoding system developed by the German manufacturer Telefunken, they had adopted differing sub-systems: China used PAL-D, as did the Soviet Union and other countries in the Eastern Bloc. Hong Kong, following Britain's lead, used PAL-I. They differed in audio carrier frequency and channel bandwidth. In other words, the color television sets designed for the Hong Kong market did not work in China. Many Hong Kong consumers, however, were unaware of the difference until their Chinese relatives switched on the televisions they had given them and complained they did not work.

There were also dishonest dealers in Hong Kong who converted PAL-I television sets to the Chinese PAL-D system without a license, or who deceived customers into buying models that they knew would not work in China. This was a quick way to make a profit, since once bulky television sets had been carried to China they were unlikely to be returned to Hong Kong, even if they malfunctioned. The Hong Kong newspapers were full of complaints against these local dealers, from consumers who had taken a television set all the way to Guangdong Province only to discover that all they could get was static.

William Mong's response was fast. He became aware of these complaints and realized that National needed to develop a PAL-D model for China in order to get ahead of the competition. Mong immediately visited Matsushita's television factory in Osaka and insisted Matsushita urgently produce a new standard model.[14] It was Misao Naka, the manager of Matsushita Electric Trading's Hong Kong Section, who accompanied Mong to the factory. Naka recalls:

> The TV systems of Hong Kong and China were slightly different. We had to come up with TV sets that worked in China. But it wasn't as easy as we had thought.
>
> "It should be possible," Mong-san insisted, and so we went to the TV factory. One after the other, engineers worked on trying to solve the puzzle. Finally, they came up with a model that worked both in Hong Kong and China with the flick of a switch. They installed a switch at the back of the TV. Although intended for China, we could also sell this model in Hong Kong if we wanted to.
>
> We tried to get ahead with innovative ideas. We tried to differentiate ourselves from our competitors every step of the way. Otherwise, they would just imitate what we had done and catch up with us.[15]

Thus, instead of simply taking the Hong Kong model and adapting it to function solely in China, Matsushita created a single television set that could meet consumers' needs and demand on both sides of the border.

National's archrival for the China TV business was Hitachi. The Hong Kong dealers for both Japanese manufacturers were fully prepared for the announcement of China's new policy of one gift appliance per person per year for Hong Kong and Macau visitors to the country, scheduled for December 29, 1978. Ten days prior to the announcement, Hitachi had already begun to run advertisements promoting its PAL-D model in the pro-China newspaper *Wen Wei Po* (文匯報).[16] Their opening line, "Notice to Compatriots in Hong Kong and Macau," read like a Chinese communist bulletin. A week later, on December 26, three days before the announcement, Shun Hing began running advertisements for the National PAL-D model in the same newspaper. By January 4, the politically loaded term *compatriot* had found its way into National's advertising slogan:

> Attention: compatriots who are planning to return home to China
>
> The picture quality of a National color TV is now even clearer
>
> Modeled and designed for the People's Republic of China
>
> You can watch this TV nationwide thanks to its PAL-D system
>
> (*Wen Wei Po*, January 4, 1979, 9)

This advertisement not only ran in pro-China newspapers but also in the more pro-capitalist publications *Ming Pao* (明報) and *Sing Tao* (星島).[17]

The advertisement provided a list of stores and trading firms in Hong Kong that had been designated by the Chinese government as their official gift stores for visitors to China. Among them were three Chinese product emporiums (國貨公司), or department stores, that exclusively carried mainland Chinese products: *Da Hua* (大華), *Zhong Guo* (中國), and *Hua Feng* (華豐). The chairman of the Communist Party of China at the time was Hua Guofeng (華國鋒), and so, jokingly, Hong Kongers took the second character from each of the three stores' names and collectively referred to them as "Hua Guo Feng (華國豐)." Many Hong Kongers, who had never entered or even been near these Chinese product emporiums, suddenly flocked there to buy appliances to take with them to China.

National's PAL-D television had another China-friendly feature: it could accommodate sudden changes in voltage. In China, voltage was officially 220, but National's advertised model could function on a minimum of 160 and up to a maximum of 240 volts. Mong explains the 80-volt operating range:

> "You see, in the Chinese countryside, where there were many factories, the voltage went down when they were in operation. It went as low as 160 or 170. But in places where there were not many factories, the voltage went up as high as 240."[18]

Mong pushed Matsushita Electric's television factory hard, telling the engineers that he needed a set that could adapt to China's wildly fluctuating voltage standards; otherwise,

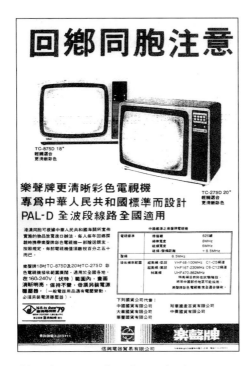

"Attention: compatriots who are planning to return
home to China" Ad promoting National color TVs
modeled for China to Hong Kongers who plan to
visit their Mainland relatives.
(*Wen Wei Po*, January 4, 1979)

they would not sell in the long run. The ad in the pro-Chinese newspapers emphasized in bold letters, "Within a range of 160 to 240 volts, the picture stays crystal clear without the need for a voltage converter."[19]

Guangzhou Service Center

National's forte was after-sales service and maintenance. William Mong saw that this was essential to gaining customers' trust in National products. By June 1979, within half a year of China implementing its "one appliance per person per year" policy, National's rivals, Hitachi and Sony, had set up service stations in Guangzhou.[20] Shun Hing followed suit a few weeks later, opening its service station in one of the city's most visible locations, right in front of Guangzhou Station.[21] In fact, while many dealers in Hong Kong found doing business in China attractive precisely because they did not have to entertain maintenance requests from end users living across the border, Mong saw things otherwise. Tommy Ho, who was in charge of the China market at Shun Hing for many years, comments as follows:

> Mr Mong paid very serious attention to our after-sales service. The first time we went to China, we did not go to promote our products but to set up a service center.
>
> In those days the government owned all the real estate, and it was not easy to rent an office. The process was very complicated, and we had to get all kinds of documents and approval from the government. We had several meetings with Chinese officials, yet we were unable to come up with an arrangement.
>
> In order to speed things up, we decided to rent four rooms on the ground floor of Liuhua Hotel (流花賓館) in Guangzhou, and turn two of these rooms into our temporary service station. It was a good location and it was quite convenient for customers.[22]

Liuhua Hotel is indeed convenient; it is located right opposite the Guangzhou terminal of the Kowloon-Canton Railway. Mong's team rented rooms that also faced a bus terminal, ensuring that their service station was visible to both customers and pedestrians.

> With the service station in place, we could issue a warranty to customers who bought our products and tell them they could go there if their National products were out of order. We also assured our customers that we would use genuine National spare parts.
>
> But, at that time, there were no qualified technicians in China. We had to send our own staff from Hong Kong to Guangzhou. Our technicians were regularly stationed there.[23]

From a short-term perspective, making a profit in the China market was easy, as products sold out almost as soon as the shipment had arrived from Japan. But for the long term, it was essential to take steps to establish the National brand identity in a country where it was still virtually unknown. Matsushita's policy had always been that it would not sell its products anywhere unless after-sales service was available; Shun Hing, therefore, decided to extend this principle to the Chinese re-export business as well.

Following the opening of the service station, "Prompt and Reliable After-sales Service" became Shun Hing's motto. Shun Hing opened a full-fledged service center in Renmin Nan Lu (人民南路), Guangzhou's premier shopping street. The service center was later relocated opposite South China Normal University (華南師範大學). The company was able to come to an arrangement with the university's Department of Engineering, whereby students could work at the center and acquire the technical skills necessary to repair electrical goods. Shun Hing later commissioned the university to operate the service center on its behalf and provided it with technical support. This lowered Shun Hing's operating costs and gave students access to the latest technology; in other words, it was a win-win situation. Shun Hing subsequently expanded its after-sales service network to other cities in southern China, including Shenzhen (深圳), Chaozhou (潮州), Dongguan (東莞), Zhongshan (中山), Shantou (汕頭), Foshan (佛山), and Huizhou (惠州).[24]

Apart from the service centers, Shun Hing organized National product shows and demonstrations in China. In 1979, the company held a series of seminars entitled "Promoting Education for the Modernization of our Motherland" in Guangzhou and Shanghai, the purpose of which was to show how electrical appliances were essential to a modern lifestyle in China. During the seminars, Shun Hing would display and demonstrate many National products, such as radio-cassette recorders, television sets, and other types of audiovisual equipment. After the seminars, they would donate these demonstration models to local universities or vocational schools, which were of course thrilled. All these initiatives helped enhance National's reputation in China.[25]

Crossing the Border at Lo Wu Bridge

Hong Kong secondary school student Henry Chan boarded the Kowloon-Canton Railway train carrying his National television set in a big cardboard box. It was unassigned seating inside the carriages. As soon as the doors opened, people rushed in, the competition for seats was fierce and many had to make do with sitting on the floor. Electric ceiling fans whirled above the passengers' heads, and the wooden benches were hard. A diesel locomotive pulled the carriages from crowded urban Kowloon, through rice paddies with grazing water buffalos, all the way to Lo Wu. Wagons transporting pigs would sometimes go by in the opposite direction, the stench forcing passengers to cover their nose with their hands.

The train eventually reached the last station on the Hong Kong side of the border, Lo Wu. Henry got off and went up to a Hong Kong immigration counter to complete the departure procedures. Carrying the television set and the heavy bag of clothing, he walked up a narrow slope, across the Lo Wu Bridge, and over the Shenzhen River that divided Hong Kong and China. This was the bridge countless Hong Kongers crossed, bearing gift appliances for their relatives in China. Some had tied as many as four television sets to a carrying pole, two at the front and two at the back. Some even lugged refrigerators across the narrow bridge.

It was a sweltering hot day, and porters came up to Henry and his parents offering to carry the television set. The Chans were determined not to use their service. Whereas most of the televisions brought in as gifts were black-and-white, theirs was color, and if it were to be stolen or damaged, they would never forgive themselves.

When Henry reached the Chinese checkpoint, he had to present his "Home Return Permit" for inspection by the Customs officials, just like a passport. The crowd at the checkpoint was so thick that Henry felt like he was suffocating. Visitors had to wait in line for one to two hours, and when their turn came, they were called into a private room for their luggage to be examined. The luggage inspection was a strict, and therefore painfully slow, process. Bags had to be completely unpacked, and items examined one by one. Each pocket was turned inside out to ensure nothing was hidden. Anything the visitors were wearing, including watches, rings, and earrings, had to be declared.

If a visitor forgot to declare a winter coat, the inspector would suspect him or her of smuggling, resulting in a fine or the coat being confiscated. To Hong Kong travelers, it felt like a police search.

When he finally made it through Customs, Henry boarded an even older train to his mother's hometown of Guangzhou. This train was, if anything, more packed than the previous one from Hong Kong. It was simply impossible to find a seat. He stood, then squatted, then stood again. The train made several stops between Shenzhen and Guangzhou, and at every station more and more passengers squeezed into the carriages. When even the few steps leading up to the carriage door were occupied and no one was able to get on, some desperate people tried to climb through the train windows, causing altercations with the passengers inside.

At last, when Henry's train pulled into Guangzhou Station, the first thing he noticed was how the colorful outfits of the Hong Kongers stood out against the gray suits of the Mainlanders. His uncle's family welcomed him at the station, and they were overjoyed to see the television set. Henry was, of course, delighted by their smiles, but he recalls, "There were just so many people, and I had to be wary of pickpockets." Henry sums up his memories of that 1979 summer holiday by saying: "Carrying that TV was just so hard."[26]

Pay in Hong Kong; Pick up in China

William Mong and the Shun Hing staff stood in the bustling Kowloon Station in Hung Hom, from where all China-bound trains departed. They carefully observed passengers and took note of the contents of the cardboard boxes they were carrying. This market research exercise would tell them which products were most in demand and which companies were manufacturing them. Mong recalls:

> Many passengers carried TVs, refrigerators, and various other things, to Hung Hom Station, caught a train to the border, got off there, and walked to Shenzhen.
>
> We witnessed this sequence of events over and over again. So we discussed this with China Travel Service and told them that our customers were having a hard time.[27]

In those days, China Travel Service, China's state-run travel agency, managed the flow of people in and out of the country. After a series of negotiations, Shun Hing, along with three of its competitors, came up with a much more convenient system: television coupons. The system worked as follows: those planning to visit China would go to one of the Chinese product emporiums where they paid for both the television set and the transportation and handling charges associated with its delivery to Guangzhou. In return, they received a coupon that served as a bill of lading. They then carried the coupon with them on the train to Lo Wu; once there, they presented it to the Chinese Customs and paid the import tax. Armed with the coupon and the tax receipt, they could claim their

"Pay in Hong Kong; Pick up in China"
Hong Kong's three Chinese product emporiums
promote their free television delivery service.
(*Wen Wei Po*, March 12, 1979)

television, which Shun Hing had transported for them from Hong Kong, at designated stores in Guangzhou. This system was called "Pay in Hong Kong; Pick up in China (香港買單，國內提貨)" and would later be expanded to encompass other cities in Guangdong and Fujian Provinces.

There were precedents to the "Pay in Hong Kong; Pick up in China" system, and they had already been put to good use by Hong Kong's Chinese product emporiums. At Chinese New Year, for example, the stores offered special 30-kilogram holiday food packages that customers could pay for in Hong Kong and pick up in Guangzhou or Shenzhen upon presentation of a coupon.

Shun Hing took the lead for National, and the agents for three other manufacturers, Hitachi, Philips, and Sharp, quickly adapted this system to include television sets. On March 15, 1979, just two and a half months after the implementation of the "one appliance per person per year" rule, all four brands started selling the China television coupons. The swiftness of the deal was due to the fact that both parties—Shun Hing and China Travel Service—were Chinese. The service was convenient, and it came with a one-year guarantee. An advertisement that appeared in the pro-China *Wen Wei Po* assured potential customers that it was also reliable, because the television set would be inspected by a technician before any exchange took place at Liuhua Hotel in Guangzhou.[28]

Shun Hing also advertised its "Pay in Hong Kong; Pick up in China" services on television, since, by then, over ninety percent of Hong Kong households owned a set. The commercial is set in a Hung Hom Station packed with luggage-laden Hong Kongers. An old man crosses the screen, heavy bags dangling on both sides of his carrying pole. The seven members of the Lee family, however, are traveling light.

> Mr Lee's friend: Well, Mr Lee, is your family going to visit your hometown? Traveling to China is tough, but why are you carrying so little?
>
> Mr Lee: Actually, we're bringing a lot with us. I have a National color TV for my mother-in-law.
>
> Wife: I'm bringing in a radio-cassette recorder for my father-in-law.
>
> Son: I've got a radio for my cousin.
>
> Daughter: I'm bringing in a calculator for my grandpa.
>
> Grandmother: Everybody will be happy with the rice cooker and electric fan.
>
> Teenager: I'm sure my cousin will love the compact camera.[29]

The ad aimed to show that, despite bringing in so many gift appliances for their relatives in China, the Lees were actually traveling light, because they were using the "Pay in Hong Kong; Pick up in China" system. The ad was in line with the "one appliance per person per year" rule, and the Lees were even seen to show consideration for their in-laws, Mr Lee buying a color television for his mother-in-law, and Mrs Lee a radio-cassette recorder for her father-in-law.

Buying appliances for relatives in China placed quite a heavy economic burden on many Hong Kongers. In 1981, the non-governmental organization, Neighbourhood Advice-Action Council, conducted a survey among lower- and middle-class families on the matter of visits to relatives in China. It asked what kind of economic impact the visits had had on them. Of those who responded to the survey, twenty-two percent stated that the trips had forced them to cut down on their own living expenses, and fourteen percent said that their financial burden had become greater.[30] Since the appliances brought in as gifts were rather expensive, they often ended up being the cause of marital disputes. It was fairly common for arguments to erupt over how much should be spent on one side of the family versus the other. For example, a wife would want to bring in a color television for her family in China, but her husband thought that it was too extravagant. For this reason, the couple portrayed in Shun Hing's television commercial tactfully directed their gifts to each other's in-laws.

Shun Hing also expanded the number of outlets authorized to sell appliance coupons. In addition to the Chinese product emporiums, the coupons were now available from China Travel Service and other designated Chinese trading companies. Without going into detail, Mong recounts the negotiations that led to the expansion:

"We looked for buyers. We went directly to the Chinese government and other units that would be able to import our products, and negotiated with them. And that was how the coupon business came about."[31]

Traveling Light with just a Coupon

In the summer of 1980, Henry's uncle in Guangzhou said that he wanted to get another color television set for one of his friends. Henry was therefore once again asked to use his quota under the "one appliance per person per year" scheme. His uncle in Hong Kong went to China Travel Service to buy train tickets. In the year since Henry's last trip to the Mainland, the China Travel Service offices had undergone a major transformation. The ground floor looked more like an electrical appliance shop than a travel agency, the display cabinets full of televisions, rice cookers, cameras, refrigerators, bicycles, and sewing machines for people to buy as gifts for their relatives in China. Several brands were represented, National among them. The train ticket counters were located on the first floor. Would-be travelers had no choice but to walk through the appliance section to get to the ticket counters, and many of them did end up shopping there. Arrangements for the "Pay in Hong Kong; Pick up in China" service were easy and done on the spot. Henry's uncle once again chose a National television, but this time he also paid for the transportation and handling charges so that he could pick it up in Guangzhou.

As a result, Henry had to carry only one piece of luggage onboard the train. He put the coupon specifying both the stock number and price of the television in his travel bag, alongside his other gifts of imported candies and soft drinks. Of this second trip, he says, "Of course, it was easy. I didn't have to carry a TV anymore."[32] Even the Customs inspection seemed less strict this time. Upon his arrival in Guangzhou, he handed the coupon to his uncle, who would use it to collect the television. In this manner, Henry "carried" a television set from Hong Kong to Guangzhou without even touching it.

Televisions found their way across the Sino-Hong Kong border in amazing numbers. In 1981, at the peak of this influx, 1.79 million sets were re-exported from Hong Kong to China. That same year, the total number of television sets imported into Hong Kong reached 2.53 million. If we base our calculations on these two numbers alone, we can estimate that approximately seventy percent of all televisions imported into Hong Kong were being re-exported to China.

In 1986, following in the footsteps of other "compatriots" in Hong Kong and Macau, Chinese immigrants from Taiwan began making trips back to China. There were no direct flights from Taiwan to China; therefore, the majority of Taiwanese visitors to the Mainland had to travel via Hong Kong. During the Cultural Revolution, many Chinese nationals whose relatives had fled to Taiwan with the Kuomintang had received harsh treatment at the hands of the Communist Party. Now, after more than thirty-seven years of separation, Taiwanese people were being allowed back in to visit their relatives, bringing with them, as gifts, appliances that they had often picked up in Hong Kong.

At the time of China's opening up to the world, the majority of electrical appliances sold in Hong Kong were made in Japan. As a result, Japanese manufacturers witnessed an unexpected flow of their appliances, along Chinese transnational networks once again, from Japan to China via Hong Kong. The system of "Pay in Hong Kong; Pick up in China" was a revolution in logistics made possible thanks to local insight: Hong Kong entrepreneurs, realizing the potential of this new transnational flow of people and goods, had taken immediate action. By 1985, China Travel Service had expanded its "Pay in Hong Kong; Pick up in China" service to include white goods, as well as sewing machines, electric fans, rice cookers, and typewriters. It had also extended it to cities such as Beijing and Shanghai.[33]

The re-export of Japanese appliances using the "Pay in Hong Kong; Pick up in China" system was officially sanctioned by the Chinese government, but there were some at Matsushita who frowned upon it as illegitimate because it violated agreements restricting the operations of individual agents to within their own political boundaries. Mong, however, countered these arguments by saying:

> "This is legitimate. We are selling these products in Hong Kong. We get money for the TV and our service. I just carry it for them as well!"[34]

The desire for modern convenience transcends national boundaries. For Mong, this transnational flow of goods was as natural as water flowing downward; some of his counterparts in Japan, however, felt that business should be conducted on a purely bilateral basis. But as the success of the gift appliance business grew, Matsushita, working in conjunction with China Travel Service's outlets in North America, adapted Shun Hing's coupon formula to cater to Chinese diasporas there.

Monkey Business

The China re-export business was a gold mine. In 1980, for example, approximately 290,000 National rice cookers were sold in Hong Kong, which at the time had a population of just 5.1 million. In other words, one in seventeen Hong Kongers bought a National rice cooker that year, an all-time record. In 1978, National released a high-end rice cooker model that not only cooked the rice but also kept it warm for up to twelve hours. Furthermore, it had a completely revamped look with a hinged lid connected to the body (Chapter 6). These innovations certainly helped boost sales figures, but the main reason for their increase was the massive flow of Hong Kongers carrying them as gifts into China. Tommy Ho, who was in charge of China sales for many years at Shun Hing recalls:

> The decade that followed was really a golden age. The rapid growth of the electrical goods industry was mainly driven by China's Open Door Policy. The first two big-ticket items to be imported into China were radios and radio-cassette recorders, followed by televisions, fridges, washing machines, and air conditioners.[35]

For Hong Kong people, modern appliances meant a better quality of life, something they wanted their Chinese relatives to enjoy as they did. And this was the determining factor for the continuous flow of appliances from Japan to Hong Kong and on to southern China throughout the 1980s. Tommy Ho recalls:

> In fact, from the time China first opened its doors in 1979, our China business went very smoothly. It was so easy for us to make a profit. [As far as several types of National appliances were concerned], we simply sold them to Chinese government-affiliated agents [such as Chinese emporiums] in Hong Kong and that's it! Products such as air conditioners were great hits with the Chinese market. We were always running out of stock. As long as we had the products on hand, we had nothing to worry about!

> After a while, Chinese buyers came to Hong Kong to purchase goods [without going through the Chinese-government affiliated agents in Hong Kong.] As soon as the deliveries from Matsushita arrived, we just sold the goods to local dealers who then sold them to buyers from China.

> The retailers in Hong Kong liked selling their goods to buyers from China even if the profit margins were lower. These sales were made in cash and they did not have to worry about collecting payment after delivery. In addition, China's importers would ship the merchandise back to China by themselves, and local dealers could save on shipping and administrative costs. Lastly, there would be no after-sales complaints, as the end users were all in China.

> Given these advantages, almost all of the local dealers in Hong Kong rushed in to take advantage of this new Chinese market.[36]

The Hong Kong home appliances industry became extremely dependent on its China business, as it offered fast turnover, large sales volumes, good profits, and few complaints from end users. It was, however, also a high-risk business.

By 1985, the year Michael Jackson and Lionel Richie brought dozens of American pop stars together to release the single "We Are the World" and raise funds for hunger relief in Africa, Hong Kong's appliance trade with China was beginning to show signs of strain. In response to the high, popular demand for electric appliances, especially televisions, China's central government made it a policy to regulate foreign imports and promote domestic production. Chinese citizens continued to strive for modern living and Japanese appliances, despite the punishing import taxes imposed.[37] As a result, they came to occupy a significant portion of China's imports and strained China's foreign currency reserve. The Library of Congress's Country Report summed up the situation as follows:

> Because of the expansion of exports in the mid-1980s, a large foreign reserve surplus, and the decentralized management of foreign trade, imports surged. Huge, uncontrolled purchases of consumer goods led to trade deficits in 1984 and 1985, resulting in the introduction of an import and export licensing system, stricter controls on foreign exchange expenditures, and the devaluation of the yuan in order to reduce the trade deficit and ensure that machinery, equipment, and semifinished goods, rather than consumer goods, were imported.[38]

For television imports, this meant that the Central Government would encourage import of color picture tubes and equipment for television production plants, while controlling imports of finished products.[39]

China's local governments began making frequent amendments to their policies on the import of foreign electrical appliances. Import taxes fluctuated wildly. False rumors regarding the introduction of new regulations abounded. Hong Kong dealers were at a loss to figure out what was really going on. On several occasions Chinese authorities had, without prior notice, suspended all imports into the country, leaving Hong Kong dealers with large quantities of merchandise sitting in their warehouses and causing them significant financial losses. Tommy Ho explains:

> In 1986, the Central Government suddenly announced strict monitoring of the import of foreign electrical goods in all provinces and cities. After the announcement, Shun Hing's Chinese purchasing agent in Hong Kong asked to terminate the contract, even cancelling the letters of credit that had already been issued. All of a sudden, Matsushita's warehouses were stacked to the ceiling with tens of thousands of color televisions. It took us a very long time to clear them all.

> That 1986 policy severely affected Hong Kong's electrical appliance industry. The Hong Kong market was too small to absorb this surplus merchandise, and local merchants suffered losses. China trade generated a good profit margin but also carried unforeseen risks.[40]

China's overall official import of color television sets plummeted from 4.96 million in 1985 to 1.37 million in 1986.[41] Kyoichi Yoshioka, working in Matsushita Trading's Hong Kong Section in Osaka, also witnessed the wild ups and downs of the China business.

> It was a complete turnaround, you know. One day, all of a sudden, the door [allowing the import of appliances] was shut, and [Shun Hing] had purchased a lot of products from us without any idea that this was about to happen. As soon as the door closed, dealers [who had placed orders with Shun Hing] just canceled them, like that. It was horrible. But we overcame all these misfortunes.[42]

Hong Kong's role as the primary gateway for the flow of Japanese appliances into China gradually diminished, and Matsushita Electric started to deal directly with China. In 1987, Matsushita set up a joint venture with a Mainland company and began manufacturing color picture tubes in Beijing. Starting in 1993, as a market-driven economy began to take root in China, Matsushita steadily expanded its manufacturing base and direct sales channels in the country. At the same time, Chinese manufacturers became more competitive and began assuming a dominant position in the domestic market, including white goods such as refrigerators and washing machines.

Hong Kongers were yet again faced with having to adapt to a new situation. In 1989, Shun Hing stopped all direct trade in appliances with China, choosing instead to act as an intermediary between Matsushita's Japanese operations and its Chinese customers. Drawing on past experience and making use of existing networks, the versatile Shun Hing helped negotiate business contracts between the two parties and in exchange received a commission. This protected Shun Hing from the risks inherent in any sudden changes to China's import policies. Its profits, however, went down significantly. As a result, Shun Hing gradually withdrew from the China trade altogether. Tommy Ho, who later went on to become a director of Shun Hing Electronic Trading, says that it was a wise decision. Many Hong Kong dealers who did not get out of the China business in time ended up going bankrupt.

> We referred to the China business as "monkey business"; we were never sure of what would happen next, and the business environment was forever changing.
>
> Our chairman [Mr Mong] always reminded us that China was not a stable market and that we should treat any business we did there as a bonus. Instead we should focus our energies on Hong Kong, which was a stable and reliable local market.[43]

Shun Hing once again concentrated on developing new products and services to meet the needs of Hong Kong consumers. Ironically, some of these products ended up on a journey of their own. They would accompany Hong Kongers in the mass exodus across the Pacific that followed the signing of the Sino-British Joint Declaration in 1984.

6

---•---

What if We Can't Buy a Rice Cooker in Canada?
Across the Ocean to Asian Diasporas

Rice Cookers sold on the top shelf of a supermarket
in New York's Chinatown, 2006.

The Sino-British Joint Declaration was signed by Chinese Prime Minister Zhao Ziyang
(趙紫陽) and British Prime Minister Margaret Thatcher in Beijing, on December
19, 1984. The prospect of the British colony being returned to China in 1997 caused
tremendous anxiety among the people of Hong Kong. Those who had fled poverty-
stricken villages in China and whose family members had suffered hardship during the
Cultural Revolution felt uneasy about their future under the Communist regime. Many
feared the worst. Thus began the mass exodus from Hong Kong to the West, in order to
obtain foreign citizenship as insurance against what might happen to the territory after
it reverted to Chinese rule.[1]

The most popular destinations for emigration were Canada, the United States, and
Australia.[2] The United States was the first choice for many, as they saw it as the most
attractive for job opportunities and education for their children. But the criteria required
to qualify for residency or naturalization in the United States were extremely strict:

relatives already living in the country, highly specialized professional skills, or a firm job offer from a US employer. These requirements created an almost impassable barrier. The number of Hong Kong emigrants to the United States showed no rapid increase after the signing, and remained stable at around 12,500 annually.[3] The British government, for its part, offered full nationality to just 50,000 highly qualified Hong Kongers and their families.[4]

Unlike the United States and the United Kingdom, Canada had a more relaxed immigration policy and accepted workers without professional skills, as well as retirees. In 1978, the Canadian government introduced a business immigration program targeted at people with a strong business background who could contribute to its economy. In 1984, the program was expanded to include three categories: entrepreneurs, investors, and self-employed persons.[5] Immigration from Hong Kong to Canada grew rapidly, from 7,696 in 1984 to 19,908 in 1989, the year of the student protests in Tiananmen Square, and to 43,651 in 1994.[6]

In the meantime, the National rice cooker, which continued to dominate the Hong Kong market, had gone high-tech. By the late 1980s, it featured a built-in micro computer chip that allowed subtle adjustments in temperature during the cooking process. Unlike previous models, these high-tech rice cookers owed their development to the contributions of female rice specialists and designers. These rice cookers had become an essential item in Hong Kong kitchens, so essential that, when Hong Kongers emigrated, many took their multifunction rice cookers with them.

The Advent of "Rice Ladies"[7]

The majority of rice cooker users had, from the onset, been women. The National rice cooker research and development team, however, did not include a female member until 1979. In this, the rice cooker was the norm rather than the exception when it came to female-oriented products. According to sociologists Masako Amano and Atsushi Sakurai, consumer items targeted at women, like washing machines, underwear, and sanitary pads, were generally designed and produced by men. These products started to reflect their customers' needs only when Japanese women began participating in their production process.[8]

In the summer of 1978, Yoshiaki Sano, head engineer of the Rice Cooker Division, embarked on the quest for a formula that turned out better rice. He began by looking for a rice specialist able to assess flavor through the application of scientific methods. In those days, the research and development team consisted of mechanical engineers trained in drawing plans, and they did not apply laboratory data to produce perfectly cooked food. This all-male group relied solely on their personal taste to evaluate the rice cooked in their machines.

Moreover, Matsushita Electric Industrial recruited all of its engineers first to the main company and then allocated them to various product divisions. The vast majority of these engineers joined the company in hopes of developing cutting-edge technology at its Research Institute, or working in one of the more glamorous audio-visual divisions. Rice cookers, on the other hand, were regarded as low-tech appliances for housewives (*okusan-yōhin*), so assignment to their research team was usually considered a disappointment. As the head engineer of the Rice Cooker Division, Sano struggled to get his young team of male engineers motivated:

> When new engineers were allocated to the Rice Cooker Division, many of them felt deflated and couldn't get over their disappointment. They would say, "Why do I have to work on rice cookers? We already have rice cookers. Is there anything else to do?"
>
> One actually resigned. Some complained and asked to be transferred to the Research Institute or another division. There were several such cases.
>
> In addition, the HQ Personnel Office wouldn't send us the best engineers. After all, our [Rice Cooker] division was considered a minor one.[9]

Sano was determined to find a rice specialist, and his quest led him to Professor Hiroyasu Fukuba, one of Japan's most respected food scientists, who had written extensively on the subject of rice. He taught at Ochanomizu Women's University in Tokyo, so naturally the candidate he introduced to Sano was a woman:

> "To me, it didn't matter whether [the rice specialist] was a man or a woman. I was simply trying to fill a void in our team."[10]

Professor Fukuba introduced him to one of his students, Takako Kuroda, a master's degree candidate in home economics with an emphasis on food and nutritional sciences.

Kuroda had extensive experience in lab research on carbohydrates. For Kuroda, a Tokyo native, the opportunity to work in Osaka came out of the blue:

> I asked Professor Fukuba one day, "Have you heard of any jobs going at the moment?"
>
> He said, "There's one if you are willing to move to Osaka. Are you interested?" He told me that Matsushita was looking for someone to conduct scientific research on its cooking appliances, and that they hadn't had much success so far.
>
> So I met Sano-san on a hot summer's day.[11]

Sano was impressed with Kuroda and was convinced that she would be able to run the new research on her own. So he asked Matsushita's HQ Personnel Office for special permission to hire her, bypassing the central allocation system. He was immediately bombarded with questions:

> "Why do you want to hire a woman? Why do you want a graduate of [Tokyo's] Ochanomizu Women's University? Why not a graduate of Nara Women's University, which is nearby?"

Yoshiaki Sano inspects a rice cooker
production line. Osaka, circa 1982.
Courtesy of Yoshiaki Sano

So I replied, "Why should I hire a Nara Women's University graduate?"

[The personnel officer] answered, "A Nara Women's University graduate can stay with her parents and commute to our office in Osaka. When she gets married, she will probably stay in Osaka. If we hire one from Tokyo, she has to move to Osaka and live alone. And who is going to find her a husband?"

I shot back, "That's not for us to worry about."

Looking back, all of this sounds ridiculous, but I really had to fight [for this position]. I insisted, "I need Miss Kuroda. She is the one."[12]

Sano was clearly starting a new tradition at Matsushita, even if it was out of necessity. Once again, the relatively low status of the Rice Cooker Division within the giant corporation forced Sano and his associates to search for innovative solutions, and this led him to hire a female professional.

Upon her graduation, Kuroda went to work for Matsushita, where she received further training in engineering. This was eight years before the implementation of the 1986 Japanese Equal Employment Opportunity Law for men and women, and the first time Matsushita had ever had a female researcher on staff, let alone one with a postgraduate degree.

Kuroda joined the all-male team of rice cooker engineers. Dressed in her white lab coat, she stood out in every aspect from her colleagues in their gray factory uniforms. She set her own agenda and conducted experiments on the relationship between the temperature the rice was cooked at and its texture, with the aim of developing a formula to enhance the flavor. The key was in when to adjust the temperature inside the appliance; this had to be done four times within a twenty- to thirty-minute period to imitate the traditional Japanese method of cooking rice in a thick metal pot over firewood. The process is explained in this old Japanese rhyme:

Hajime choro choro

Naka pappa

Butsu butsu iu koro hi wo hiite

Hito nigiri no wara moyashi

Akago naitemo futa toruna[13]

Start with a low flame	[low]
Bring it to a vigorous boil	[high]
Turn it down when the pot whistles	[medium]
Throw in a handful of straw	[high]
Never take the lid off	
Even when your little one cries out for rice.	

Tokyo-Edo Museum exhibit recreating a late-1920s Japanese kitchen and featuring the traditional metal pot (*kama*) used to cook rice.

Kuroda worked tirelessly on the correct timing for the low-high-medium-high flame formula. Her formal training in food science allowed her to make subtle adjustments to every step of the cooking process. When the rice was ready, she used a tailor-made scientific device to measure the consistency. She discovered that, to ensure the ideal texture, it was necessary to bring the rice to the boil faster. Based on the results obtained in this manner, Kuroda's mechanical engineer colleagues developed a computer program that could automatically regulate the temperature inside the cooker.

However, because no scientific test can effectively replace the human sense of taste, this experimentation with different timings and temperatures involved tasting bowl after bowl of steamed rice every day. National used to advertise that the research and development of every one of its new models required three tons of rice. The female engineers who were subsequently hired to replace Kuroda in the rice cooker team eventually became known informally throughout the company as the "rice ladies."[14]

The National "rice ladies" carry out taste tests and try out different recipes. Osaka, 1983.
Courtesy of Panasonic

It was not just the technology that was innovative. The rice cooker was also given a complete makeover by a young female designer: the hinged lid had a handle and was connected to the main body of the appliance, which featured a floral pattern. It was feminine, rounded, and almost Hello Kitty cute, unlike previous rice cookers that looked more like mechanized versions of traditional pots and pans. Now the rice cooker could be carried by its handle like a handbag.

National named its new line *mai-con denshi jar* (micro-computerized electronic jar). *Mai-con* was a buzzword for home appliances. Unlike the Sony Walkman portable cassette player, National rice cookers were not given a nickname for the Japanese market but acquired one in Hong Kong.

A Rice Cooker Named after a Chinese Beauty

In November 1979, the cute rice cooker made its appearance in stores across Hong Kong. Although the localized model did not have a built-in microchip, it was intelligent enough to not only cook the rice but also keep it warm for up to twelve hours. The "keep warm" function automatically switched on as soon as the rice was cooked. It also had a non-stick coated inner pan, which Shun Hing advertised: "You don't waste a single grain. Easy to clean, hygienic and convenient."[15] To distinguish this new high-end line from the classic model with a windowed lid, William Mong gave it the nickname *Saishi* (西施) in Cantonese, *Xishi* in Mandarin.

Saishi was a famed beauty in ancient China. In the Spring and Autumn Period (from the late eighth century BC to the early fifth century BC), two neighboring states, Yue (越) and Wu (吳), were at war. After losing a battle, King Goujian (勾踐) of Yue sent Saishi as a tribute to King Fuchai (夫差) of Wu. Legend has it that Fuchai, bewitched by Saishi's great beauty, lost all interest in affairs of state, and, under her influence, made several decisions that led to the decline and eventual fall of Wu.[16]

But why did Mong name this rice cooker model Saishi? "Because it was beautiful," he answers simply.[17] That is how this new line, its cute design originally targeted at young Japanese housewives, came to acquire the name of a famed Chinese beauty.[18] The first Saishi ad, featuring two models dressed as Saishi and King Fuchai, puts particular emphasis on the appliance's eye-catching design:

National Keep Warm Electronic Rice Jar "Saishi"

12-hour Keep Warm function

The "Saishi" Flower's Delicate Beauty Adds Charm to its Appearance[19]

Take Part in Our Coloring Competition for Your Chance to Win a "Saishi"

(*Ming Pao*, November 3, 1979)

There were three kinds of design for the body: jade green and rainbow orange, which were in keeping with the vivid striped patterns of the 1970s, and rose red, which had a floral pattern. All three added a feminine touch to the kitchen. To highlight the new colors and patterns, Shun Hing organized a competition in which participants were asked to color in a picture of a model dressed like the legendary beauty, and gave away thirty Saishi cookers to the winners.[20] The new colors were a marked departure from the traditional white enamel of earlier models and were designed to attract younger, more fashion-conscious customers. The Saishi model proved so popular in Hong Kong that its name became synonymous with the high-end thermal rice cooker.

Let Me Hear the Whistling of Steaming Rice

In 1985, a congee-making function was added to the Saishi model. Ten years had passed since the congee cooking trials at Mong's summer house in Ito, Japan, which had resulted in the production of a multifunction rice cooker with a bright orange enameled pot (Chapter 1). This time, the slow-cooking function, complete with an analogue timing device, was added to a Saishi thermal rice cooker with a floral-patterned pastel pink body.

Users were able to adjust the consistency of the congee by using the timer. The cooking function could be set to last for up to four hours, the time needed to produce mushy, Cantonese-style congee, versus the one hour needed for the smooth Chiu Chow-style congee common to the eastern part of Guangdong Province.[21] It also functioned as a slow cooker, ideal for making savory Chinese soups and sweet bean desserts.

In addition, there was great progress in taste. The rice cooker was designed to reach boiling point quickly without burning the rice, thereby greatly enhancing its flavor. It was a product of which the employees in what was formerly the Rice Cooker Division, now the Cooking Systems Division, were justifiably proud.

Ad featuring the Saishi rice cooker that Mong named
after the legendary beauty of ancient China.
(*Ming Pao*, November 3, 1979)

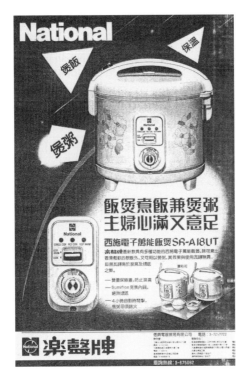

The next generation Saishi model allowed users to
manually adjust the cooking time
for Cantonese-style congee.
(*Oriental Daily*, January 18, 1988)

They showed Mong a prototype and conducted a cooking demonstration for him. He watched their actions as if he were an eagle circling its prey. Then, he said something totally unexpected:

> Let me see more steam. Let me hear that sweet sound the rice cooker makes when it is cooking congee. It can't be silent. The steam starts whistling when the congee is cooking. Let me hear the whistling of steaming rice.[22]

Technically, there was nothing wrong with the rice cooker, but the amount of steam generated was insufficient for it to produce a whistling sound as it escaped from the pot. Mong wanted to make the process of cooking congee a visual and auditory experience. People needed to hear that the rice was being cooked, in the same way that the glass viewing pane allowed them to see it.

The amount of steam produced was not a consideration for Matsushita because the types of pot used to cook rice were different. While traditional Japanese cooking pots had a solid wooden lid, Cantonese clay pot lids had a small hole through which steam could escape, making a whistling sound in the process. For Hong Kongers, this sound was a reassuring sign that dinner would soon be served. Some of the Hong Kong university students who spend a year on exchange programs in Japan and buy rice cookers during their stay say they find the Japanese models too quiet and they miss the whistling of National's Hong Kong models.

The Cooking Systems Division carried out trial after trial. Masayuki Nakano was in charge of international sales at the time, and he witnessed the difficulties faced by the division's technical staff.

> "The engineers had a hard time with this too. Mong-san asked them to make the steam more visible to show that the congee was being cooked. In the end, to achieve this, they put a sensor on the lid."[23]

The sensor the engineers fitted on the lid regulated the amount of steam that could escape from the pot. Shun Hing advertised this multifunction Saishi as "Everything a housewife needs." The ad goes on to claim that:

> National's newest Saishi multifunction all-purpose Warm Jar cooks perfect rice and congee every time, giving you the same results as a traditional Chinese clay pot, but without the risks of water overflowing or burnt rice.
>
> Pre-set timer for up to 4 hours lets your congee cook by itself.[24]

The National rice cooker team and Mong continued to use the interactive approach that they had established in 1960 with Mong involved in every step of the development and manufacturing process. This was particularly the case when it came to models that cooked congee. Mong would not approve a product until he had monitored every single stage of its development, from planning to mass production. He would go so far as to check the consumer catalogues used to promote rice cookers in Hong Kong. "Isn't this congee too watery?" Mong was looking through the rice cooker catalogue that had arrived from Osaka and was unhappy with the consistency of the congee in the illustrations. To him, it did not look like Cantonese congee. Even Takekazu Nishiwaki, who had been in charge of the overseas sales of rice cookers for many years, was surprised by the attention to detail of Shun Hing's charismatic managing director.

> Well, I didn't expect Mong-san to do this.
>
> Mong-san is the big boss. We thought that we could let his staff handle things and we didn't consult him. Understandably, he was angry.[25]

The collaborative Shun Hing and Matsushita rice cooker teams spared no effort, expending time and energy on matters that other market competitors considered minor. The Hong Kong side was attentive to even the smallest details, and the Japanese side was careful never to dismiss local input. Rather, the Matsushita employees would listen carefully to what Shun Hing had to say, thinking, "If that's what's needed in Hong Kong, we have to do it," and endeavored to take local considerations into account.[26]

The multifunction Saishi model became a bestseller. It cooked Cantonese congee to the right consistency without fail, which was, of course, its most essential feature. The timer, which allowed customers to check on and adjust the cooking process, was also a welcome new addition. The seeing, hearing, and manual adjusting of the appliance's cooking functions were reassuring to customers and convinced them that it really worked. By the late 1980s, the Saishi model with congee function had become an essential item in Hong Kong kitchens, so essential that, when Hong Kongers began to emigrate to Canada, Australia, and other countries following the signing of the Sino-British Joint Declaration, many Saishi rice cookers went along with them in their luggage.

Across the Pacific with Hong Kong Immigrants

Soon after their marriage in 1990, Mr and Mrs Pang decided to move to Vancouver, where Mr Pang had spent his university years. Both accountants, they left Hong Kong without any hesitation; they liked Canada's clean air and green environment. There were many things they wanted to take with them, but in the end they brought along only four pieces of luggage, all that they were permitted under the airline baggage allowance. They packed clothing, bedding, plates, utensils—and a multifunction Saishi rice cooker that a relative had given them as a farewell gift. Saishi was a popular wedding as well as farewell gift. The Pangs decided to include it in their luggage because they would need to cook rice from the very first day of their new life in Canada.

This multifunction rice cooker was indeed a National, a model that Mong's company, Shun Hing Electronic Trading, had imported specifically for those consumers leaving Hong Kong for North America. In Hong Kong, the electricity voltage was 220, while in North America it was 110. If Mr and Mrs Pang had taken to Canada the model they used in Hong Kong, it would not have worked.

Many Hong Kong people who were about to emigrate wanted to take multifunction rice cookers with them. Some worried, "What if we can't buy a rice cooker in Canada?" Some thought it was cheaper to get one in Hong Kong, and some saw extra space in their containers and thought, Why not? These consumer voices reached Shun Hing, and soon appliance stores in Hong Kong began to carry 110-volt models. In 1988, just before Christmas, the popular Chinese-language newspaper, *Oriental Daily* (東方日報), carried an ad with pictures of nine National Saishi rice cookers:

National

Saishi Electric Warm Jar

Cooks Congee, Cooks Rice

Praised by Every Family

(*Oriental Daily*, December 22, 1988)

William Mong. Hong Kong, 2003.
Courtesy of Shun Hing Group

Of the nine multifunction rice cookers advertised, eight were available in both 110- and 220-volt versions. Since Shun Hing was also Matsushita's sole agent in Macau, where voltage was 110, it could officially import 110-volt rice cookers; the majority, however, ended up being bought in Hong Kong and carried to North America. Kenneth Man, in charge of rice cooker sales for Shun Hing at the time, explains that, in the late 1980s, when the number of immigrants to Canada was showing a sharp increase, the 110-volt models accounted for approximately ten percent of all sales in the territory.[27]

Later, the news that the Saishi model could be purchased in Canada spread, and sales of the 110-volt rice cooker started falling in Hong Kong.[28] In the meantime, Lok Seng Pai (樂聲牌), the Chinese trademark Shun Hing had come up with for the National product line in the 1950s, had accompanied Hong Kongers across the ocean to Canada. By 1990, Canada's ethnic Chinese population had grown significantly, exceeding 500,000 people.[29] Newly arrived immigrants from Hong Kong continued to use the familiar name informally when referring to National appliances, as did stores catering to the Chinese diaspora. Finally, Matsushita asked for Mong's permission to use the Chinese Lok Seng Pai brand name in Canada, which he happily agreed to.

After the initial exodus, the flow of people across the Pacific evolved into a two-way process and gave rise to a new phenomenon, that of the *tai hung yan* (太空人), or "astronaut." The term was used to refer to Hong Kongers who, having gained residency or citizenship in Canada and the US, returned to Hong Kong for short or, in some cases, extended periods to live and work. Mr and Mrs Pang, who became naturalized Canadians in 1994, were among those who elected to return to Hong Kong in 1998, a year after the handover. They wanted their children to get their primary and secondary schooling in Hong Kong.

In the mid-1980s, the classic white-bodied rice cookers were already widespread among the Asian diasporas in North America. The massive flow of new migrants from Hong Kong, however, created a market in Canada for a high-tech rice cooker whose functions and design were similar to those produced for the Hong Kong market. "The design process starts in Hong Kong," says Tomoko Sasakura, Overseas Products Planner in the Cooking Systems Division of Matsushita Electric.[30] She explains how, even now, the development of rice cooker models for the "oriental market," or Asian diaspora, begins in Hong Kong. Whenever a product design has to be modified or improved, designers will head for Hong Kong to conduct market research. They will then create new patterns, choose colors, and further refine their design through input from the Hong Kong side.

> When we go for a floral pattern, for example, we ask the Hong Kong side for their input first. Then we take it to other consumers like the oriental market in North America. When a product sells in Hong Kong, it sells in North America, too.[31]

In this way, the latest rice cooker models followed Asian migrants. But the flow of rice cookers from Asia to the West was by no means a new phenomenon. Since the launch of the automatic rice cooker in 1955, it has followed many Asians around the world.

Cooking California Rice in Copenhagen

A rice cooker is often considered vital to the survival of Asians living abroad. As of spring 2008, there are sixteen Japanese players in American Major League Baseball teams. Two of them, Daisuke Matsuzaka and Hideki Okajima, are pitchers for the Boston Red Sox. When they moved from Tokyo to Boston, they brought one thing with them: a rice cooker. Matsuzaka takes his rice cooker along when his team plays away from Fenway Park, so that he can cook low-fat Japanese food in his hotel room. A rice cooker also accompanied Okajima on trips made when he was a rookie in 2007. *The New York Times* reported his struggle to come to grips with American culture as follows:

> And during the first month of the season, not yet with a translator or English-language skills to order from room service, Okajima brought a rice cooker on trips, often cooking and eating alone.[32]

Rice cookers have been a source of comfort for Japanese working overseas for the last five decades.

In the spring of 1961, Shigeru Yoshida, a Japan Airlines employee who shares the name of the Japanese prime minister who signed the San Francisco Peace Treaty, was assigned to the airline's newly opened office in Copenhagen, Denmark. Japan Airlines was about to launch a polar route from Tokyo to Paris, via Anchorage, Copenhagen, and London. The new service would operate twice weekly and was scheduled to start on June 6, 1961.[33] Yoshida, who had trained as an army pilot in Manchuria (now northeastern China) during World War II, was the airline's first Copenhagen station manager. As was common practice among his colleagues when assigned overseas for the first time, Yoshida left his family in Tokyo, but he did take a Toshiba rice cooker with him.

> When I was assigned to Copenhagen, I went alone, because my family would have slowed me down in a foreign environment. But I wanted to eat rice with my meals. So I hand-carried a rice cooker.
>
> After the start of our polar route service, most of the Japanese businessmen assigned to Europe carried rice cookers with them. We were able to buy other appliances in Europe, but not rice cookers. We simply had to bring one with us.[34]

There is an old Japanese saying that goes "Men should not be in the kitchen (*Danshi chūbō ni hairu bekarazu*)." Traditionally, cooking was not considered a man's domain, and rice was especially challenging: it is necessary to get the heat just right and keep adjusting it for about thirty minutes. A rice cooker, however, ensured that rice was cooked properly. The rate of rice cooker ownership in Japan was eighty-eight percent in 1964, so the rice cooker became an essential item for Japanese posted overseas.[35] Armed with a rice cooker, an elite Japanese salaryman could prepare rice easily, even when far from home.

Yoshida bought his rice at a mom-and-pop grocery store near his house in the town of Kastrup, near Copenhagen Airport. He was one of the few Asians living in this suburban neighborhood; the majority of the inhabitants were Danish, or from another Scandinavian country.

> This was 1961 and 1962, before companies had really started to globalize their brands, so the town had no American-style supermarket or drug store. In my neighborhood, there were only a few family-run stores: a grocer, a butcher, and a fishmonger.[36]

Of the different varieties of rice available, Italian short-grain came the closest to Japanese rice. So, for a while, Yoshida prepared Italian rice in his Toshiba cooker. One day, a crew member stationed in Copenhagen gave him some good news. California rice, a Japanese variety grown in California, was available in Anchorage, and it was just like rice from home. For the next year or so, crew members flying regularly between Anchorage and Copenhagen brought with them pillow cases stuffed full of California rice, ensuring Yoshida had a steady supply for his personal consumption.

In the meantime, an import-export company in Kent, England, which specialized in Japanese food, discovered that Japanese expatriates living in Europe were willing to pay handsomely for California rice. So, it began importing rice from the United States and distributing it to retailers across Western Europe.[37] By 1962, California rice had made it onto the shelves of Yoshida's neighborhood grocer. The fishmonger next door kept live flounder in a tank, which was perfect for sashimi. Yoshida wanted the flounder skinned according to his specific instructions, but the shopkeeper did not understand English. So, he called his English-speaking assistant, Ms Olsen, to interpret for him. This ultimately made it possible for Yoshida to enjoy a feast of flounder sashimi, cucumber salad, and steamed rice from California, in Denmark.

Yoshida was later transferred to London, and, again, his rice cooker went with him. When he was assigned back to Tokyo in 1965, however, a Japanese astronomer working at an observatory in the Dutch city of Utrecht asked Yoshida if he could leave the rice cooker behind for his family. He was happy to do so and before his departure arranged for his Toshiba rice cooker to be shipped from London to Utrecht. For his subsequent postings to Rome and Seattle, Yoshida was accompanied by both a National rice cooker and his family.

According to the Japanese Ministry of Foreign Affairs, the number of Japanese nationals residing overseas had reached 1 million in 2005, approximately forty percent of whom were Japanese businesspeople (235,171) and their family members (182,029).[38] Koichiro Hioki, a professor of business management at Kyoto University, argues that rice cookers have been essential to the globalization of Japanese business. He goes so far as to say that it would have been impossible for Japanese corporations to post their salarymen overseas without rice cookers.[39]

In fact, a rice cooker remains at the top of the list of items to bring along on overseas postings. An online store popular with Japanese nationals preparing to relocate, "Device Net for World Mobilers," for example, stocks both 120- and 220-volt mid-range rice cooker models and somewhat disingenuously states on its website that "Rice cookers are especially difficult to get overseas. We recommend that you take one with you from Japan."[40]

Cooking in Secret at a British Boarding School

Another group of people who find comfort in a bowl of rice are Asian students living abroad. In dormitories, where cooking facilities are often limited, Asian students use and abuse rice cookers. They not only use rice cookers to steam rice, but they also boil water, warm canned food, and, at the University of Hong Kong, some even fry fish in them. On this highly creative use of a rice cooker, a former National "rice lady," now director of the Cooking Appliances Business Unit (originally known as the Rice Cooker Division), Machiko Miyai, comments, "Well, it is possible to fry fish in a rice cooker. But I'm afraid this will shorten its life span."[41] Yet for Asian students unable to get used to foreign food, or who have grown tired of dorm food, the rice cooker is a savior; it is versatile, and compact enough to sneak into any dormitory.

Shortly before Christmas 1973, at a boarding school in Shropshire in central England, Form 5 student John Yao, who had been in the country for just three months, received a package from Hong Kong. John ate three times a day in the school's dining hall but had had a hard time adjusting to the local English food. He missed home-cooked Chinese meals, but his boarding house did not even have a pantry in which to store food, let alone cook it. The package was from his father who ran a neighborhood store in Kwun Tong (觀塘), in East Kowloon. Inside a recycled Sunkist orange cardboard box, John was overjoyed to find a National rice cooker and some food from home.

John secretly started cooking rice at weekends. Since he shared a room with nine other classmates, including an Iranian, a Japanese, a Thai, and several English boys, cooking during the week was not an option. But on weekends and during the holidays, he would skip meals in the dining hall and turn on his rice cooker. His treat was steamed rice flavored with the cured Chinese *lapchong* sausages that his parents occasionally sent from home. He usually cooked for himself, but he sometimes treated his friends.

The sweet smell of rice from John's cooker spread to the hallways, as did the rumor that John Yao, the Chinese boy in Form 5, had a strange machine in his room that cooked rice. Some students asked whether they could borrow it, a request he politely refused, because "it was a gift from my dad. I didn't feel comfortable lending it to others."[42] But one day, a Form 7 English student, who was also a prefect, approached John and asked, "May I borrow your rice cooker?" The student had heard about John's rice cooker, and John could not turn him down, because "he was a prefect. He was in a position to punish me if I did anything wrong."[43] So he reluctantly lent it to him.

When the rice cooker was returned to him, however, John was extremely upset to discover that its inner pot had been stained bright yellow. The prefect had cooked curry-flavored rice in it, and no matter how many times he had washed it, he had been unable to get rid of the yellow stain. The prefect was apologetic, but there was nothing he could

John Yao in England, mid-1970s.
Courtesy of John Yao

do. So, there and then John made the decision that, since the rice cooker was no longer brand-new, he would start lending it to other students. Several English boys asked to borrow it, as did his Iranian roommate.

John also began cooking various other things in his rice cooker, including instant noodles. Whenever he went to a Chinese store, he picked up packets of Japanese instant noodles, *Demae Iccho* (出前一丁), that were also popular in Hong Kong. First, he used the rice cooker to boil some water, to which he added the noodles and other ingredients. Once the mixture had been brought back to the boil, he stirred in the soup mix, and the noodles were ready to eat. His rice cooker also performed various other duties, such as heating canned baked beans and reheating takeouts.

After completing Form 7, John moved to London to study building technology at a college in the city. He shared a flat with his brother, who had studied in Toronto, his sister, and a few other Chinese friends. This time, John's father sent them a much bigger rice cooker, and they took turns cooking meals for the entire household. John went on to pursue a postgraduate degree at London Polytechnic, following which he returned to Hong Kong and joined a curtain wall façade company. When he got married and moved to a flat in Tai Po (大埔), in the New Territories, in 1987, one of the house-warming gifts given to him by a colleague was the National Saishi rice cooker with a congee-making function.

UNESCO's *Global Education Digest 2007* estimated that 981,095 students from Asia were studying at tertiary educational institutions in other parts of the world and that, of these, nearly sixty percent were in North America and Europe.[44] This figure is for tertiary institutions only; it does not include the number of high school students enrolled at overseas boarding schools, for example. For many of these young people living far from home, a rice cooker not only steams rice, but it also functions as a safe, portable kitchen.

Returning Home with a Rice Cooker

The flow of rice cookers has not been limited to movement from East to West, or from home to a foreign land. Many migrant workers use part of their salary to buy a rice cooker in the country where they are based and then take it back home when they leave. This includes some of the 1.56 million Filipinos who work overseas.[45] In Saudi Arabia, where one in five Filipino migrant workers is employed, there has been a steady demand for rice cookers. In the early 1990s, Filipino domestic helpers actually approached National with a request that they provide back home in the Philippines repair and maintenance services for rice cookers purchased abroad.[46] Upon investigation, National learned that a significant percentage of customers purchasing rice cookers in the Middle East were Asian migrant workers. These included not only Filipino but also Indian and Pakistani workers living in Saudi Arabia, the United Arab Emirates, and Kuwait, who bought a rice cooker there and then carried it back to their homeland when they left. In 1992, in response to the Filipino domestic workers' request, National's sales teams in the Middle East and the Philippines got together to set up an international maintenance service in the Philippines; they even ran an advertising campaign across the Middle East to promote it. "We wanted to assure those [Filipino] customers," says Masayuki Nakano, in charge of international sales at the time, "that maintenance services for their [gray market] rice cookers would be provided."[47]

Today, one of most frequent questions that customers ask Panasonic in the Philippines remains, "Do you accept foreign imported models for repair?" And the official answer is, "We do accept imported National Panasonic products for repair but subject to Service Manual and Spare Parts availability."[48] In addition, unlike other sites in Asia, Panasonic's customer service website in the Philippines has a separate section dedicated to "gray market" appliances.[49]

Asian women hired by night clubs overseas are another group of migrant workers who buy rice cookers abroad and then bring them home. In the early 1980s, a substantial number of Taiwanese bar hostesses were working in Japan. During their stay, they often purchased rice cookers with a built-in microchip, which were then relatively new to the market, and took them back to Taiwan. While rice cookers were readily available in Taiwan, there were many more high-end rice cooker models to choose from in Japanese stores, and thus they made popular gifts for relatives and friends.

A Japan Airlines employee regularly assigned to the China Airlines check-in counters at Haneda Airport between 1983 and 1985 describes his struggles with Taiwanese bar hostesses and their excess luggage:

> I was constantly engaged in a battle over baggage. [Taiwanese bar hostesses] carried a lot of electric appliances as gifts for their families. Most of them carried a rice cooker, and some also carried a sack of rice. [So their baggage often exceeded the twenty-kilogram limit] but they didn't want to pay for excess baggage. But with so much stuff, I just couldn't let them off. So, whenever I was assigned to a China Airlines counter, I spent all day arguing with them.[50]

Japanese rice cookers have been popular gifts among Asians since the 1960s. As discussed in Chapter 1, Wong Kar-wai's movie *In the Mood for Love* features a rice cooker brought back as a gift from Japan to Hong Kong in 1962: a Hong Kong businessman working for a Japanese trading company gives it to his wife, played by Maggie Cheung.

Prior to South Korean manufacturers developing their own local version, rice cookers bought as gifts in Japan were also extremely popular in South Korea. In April 1969, Japan Airlines launched its service between Fukuoka (福岡) and Pusan (釜山). On most flights the belly of the aircraft was completely full of Japanese electrical appliances, including rice cookers and, occasionally, washing machines, purchased by wealthy Korean tourists.[51]

Highflyers were not the only ones responsible for this transnational flow of appliances from Japan to South Korea. In the 1970s, the National Rice Cooker Division found that the volume of rice cooker sales in Yamaguchi Prefecture (山口縣), at the southern tip of Honshu Island, was unusually high. Upon investigation, they discovered that large numbers of rice cookers were being bought there and then ferried to Pusan on passenger and fishing boats. This was happening at a time when South Korea had a strict protectionist trade policy in place, and National was unable to export rice cookers directly into the country. Yet despite this, Japanese rice cookers found their way in.[52]

In addition to genuine tourists, there were plenty of Korean peddlers, usually middle-aged, or older, women, who traveled to Yamaguchi by ferry, bought Japanese products, and then carried them back to Pusan to sell. In the late 1970s and early 1980s, their staples were rice cookers and radio-cassette players. There were also Korean fishermen, who, having unloaded their mackerel catch in the port of Shimonoseki (下關), filled the empty holds of their fishing boats with Japanese appliances, including rice cookers, for the trip home. Shimonoseki lies almost directly across the Korea Strait from Pusan and is one of Japan's two maritime gateways to Korea, the other being Fukuoka. The flow of rice cookers passed through these two ports to Pusan in the 1970s and 1980s, just as it had through Hong Kong and Shenzhen to China, following the implementation of the Open Door Policy in 1979. In the mid-1980s, the most sought-after Japanese rice cookers in Korea were those manufactured under the Zojirushi brand, with its distinctive elephant logo.

But by the 1990s, South Korean brands had succeeded in developing their own localized rice cookers. South Korean models are a cross between a traditional rice cooker and a pressure cooker; they prepare softer rice, and a Korean favorite, "mixed grain rice," which usually includes barley, beans, or millet. South Korea's leading manufacturer, Cuckoo, currently offers a pressure rice cooker with ten separate function buttons: it cooks congee, brown rice, and *samgaetang* chicken soup with ginseng and glutinous rice; it also stews beef spare ribs and chicken. And to cater to the latest fad among health-conscious consumers, Cuckoo's newest model includes technology to make brown rice germinate before cooking it, to increase its nutritional value. Cuckoo rice cookers come with conventional white bodies as well as bright red ones, a color never on the menu for Japanese manufacturers. These South Korean models have gradually taken on the aura of prestige once accorded Japanese rice cookers, and owning one is a symbol of wealth across the border in North Korea.[53]

In Tandem with Soy Sauce

Many rice cookers followed a mobile population, moving from one country or continent to another. The flow of rice cookers to Asian diasporas in the West was not always a natural process initiated by consumers, however; it was often the result of a deliberate sales strategy on the part of the manufacturer. In North America and France, the National rice cooker team actively worked with local agents to develop the Asian diaspora markets. These agents were often nationals of Asian descent, whose families had left their homeland to settle in a foreign country. In both the United States and Canada, Matsushita launched its rice cooker business through agents who were second-generation Japanese-Americans (nisei).

Matsushita Electric Trading exported its first overseas lot of 720 rice cookers to the United States and Hawaii in 1957,[54] initially targeted at cities with sizeable Japanese communities, such as Los Angeles and Honolulu. The company looked for an agent in Los Angeles, and turned to George Nozawa, a staff writer at a Japanese-language newspaper, for advice. Nozawa gave the rice cooker a try, immediately saw its potential, and became Matsushita's rice cooker agent in the United States. The rice cooker business, however, had a rocky start: many units malfunctioned and had to be returned but, more importantly, some consumers simply could not figure out how to use them. There was even a case of someone putting a rice cooker on the kitchen stove and heating it until nothing was left but a blackened shell.[55] Nozawa struggled with having to explain to customers exactly how this new invention worked, a situation Mong faced just a few years later in Hong Kong (Chapter 1).[56]

Matsushita established its own distribution company in the United States in 1959 and, because National had already been registered as a trademark by other firms, sold its wireless product lines under a new brand name created specifically for the American market, Panasonic. Since none of the trademark holders had registered its use for rice cookers, however, Matsushita was able to continue selling them under the original, and more recognizable to Asian-Americans, National brand name.[57]

As far as the distribution of its Panasonic line was concerned, Matsushita focused predominantly on mainstream outlets, such as department stores like Macy's, and appliance retailers. The company realized, however, that rice cookers were more of a niche market product and decided that it would make more sense for them to be sold in Asian grocery stores, alongside California rice, soy sauce, and instant noodles, rather than in electrical appliance shops, next to transistor radios, television sets, and toasters. It therefore elected to put the distribution of rice cookers in the western United States, in the hands of Japanese-American, George Nozawa.

The turning point in the rice cooker's fortunes came when Nozawa, in an effort to reach out to Japanese communities across eleven states, hitched a ride on the back of the Japanese food distribution network. He established a partnership with the Japan Food Corporation, a Los Angeles-based distributor of imported food items from Japan which, in 1969, had become a subsidiary of Kikkoman (萬字醬油), the leading Japanese manufacturer of soy sauce. In tandem with Kikkoman, classic-design National rice cookers found their way into the homes of the Japanese, Chinese, and Southeast Asian diasporas, as well as Asian food lovers throughout the western United States.[58]

In 1984, Nozawa Trading celebrated 1 million National rice cookers sold in the United States.[59] Nozawa eventually went on to acquire the American distribution rights for Zojirushi's rice cookers.[60] At the same time, in Canada, the distribution of National rice cookers followed a similar route. Through the efforts of Japanese-Canadian Charles Hiroshi Kadota, rice cookers appeared on the shelves of Asian grocery stores and supermarkets all over the country.[61]

Across the Atlantic in Paris, National rice cookers were being sold alongside Vietnamese fish sauce. This was due to the efforts of Mr Nguyen Thanh Nam, a Vietnamese refugee who had been Matsushita's agent in Saigon. During the Vietnam War, there had been a steady demand for three Japanese products in South Vietnam: instant noodles, transistor radios, and rice cookers. Instant noodles fed both soldiers and civilians, radios kept them informed, and rice cookers were on the list of US emergency relief supplies. Yūki Ogasawara, in charge of international rice cooker sales at the time, recalls how, in 1967, he was surprised to receive orders from war-torn Vietnam:

> We received orders for rice cookers from Vietnam during the war, when I thought there couldn't possibly be any business. I heard that when the US military were preparing to provide emergency supplies, they asked [the Vietnamese people] what they wanted. They supposedly asked for firewood to cook rice. So the solution was rice cookers, because it was actually easier for [the US army] to generate electric power than it was for them to provide firewood.

> So whenever the US military were getting ready to provide emergency supplies, we received an order. At one point, we were supplying 2,000 or 3,000 rice cookers a month.[62]

The Vietnamese agent for these deals had been Mr Nam, who fled to Paris with his family after the war ended. Matsushita Electric Trading already had an office in the capital and an established French distribution network, but it appointed him as an agent for its rice cooker line, with the explicit purpose of reaching out to the country's Asian diasporas. So it was that, throughout the late 1970s and early 1980s, with the help of a Vietnamese immigrant, National rice cookers made their way into Asian grocery stores across France and the European continent.[63]

Where there are Asians, there are rice cookers. And when Asians moved around the world, their rice cookers followed. Asian businessmen carried their rice cookers to and from their overseas postings; international tourists brought them back as souvenirs; and unauthorized intermediaries, such as peddlers, found ingenious ways of getting them across national borders. In the West, hyphenated Asians championed the rice cooker, spreading word of its convenience to the diasporas, and took the lead in building on existing distribution networks that ran along ethnic lines. Meanwhile, as rice cookers started to gain a following outside Japanese and Chinese communities and penetrate new markets, they began to steam, stew, and bake in ways their original Japanese manufacturers had never anticipated.

7

Only They Would Know
Globalizing Rice Cookers through Local Insight

The rice cooker originally developed in Thailand that bakes a cake
at the touch of a button. Hong Kong, 2003.
Courtesy of Shun Hing Group

In 1976, a young Japanese diplomat was sent to the Chinese University of Hong Kong for language training. He lived on campus, attended Mandarin classes at the New Asia Yale-in-China Language Centre in the morning, and played tennis in the afternoon. That autumn, a Hong Kong Chinese student, Samuel Lee, invited him and a few other friends to his dorm for dinner.[1] When the young Japanese diplomat walked into Samuel's room, however, the only cooking appliance he could see was a classic white-bodied rice cooker. This naturally made him wonder whether their dinner was going to consist of anything more than plain steamed rice.

More than thirty years later, the diplomat still vividly remembers what he observed over the next fifteen minutes. When the rice was almost ready, Samuel opened a can of Chinese stewed beef. He put the can on a plate, lifted the lid off the rice cooker, and laid the plate on top of the rice. After Samuel had checked through the glass viewing pane and made sure that the beef was nicely steamed, he removed the plate and then distributed the rice into enough small bowls for everyone in the room.

The pot was now empty but for a few grains of rice still sticking to its sides, and Samuel proceeded to pour in hot water, which he brought to a boil. He threw in some diced tomatoes, added salt and pepper, and slowly poured in a couple of beaten eggs. He gave the liquid a final stir with a rice paddle and finished it off with a few drops of sesame oil. Egg-drop tomato soup with a sprinkling of rice was now ready to serve. All Samuel needed to prepare this three-dish meal was his rice cooker and a rice paddle.

This one-pot cooking method had the effect of a magic trick on the young Japanese diplomat, whose future postings would include Deputy Consul General in Hong Kong:

> I was truly amazed because I took it for granted that the rice cooker was just for cooking rice. It didn't even occur to me that it could be used for other things. It was shocking because this [experience] made me realize how I really couldn't compete with the Chinese when it came to thinking outside the box.[2]

The Japanese diplomat, however, is not alone in his conception that rice cookers are designed to perform only one function. While it is technically possible, not to mention energy efficient, to steam red meat and make soup in a rice cooker, it is hard to imagine a Japanese student steaming *teriyaki* beef or making *miso* soup in one. These are indeed extreme examples, but the diplomat's story illustrates how the Japanese and Hong Kong Chinese tend to conceptualize rice cookers differently. While many Japanese have traditionally regarded the electric rice cooker as an appliance that should be used to steam rice and nothing else, many people in Hong Kong, and indeed in other parts of the world, treat it as a multipurpose cooker.

For instance, when, in 2003, Shun Hing introduced a National rice cooker that baked a golden cake at the touch of a button, it became an instant hit with Hong Kong consumers. It was so popular that Shun Hing requested a cake-baking function be incorporated into all higher-end models; none of Matsushita's Japanese domestic models have it.

Conversely, there are models that are only available in Japan: super high-end rice cookers that cost over ¥100,000 (US$1,000) each. For these, the Matsushita "rice ladies" developed high-temperature steaming technology and a special inner pot coated with fluorine and diamond dust. This was not done to add sparkle but for scientific reasons, as the combination allows the heat to circulate more vigorously inside the pot, resulting in perfectly steamed rice. What the Japanese mean by "perfectly steamed rice," is rice, usually a domestic variety, that is pearly, moist, and yet fluffy—each grain of rice distinct from the others. The smell emanating from the pot also offers an important clue. When National "rice ladies" carry out taste tests, they sniff each pot of rice: only if it smells sweet is it perfectly steamed.[3] Since regular family meals must include a bowl of rice, a high-end rice cooker is a worthwhile investment for many Japanese families. The first female director of Matsushita's Cooking Appliances Business Unit (formerly known as the Rice Cooker Division), Machiko Miyai, describes Japan's obsession with perfectly steamed rice:

> The Japanese domestic market is unlike the rest of the world. With the introduction of IH (induction heating) [in 1988], the average price for rice cookers increased dramatically. It went up again in 2003, when our company introduced [high-temperature] steam-type models. Then, one of our competitors introduced a ¥100,000 model, raising the average price even further. Japanese [consumers] are prepared to spend enormous amounts of money to have superb rice.[4]

In fact, the average price of National/Panasonic rice cookers sold in Japan is more than three times that of rice cookers sold outside Japan. In 2006, National/Panasonic sold over 3 million rice cookers worldwide. While only forty-one percent of them were sold in Japan, they accounted for seventy-two percent of the company's net profits for this particular appliance. Miyai explains how the research and development of new rice cookers for the Japanese and international markets has gone in two separate directions:

> We might say that the Japanese market is unusual. [Many of our Japanese consumers] believe that the rice cooker is purely for steaming "white rice" and refuse to cook anything else in the pot.

> But to develop overseas models, we have to see the rice cooker not just as a pot for cooking rice but also as a versatile multi-cooker. Otherwise they won't sell.[5]

Machiko Miyai, National's third "rice lady"
and current director of the Cooking Appliances Business Unit.

Miyai joined Matsushita's research and development team as the third "rice lady," in 1983. From her very first day as a "rice lady," her managers kept reminding her that the team's goal was to create models that were capable of meeting local needs in a global market. She was instructed to make the motto "Open up a world map when you work" her own. Habits she developed as a "rice lady" are so ingrained that she still sniffs every bowl of rice before eating it. In her current role as director of Matsushita's Cooking Appliances Business Unit, when she devises global market strategies, she abides by the localization approach that her predecessors developed through their partnership with William Mong.

Iranian Rice with a Crust

As seen in earlier chapters, National's quest to localize rice cookers started with Hong Kong in 1960. By the late 1960s, it had seen its products spread across Asia and on to Asian diasporas in Europe and North America. The next step was to target other communities where rice is commonly consumed. The company learned from United Nations statistics that 112 countries around the world produce and consume rice. Its goal was to reach all of them.

To do so, the National team used the localization process established with William Mong in Hong Kong. Once the rice cooker team found a promising market, an engineer would visit the country and ask local inhabitants what varieties of rice were popular, how they cooked their rice, and what kind of design and color appealed to them. They would then work with local taste advisors to make sure the cooked rice dish they produced was authentic. Local interpretations of taste, design, and color were respected, without imposing a Japanese interpretation. Once the design phase was complete, they would develop a local recipe book and conduct cooking demonstrations in culturally appropriate locations.

Iranian rice posed a new challenge for the rice cooker team when, in 1966, it took on the task of developing a model for Iran.[6] Iran would seem like rather an unlikely candidate for market expansion, but under the Shah the country was busy pursuing a number of modernization programs known collectively as the "White Revolution."[7] The latest consumer products were very much in demand, and there were no electric rice cookers available.

Company legend has it that a Matsushita man was flying over Iran on a business trip to sell electric heaters when he suddenly spotted green rice paddies in the middle of a desert. He was truly excited to find rice in such an unexpected place, and upon his return to Osaka reported what he had seen to the Rice Cooker Division. They soon learned that rice was a staple food for many Iranians.[8] They looked at the UN statistics and found out that, in 1965, the country's annual rice yield stood at over 1 million tons. Iran ranked twentieth in the world in rice production and was the second largest producer in the Middle East after Egypt.[9] This is what led to the birth of the Iranian model.[10]

Another, less romantic, version of the story is that Matsushita's local agent in Teheran, Mohamed Fard Ghassemi, had become aware of National's popular rice cookers, which were occasionally re-exported to Iran from Hong Kong. He saw potential for them in the Iranian market and requested a model that cooked rice with *taddig*, Persian for "bottom of pot."[11] Iranian long-grain rice, when cooked in the traditional way, is fluffy on top with a layer of golden crust on the bottom. Iranians consider the crispy layer a delicacy, and at dinnertime will turn out an entire pot of rice on a plate and offer the golden crust to the guest of honor.

Once again, the request from a local agent, this time for a rice crust, was beyond the realms of the engineers' imagination. The rice cooker had gained popularity among the Japanese and Chinese because it cooked rice conveniently and consistently without burning it; but this time the engineers needed to come up with a machine that could brown the rice until it formed a golden crust as crisp as Japanese rice crackers. The Iranians added cooking oil to the pot to achieve this result. Some used vegetable oil, some *ghee* (clarified butter), and others melted animal fat; but, for the Japanese engineers, adding any kind of oil was an alien concept. Traditionally, for the Japanese, a rice pot is purely for steaming; a separate pan must be used if oil is involved in the cooking process.

The elaborate Iranian recipe intrigued Tatsunosuke Sakamoto, the first director of the Rice Cooker Division. "If Iranians spend that much effort cooking rice and treat rice with that much care," he told his staff, "they would surely find our rice cooker useful."[12] The rice cooker team looked for an Iranian advisor to teach them authentic recipes and comment on their version of *taddig*. Ghassemi, Matsushita's agent in Teheran, unlike Mong, could not travel to Osaka himself. So, Matsushita Electric Trading located a Iranian merchant in Kobe, Rouhollah Momtazi. Initially, he showed no interest in the rice cooker project but agreed to let his wife participate in its development. Engineer Yoshiaki Sano and Matsushita Electric Trading staff visited the couple's mansion in Ashiya, an upscale Kobe neighborhood modeled after Hong Kong's Victoria Peak. Mrs Momtazi showed them, speaking in her limited Japanese, how to cook rice on the stovetop by adding vegetable oil and placing sliced potatoes on the bottom of the aluminum pan. Once it was cooked, she scooped up the rice and potato crust from the pan, and served them in a heap with the broken up *taddig* on top. This rice and potato dish was just one of many Iranian rice recipes, but Sano and the team followed it faithfully, almost too faithfully:

> We believed that we had to put potato slices on the bottom of the pan, and so we always put them there. To us, this was the only correct way we knew to cook Iranian rice. But later, through our exchanges [with Mrs Momtazi], we realized that the potato was optional, not essential.[13]

Sano and his team discarded the potatoes, adapted their technology, and came up with a prototype that steamed rice automatically and, with the extra push of a button, allowed it to be browned manually. They visited Mrs Momtazi and cooked the National version of the Iranian *taddig*. But when Mrs Momtazi served her own authentic *taddig*, the difference was clear: National's version tasted nothing like the original.[14]

The rice cooker team ordered long-grain rice in large woven sacks from the Momtazis' trading firm and went on with their experiments, further adjusting the temperature as well as the timing for browned rice. Sano, a staff engineer at the time, led the experiments. He first tried using a regular aluminum inner pot, but the *taddig* stuck to the bottom and had to be scraped off. He later introduced a fluorine-coated nonstick version, which helped to turn out a smooth unbroken golden crust. Sano presented Mrs Momtazi with one refined prototype after another, but it was not until more than a year later that she finally rated National's *taddig* as authentic.

Then it was time to adapt the design of the rice cooker body to conform to Iranian tastes. In the late 1960s, most rice cookers had white enamel-coated bodies that sought to mimic the delicate porcelain of a Japanese rice bowl, but the team developed an alternative Iranian model in shining silver. The price was intentionally set high to distinguish it from the traditional pots and pans sold in the bazaar, and it cost twice as much as a traditional white rice cooker.[15]

When Matsushita's Iranian rice cooker made its debut in 1967, there was another adjustment the sales team in Teheran was compelled to make. Following William Mong's successful sales calls to housewives in a Hong Kong public housing estate, the door-to-door approach had become part of National's rice cooker sales strategy in other international markets. But in this Muslim country it was out of the question for an all-male sales team to visit housewives in their homes and carry out individual product demonstrations.

The man responsible for overseas sales of rice cookers at the time, Yūki Ogasawara, recalls:

> Iran was one of the few countries where our salesmen couldn't go door-to-door. We were told house calls were simply not an option.

National/Panasonic rice cookers developed for the Iranian market.
Teheran, 2007.
Photo by Ryūzo Sakamoto

> When I visited Teheran, I couldn't even greet our agent Mr Ghassemi's wife. I
> was invited to a dinner at his house, but she didn't come out to see us. Even the
> servants who served us our meal were men.[16]

So instead, the sales team came up with the idea of home parties, a marketing strategy
made popular by the American brand Tupperware.[17] At a typical Tupperware party, women
would gather for food, drinks, and a private show of the company's plastic containers.
Applying this approach to the new Iranian rice cooker, Matsushita's local agent targeted
wealthy housewives and set up home parties during which he would demonstrate the
appliance's ability to produce beautiful *taddig*. Whenever the salesperson emptied the
rice out of the non-stick pot onto a plate, with a smooth crust as golden as that of an
apple pie, the assembled guests would cheer.[18] The agent would take orders for delivery
at a later date.[19] The sales team also organized numerous cooking demonstrations at
department stores and women's clubs.[20]

In the years that followed, the rice cooker team worked on refining the cooker's
browning technology until it succeeded in making the process fully automatic. The team
also added an analogue device that allowed users to brown the crust to their liking, dark
or light, just like a toaster. The National Iranian rice cooker became a bestseller: by 1974,
its monthly sales figure had reached 10,000 units, a mark of success for the company in
international sales. In 1975, Matsushita built a factory in Isfahan, a town in central Iran,
and began to produce rice cookers locally.

A Recipe for Diversity

The National rice cooker team continued to gather diverse varieties of rice through
its overseas sales offices, agents and the Japan External Trade Organization (JETRO),
adapting the classic white rice cooker models to conform to local specifications, and
shipping out prototypes to as many rice-producing countries as possible. Some were
in political turmoil and were not ready to establish a trade relationship. Some countries
responded that the cooked rice did not suit local tastes. Some did not respond at all. Some
localization attempts, like a rice cooker for Italian *risotto*, for example, were initially
abandoned. The National engineers believed it was technically possible to develop a
risotto cooker, but the lack of enthusiasm shown by potential consumers in Italy for this
product meant there was no support for its costly research and development. Spanish
paella, however, was one dish whose taste the rice cooker technology was unable to
replicate, as a shallow, flat pan was needed to produce its crunchy texture.

The rice cooker team also considered adapting the rice cooker for rice eaters in
Latin America. In fact, National's conventional rice cooker made a fairly authentic *arroz
con pollo*, a dish composed of rice, chicken, tomatoes, and red bell peppers. The sales
team saw Brazil, with its 150,000-strong Japanese diaspora and their descendents, as
a logical target.[21] But when the team investigated importing rice cookers into Brazil,
due to the government's protectionist trade policies, they came up against the prospect

of having to pay a massive import tax, effectively quadrupling their sales price. This made the proposition of creating and sustaining a rice cooker market in Brazil simply untenable.

To globalize its rice cookers, National not only developed the new technology needed to replicate exotic rice dishes but also created accessories that transform the basic model into a versatile cooker. As we saw in Chapter 1, the World Series model, developed in 1960 with input from William Mong, remains the most popular model, for sale in forty-five countries and regions around the world. In the Indian market, for example, this basic rice cooker is sold as an "automatic cooker," with a clear steaming basket mounted on top of the non-stick cooking pan. It works just like a Chinese bamboo steamer and cooks vegetables and other food economically, using the steam rising up from the cooking pan below. The clear steaming basket has been popular not just in Hong Kong and India but in the United States, where health-conscious consumers use it for steaming vegetables such as broccoli and carrots.

Another popular accessory in India is the "two-dish separator pan," which can be fitted into the top of the original pan and used to cook two dishes simultaneously: rice below and curry, soup, or stew above. It basically functions along the same principle as the ceramic plate used by the Chinese University student to warm his can of stewed beef. Of course, if curry is cooked in the two-dish separator pan, it is likely to stain it bright yellow, but it can easily be replaced. The rice cooker sales team ensures spare accessories are carried by retail outlets in India; it also admits that cheaper knock-offs are widely available. Its views on this issue, posted on the official National website in 2003, illustrate the team's open-minded approach to the sale of these imitation models:

> It is problematic that there are unofficial copies of our accessories in the market, but this is also proof of how popular the "World Series" is. There is demand [for these accessories], and selling imitations has become big business, because every family has a rice cooker. It shows that the "World Series" is a standard item.[22]

A genuine National "World Series" rice cooker. Bangkok, 2009.
Courtesy of Ratana-Ubol Kanokwal

In addition to the two-dish separator pan, consumers can choose from models with three types of lid: all glass, part glass and part aluminum, or all aluminum. And in line with the tradition started in Hong Kong in 1976 with the multifunction rice and congee cooker, each model comes with a starter booklet that includes local recipes. In India, the National automatic cooker is sold with recipes for *biriyani*, curry, and rice pudding.[23] These accessories are integral to Matsushita's attempts to develop a main rice cooker body that is standard worldwide yet caters to specific local needs.

The Rice Cooker Division has stuck to the deceptively simple principle of asking local distributors and consumers for their input and respecting local tastes. This, however, is not something that comes naturally to many Japanese. Rice is often upheld as a symbol of national pride: Japanese domestic rice is regarded as superior and better-tasting than any other foreign variety, and this distinction between Japanese rice and "foreign rice (*gaimai*)" can be a source of chauvinism and discrimination.[24]

The National rice cooker team, however, learned early on that it would not be able to globalize its rice cookers if it tried to impose the Japanese ideal of "perfectly steamed rice" on customers in other countries. Furthermore, when the National rice cooker team heard of the highly creative uses its rice cookers had been put to by consumers around the world, instead of rejecting them as "heresy," wherever practical, it added them to the rice cooker's official repertoire and turned them into business opportunities. Starting in 1960, through its partnership with William Mong, the rice cooker team learned to be adaptable; it became aware of differences in "rice culture" and established guidelines for designing, manufacturing, and marketing models that cooked what local people wanted for their dinner.

In 2001, the National Rice Cooker Division took its interactive approach to localization one step further in Thailand. It went beyond just listening to local opinions; it actually hired a couple of Thai "rice ladies" who had studied home economics at a local university, to develop rice cookers that would appeal to local sensibilities. The mission for the Thai "rice ladies" was to conduct research and develop ideas for mid-range rice cookers.

You Can Have Your Cake and Eat Rice Too

The idea of baking a cake in a rice cooker has been around for over forty years and it has, in effect, always been technically possible to make a cake using even the most basic model. It is a practice, however, that has never become mainstream in Japan. The explanation for why Japanese housewives refuse to bake cakes in their rice cookers is exemplified by a classic case of failed cross-cultural marketing. The case is recounted by George Fields, an Australian-Japanese market researcher who contributed to the import of numerous American products into Japan.[25]

In 1965, the American corporation General Mills was looking to expand sales of its Betty Crocker cake mix beyond the West, and identified Japan as a potentially lucrative market. The consumption of Western-style cakes was on the rise in Japan, but the

Japanese tended to buy them rather than bake them at home. So General Mills formed a joint venture with the Japanese confectionery manufacturer Morinaga and started exploring ways of entering the market. Upon learning that most Japanese kitchens did not have an oven, the General Mills' lab in Minneapolis adjusted the ingredients of the cake mix to make it suitable for baking in a rice cooker, an appliance owned by 87.7 percent of all Japanese families in 1964.[26]

In 1966, General Mills-Morinaga launched their vanilla and chocolate-flavored cake mix under the name "Cakeron," yet another Japanese English name that sounds cute but does not mean anything. After some initial success, however, orders failed to materialize. To find out why, Fields conducted several focus group interviews. The conclusion was that there was nothing wrong with the cake mix: it was not too sweet, not too dry, and its advertising campaign was just fine. But the problem, according to Fields, was that "psychologically, the cake mix ran the danger of contaminating the rice."[27]

Fields quoted housewives voicing their concern that the vanilla and chocolate flavors would effectively contaminate the cooking pot. The question was not whether they could get rid of these flavors during the washing process but whether they even dared to take such a risk with their rice cookers in the first place. To illuminate the cultural significance of this issue, Fields compared the Japanese rice cooker with the English teapot, and wrote, "The closest analogy I can think of for a Japanese housewife making a cake in a rice cooker is for an English housewife to brew coffee in her teapot."[28]

Residual smell is indeed a major concern not only for the Japanese but for anybody who uses a rice cooker to cook anything other than rice. But the necessary addition of butter into the cake mix, and therefore the cooking pan, was probably another insurmountable cultural barrier for rice purists. A 50-year-old Japanese writer, upon hearing that the National rice cooker with a cake-baking feature was popular in Asia, exclaimed in disbelief:

> "To me, rice is sacred. I don't want to cook anything greasy in my rice cooker."[29]

She would not even cook the popular Japanese rice casserole with chicken and root vegetables in her rice cooker because it involves chicken fat. In fact, many of the older generation share her view.

In the book, *Rice as Self*, anthropologist Emiko Ohnuki-Tierney explores the cultural significance of rice in Japan.[30] She notes that, contrary to the common belief that throughout history rice has been the staple food for all Japanese, regardless of their social rank, until the late nineteenth century it was, in fact, available only to "the elites—emperors, nobles, warriors, and wealthy merchants."[31] Rice farmers produced rice, but they could not afford to consume it. Rice, however, has always been the most sought-after food and plays an essential role in many Japanese imperial and folk rituals, festivals, and celebrations.[32] For religious rituals, rice is used when making offerings to the gods, to imply commensality between gods and humans, and is shared at feasts. Ohnuki-Tierney goes so far as to argue that each grain of rice has a soul, *nigitama* (和

魂), "the positive power of divine purity," and therefore rice is "more than an offering to the gods for consecration; every grain of rice *is* a god."[33]

In Japan, white rice is traditionally held up as part of the Japanese cultural identity, while any type of oil or fat, especially animal fat, is associated with non-Japanese qualities. In the 1960s, butter still had foreign or exotic connotations, and anything (or anybody) perceived as Western was referred to as *bata-kusai*, "smells like butter." The notion of "them" and "us" lies at the heart of this concept. While it can be used as a compliment, it also hints at an invisible barrier between what is considered to be Japanese and what is not. This carries through to the kitchen, resulting in separate pots for rice and any other food that involves oil.

For many Japanese housewives, the rice pot is still sacred. Besides oil, even rice vinegar, an essential ingredient for sushi, is barred from the pot. Given this psychological barrier, Cakeron failed to win over the Japanese market, and the alliance between General Mills and Morinaga was dissolved. Although some Japanese housewives do use their rice cooker to bake cakes, making their own adjustments to timing and recipes, it remains a practice that has never really caught on in Japan.

It was in Thailand in 2003 that the idea of baking a cake in a rice cooker resurfaced. In 2001, the 22-year-old, fresh graduate Jarapat Reainthippayasakul joined Matsushita's subsidiary in Thailand. Trained in home economics at a local university, she became the first non-Japanese "rice lady." She was assigned to conduct research on new cooking functions that would cater to local tastes. In Japan rice is steamed; in Thailand, it is boiled in a large amount of water, the water is drained off, and then it is steamed. In other words, Thai consumers had been cooking their staple food not only with imported rice cookers but also using an imported cooking method. The Thai "rice lady" set herself the task of reproducing the traditional taste of boiled rice in a rice cooker.

Boil-drain-steam: the traditional way of cooking rice in Thailand.
Bangkok, 1960.
Courtesy of Sadayoshi Sakamoto

First, Reainthippayasakul developed a program for cooking brown rice, a type of rice that had become increasingly popular among health-conscious Thai professionals. The program for short-grain brown rice was a standard function for most mid- to high-range models, but there was no program designed specifically for the long-grain rice available in Thailand. Then, she went on to suggest producing a rice cooker that automatically baked a cake. Just as General Mills had discovered when promoting baking culture in Japan in the mid-1960s, an oven was out of reach for most Thais. One difference, however, was that, by 2003, although baking remained the domain of the privileged, many supermarkets in Bangkok carried cake mixes.

When the new model was complete in 2002, it turned out a golden cake in forty minutes. National advertised it as the world's first model to incorporate a "cake" function, and button. The color of the rice cooker body also reflected Thai tastes: both models came in shimmering crystal pink and crystal silver, evoking shades of glossy nail polish. To the Japanese eye, the colors were too lurid to be considered a cute addition to the kitchen. But consumers in Thailand thought them attractive and upmarket, as did consumers in Hong Kong, which in early 2003 was in the grip of the devastating SARS crisis.

Facing Adversity Together during SARS

The Matsushita-Shun Hing collaboration not only helped both companies expand their business during periods of economic growth but also enabled them to weather less auspicious times. March 20, 2003, marked the beginning of the US-led invasion of Iraq. The Presidential Palace was blown up, and speculation was rife as to the fate of Saddam Hussein. At the same time, Hong Kong was engaged in another battle: the battle against SARS (Severe Acute Respiratory Syndrome). By the end of the epidemic, Hong Kong saw 1,755 people infected by the virus, and 299 die.

As the US-led Task Force marched on Baghdad, an increasing number of Hong Kongers wore masks when they went out to protect themselves from this mysterious virus. On March 25 and 26, the Kowloon-Canton Railway (KCR), whose trains had once carried thousands of gift appliances from Hong Kong to China, distributed 120,000 free face masks to passengers at its stations. KCR officials appealed to anyone with cold or flu symptoms to wear a mask when traveling by train. Within seven days, the number of infections in the city had doubled, and the question on everyone's lips went from "Do you really need to wear a mask?" to "Are you safe without one?"

At a classical music concert in City Hall, a soprano sang Rachmaninoff's "Vocalise," naturally without a mask; but behind her, forty percent of the string players, dressed in their formal black attire, wore masks. Then, in the rows behind them were the wind instrument players, who, like the soprano, could not cover their mouths. Looking back, it seems like a scene from a late night comedy show, but one could sense the fear creeping up on members of the audience, even among those wearing masks. On March

28, the Rolling Stones announced the cancellation of the Hong Kong leg of their concert tour. The following day, all schools in the city were closed.

Hong Kong never sleeps, or so it had always seemed. As the fear of SARS took hold, Nathan Road, with its giant neon signs, was almost deserted. On empty sidewalks, old newspapers fluttered about in the wind. A 40-year-old academic, who had as a child been thrilled by the sweet smell of rice cooker steamed rice, told his colleagues he had never seen Tsim Sha Tsui look so abandoned. When the Japanese Imperial Army occupied Hong Kong during World War II, it proclaimed martial law. He had grown up listening to stories of how people were afraid of walking the streets at night, lest they be caught by Japanese soldiers. Then he added with a sigh, "But this time, there are no soldiers. The invisible killer is SARS."

The SARS crisis did unexpectedly benefit Shun Hing's business. The virtual state of citywide quarantine in which Hong Kong residents found themselves created a surge in the demand for luxury goods. Fear of infection prevented most Hong Kongers from going out, eating out, and traveling out of the territory. During the four-day Easter holiday, it was customary for those who could afford it to go sunbathing in Phuket, unwind in Bangkok, or go shopping in Tokyo. This time, however, they were forced to spend their holidays at home, partly out of concern over retaliatory terrorist acts linked to the war in Iraq, and partly to avoid sharing an aircraft cabin with other potentially SARS-infected passengers. In addition, any mention of Hong Kong overseas evoked uneasy reactions, and tourists from the city were made to feel unwelcome wherever they went. In April 2003, almost one in three scheduled flights out of the city was canceled. Airline passenger numbers decreased by 68.9 percent when compared to April 2002, translating to a drop of approximately 2 million, in a city with 6.8 million inhabitants.[34]

Those who had been forced to cancel their holiday travel plans were left with extra cash in hand. As a result, National/Panasonic saw an unexpected boom in sales of its luxury home appliances. Many people were spending hours watching television at home, prompting them to put their names on a waiting list for flat-screen plasma televisions. Another surprise hit was the electronic massage chair. Kyoichi Yoshioka, a former Hong Kong section manager and director of the China and Northeast Asia Sales Office recounts:

> During the SARS [epidemic], between April and June, you would have expected sales figures to drop, but SARS actually boosted our sales. We received an unbelievably high number of orders for the Momi Momi massage chair.[35]

Momi Momi, literally "massage massage," is a high-tech lounger that scans a user's body and then adjusts its pressure points automatically. It is a luxury item; each chair weighs over 60 kilograms (130 pounds) and even the most economical model costs HK$12,340 (US$1,582), more than the starting monthly salary of many University of Hong Kong graduates.

In April 2003, out of the blue, over eighty of these massage chairs were snapped up weekly, and Shun Hing promptly ran out of stock. The factory in Japan was completely unprepared for this sudden surge in demand. Mother's Day and Father's Day were still to come, so Shun Hing needed more massage chairs immediately. The then-75-year-old CEO, William Mong, made a phone call to the factory in Japan and emphatically told them: "We need the massage chairs right now. The market demands them."

The solution was to ship the massage chairs by air, as opposed to sending them by sea freight, as soon as they had been packed by the factory in Japan. But does it make good business sense to ship chairs weighing sixty kilograms by air? Mong responds, "You have to seize the opportunity and do business when the timing is right. So, we usually don't [ship products by air], only when it's absolutely necessary."[36] After intense negotiations, Matsushita agreed to pay for the chairs to be air freighted, and went ahead with the deal, knowing that it would initially lose money. But why did Matsushita agree to such an impossible order? Yoshioka explains:

> When Mong-san puts in an order for our products, he sells them all and never returns any of them. When we put out a new product, he develops a market for it. And when the business is rocky, he doesn't turn away but sticks with us. These are the dynamics of our relationship.[37]

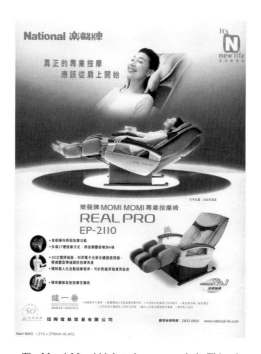

The Momi-Momi high-tech massage chair. This ad
appeared in selected Hong Kong newspapers during
the SARS epidemic of 2003.
Courtesy of Shun Hing Group

The ability to respond quickly to market changes is a fundamental characteristic of Shun Hing's business and is the result of solid local knowledge and being given autonomy in the decision-making process. Shun Hing's local insight, versatility, and extensive network have ensured that Matsushita's products move swiftly. The company has tried not to impose its own way of thinking and has been open to Shun Hing's suggestions, no matter how outrageous they may have seemed at times.

Kunio Nakamura, Matsushita's CEO between 2000 and 2006, who attended the Shun Hing Group's fiftieth anniversary celebrations in November 2003, explains the dynamics underpinning Matsushita's partnership with Shun Hing:

> We aim to build a win-win partnership between the manufacturer and the distributor: the distributor listens to consumers, makes suggestions for product enhancement, and meets his sales targets; the factory explores every possible option and caters to the market's needs. Mr Mong, who has earnestly upheld his end of the bargain [as the distributor] for half a century, is our role model. It is no exaggeration to say that Mr Mong was the driving force behind our international sales expansion.[38]

An Influx of Made-in-China Appliances

Hong Kong was once the gateway to Asia. A free port whose favorable customs regulations facilitated the flow of goods into and out of the city, Hong Kong was in a privileged position compared to the rest of Asia, where trade protectionism was the norm. Imported home appliances not only stayed in the territory, greatly enhancing the

Shun Hing's Fiftieth Anniversary Celebration at the Hong Kong
Convention and Exhibition Centre. Kunio Nakamura,
then-president of Matsushita, is third
from left. November 7, 2003.

lifestyle of the local residents, but they were also re-exported to other Asian countries and carried into China as gifts for relatives As the Chinese proverb goes, "water flows downward," and these symbols of modern living found their way to markets where there was a demand for them.

As a consequence of the huge increase in the number of Chinese and foreign-operated factories manufacturing these goods on the Mainland, however, the direction of that flow has changed: what was "Hong Kong to China" has become "China to the rest of the world." In 2003, Toyofumi Hirata, Matsushita's general manager, Consumer Products Sales, China and Northeast Asia, who has covered sales in Hong Kong since 1987, had this to say about the change of direction in the product flow:

> Hong Kong not only had its own, domestic market, but it also had access to the Chinese market. Even before China [opened up], Matsushita's products were already being re-exported to the Middle and Near East and to other parts of Asia via Hong Kong. That's why the Hong Kong market was so huge.
>
> Then, it lost the China market. Instead, Chinese-made home appliances started to appear in Hong Kong stores. In China, materials and labor are cheap, so the price of National and Panasonic products manufactured in China is cheap too. That's why several of our products have ended up on Hong Kong's [gray] market.[39]

In other words, the tide has turned; Hong Kong, once a re-export hub for Japanese appliances, is now an export market for Chinese ones. Along with products entering Hong Kong by official routes, products made for China's domestic market often find their not-so-official way in as parallel imports. Consumers are usually unable to tell the products apart. This causes problems for officially appointed agents who are forced to match the lower prices charged for parallel imports, in order to remain competitive. For example, Saishi rice cookers destined for the Hong Kong market are mostly manufactured by a factory in Thailand. Matsushita, however, manufactures its Saishi for the China market in Hangzhou (杭州). Both find their way into Hong Kong, the first through official channels, the second as a parallel import, and ironically end up competing with each other, predominantly on price.

The global rice cooker market is also experiencing massive changes. Japanese rice cooker manufacturers, who enjoyed a virtual monopoly for decades, are seeing their market share eroded by Chinese and Korean manufacturers, selling their own brands or acting as OEMs (original equipment manufacturers) for Western brands. According to an estimate issued by the Japan Electrical Manufacturers' Association, in 2006, annual sales of rice cookers stood at 43 million worldwide. China topped the list, with sales of over 21 million, followed by Japan, Korea, Thailand, and Indonesia.[40] In market share, National/Panasonic ranked fourth largest, and remained the most global in reach. Chinese manufacturers, however, held the top three rankings, thanks to their dominance at home, and their overseas market share also showed signs of rapid growth.

The influx of Chinese rice cookers has triggered a price war. In the United States, for example, a 5.5-cup basic Panasonic model with a recommended retail price of US$24.95

faces competition from a 6-cup Chinese OEM model that costs just US$12.99.[41] In a bid to differentiate its products and avoid having to compete purely on price, Matsushita has formulated the strategy of adding special, localized features to its mid-range and high-end models. It was with this aim in mind that the two Thai "rice ladies" produced their first hit model in 2003: a rice cooker that bakes a cake at the touch of a button. The higher-end rice cookers developed by the Japanese "rice ladies" are also aggressively promoted. The IH models featuring an inner pot coated with diamond dust retail for over HK$2,000 (US$230), and yet in Hong Kong they are immensely popular. They sell more than 1,000 units a month, making the territory the biggest luxury rice cooker market outside of Japan.

Despite the massive influx of Made-in-China home appliances, National/Panasonic occupies nearly fifteen percent of the home appliances market in Hong Kong, and its rice cookers account for almost sixty percent of all rice cookers sold.

Using is Believing

In the spring of 2003, Matsushita Electric decided to consolidate its overseas brand names under Panasonic and to stop using National. In Hong Kong, the Chinese version of the National name, Lok Seng Pai (樂聲牌), was kept, but the English brand name for rice cookers changed to Panasonic. The name may have changed, but the dedication to localizing the end product has not. Mong and his successor as managing director of Shun Hing Electronic Trading, his son, David, continue to look for new ways of adapting the rice cooker for the Hong Kong market. Even now, in his ninth decade, William Mong persists in his quest to design an appliance capable of making several different kinds of congee to cater to the tastes of Hong Kong's regionally diverse Chinese population:

> There are all kinds of rice cookers now. But there is still room for improvement as far as the one that cooks congee is concerned. That's because the way Chinese people like their congee is different, depending on which part of China they come from; there is a big difference between Cantonese and Shanghainese congee. The way congee tastes in Chiu Chow is also different.

> It's not that it tastes bad. When it comes to customer satisfaction for rice and congee [cooked in a rice cooker], customers are happiest with the rice, which probably gets a ninety-five percent [customer satisfaction rating]. If you'd allow me to give my own rating for the congee, I'd say it's about seventy percent.[42]

Some of Matsushita Electric Trading's former employees in Japan admit to being surprised by Mong's obsession with rice cookers, as they always considered them to be "rather minor items." To them it is clear that Mong has made his money from the sale of audio-visual products such as televisions and radios, not from rice cookers. Mong counters:

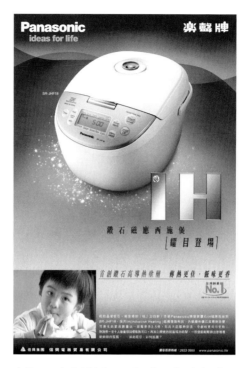

A Panasonic Saishi rice cooker featuring induction
heating (IH) and a diamond-coated inner pot.
Hong Kong, 2005.
Courtesy of Shun Hing Group

"Well, wireless products were more profitable, of course.

But I was the one who laid the foundation for the success of the rice cooker in
Hong Kong. Even now, National is the number one brand of rice cooker in Hong
Kong."[43]

It should be added that, of all the divisions at Matsushita, the rice cooker team was the
most open to Mong's suggestions and involved him in every step of the localization
process. It seems that this partnership was something that he truly enjoyed and was
proud of.

David Mong carries on his father's efforts to make the Saishi model more versatile.
Born in 1962, David grew up watching his parents thoroughly test every single product
sample before it was allowed to go on sale, and he similarly refuses to compromise on
attention to detail. One day in January 2003, when asked why a piece of cake had been
delivered to his desk, he responded that it was part of his research. "I'm having a cake
baked this way every day," he said, his finger pointing at a rice cooker catalogue.

The cake had been made using the rice cooker model developed by the Thai "rice
lady." And although it may have baked cakes that were delicious by Thai standards, this

did not necessarily mean that they would appeal to Hong Kongers. David Mong was therefore carrying out his own tests on the model that was about to be launched in Hong Kong:

> We are a marketing company. We are marketing products for Panasonic in Hong Kong. So my philosophy is "using is believing." You have to use the product and then you understand how good it is. I always ask my staff to use the product.[44]

Like his father, David goes about the testing of his latest appliances with the zeal of a missionary. Every day since he received a prototype of the new cake-baking model, he had had his rice cooker sales team use it to bake a cake. Every afternoon, Shun Hing's pantry turned into a baking lab. The head of the sales team, Elvina Li, was not a particularly good cook, but, as David explains, that proved to be an asset during the testing process:

> First, we asked people who are good at baking cakes to test the product. That way we could be sure that it worked. Then we asked people who are not that good at cooking, like Elvina, to try it out. It still worked. That meant that using it to bake a cake was as simple as cooking rice in it. Just follow the recipe, press the button, and thirty minutes later you have a great-tasting sponge cake.[45]

"That meant," Elvina adds with a smile, "that it is very user-friendly."

David and his team experimented with various cake mixes, flour, and eggs sold at local supermarkets, to which they added local water or, occasionally, unsweetened condensed milk, a long-time Hong Kong favorite:

> We baked many cakes, adjusting the amount of water, eggs, and flour each time. As we were planning to carry out product demonstrations in department stores and electrical appliance shops, it was important to make the cake look good and taste good.[46]

David Mong. Hong Kong, 2003.
Courtesy of Shun Hing Group

David invited other employees to taste the results, asked for their comments, tried it out at home with his family, and continued to make small adjustments to the recipes the team was testing. They also tried different flavors, including chocolate, coffee, and green tea. At first, the cakes were too sweet, and they struggled to achieve the taste they were looking for. After a whole month of trials, however, they finally felt they had come up with recipes that would appeal to their Hong Kong customers. They attached a small booklet to the new model, containing tested recipes adapted from those developed by the Thai "rice ladies."

Just before Chinese New Year in 2003, the cake-baking model made its debut in Hong Kong stores as the latest Saishi rice cooker. The ad depicted a cartoon sumo wrestler holding up a plate with a golden brown cake on it, and proclaiming in English, "Baking cake is so easy and simple." In addition to cake baking, it came with five other functions, all activated at the push of a button. These included "Rice Cook/Steam," "Brown Rice," "Keep Warm," as well as one-hour "Porridge" and three-hour "Congee" modes. It also had a steaming basket. Understandably, the ad emphasized how multifunctional the new rice cooker was:

> Versatile: Cooks many dishes automatically thanks to a built-in microcomputer.

In fact, the Chinese version of versatile used in the ad, "多才多藝 (gifted in many ways)," is more than just a description of the latest rice cooker model; it also captures the essence of William Mong's partnership with Matsushita and its National rice cooker team. Its open-minded approach and willingness to go beyond the limits of its own cultural boundaries led to the localization and then globalization of a small electrical appliance that has transformed the lives of Asians all over the world. By accepting the value of local insight and understanding that the rice cooker needed to cater to local tastes for it to sell outside of Japan, the National team managed to produce a versatile appliance that is constantly evolving to suit the diverse needs of its customers.

The cake-baking model immediately became a bestseller. It was so popular that the factory in Thailand began shipping the new rice cookers to Shun Hing by air rather than surface freight, just to save seventy-two hours in the delivery time, such was the demand. The territory's sales target was originally 2,000 units per month, but by March 2003, in the midst of the SARS epidemic, the cake-baking model was selling by as many as 5,000 a month. The head of the sales team, Elvina Li, was overjoyed:

> It was like a dream come true. All the salesmen told me it was like a dream. But it was true. And they couldn't understand why housewives like cake so much, because the salesmen, all of them, were men.[47]

Perversely, another way of gauging a product's popularity in Hong Kong is not only whether or not it has been copied but also how closely the copy resembles the original. The cake-baking Saishi was replicated almost as soon as it was launched, right down to the silver nail polish shade of the pot, by a Chinese manufacturer, and openly sold at a major Hong Kong supermarket chain.

The price for a genuine National 5.5-cup model was fixed at HK$628 (US$85), nearly seventy percent more expensive than the basic, single-function Saishi rice cooker. Versatile appliances, however, appeal to Hong Kongers, even if they rarely use all the features provided. Back in the 1980s, for example, a National office phone with a busy keypad outsold sleek American and European models. The National model had six keys just for outside lines, but Hong Kongers preferred this set-up to having to press "9" or "0" every time they wanted to make an outside call.[48] In this fast-paced city driven by money, less is not always more.

Following its success in Hong Kong and Thailand, Panasonic made the new model available in Indonesia and Malaysia, where many housewives practice the traditional boil-drain-steam method of rice cooking. The model was also distributed in Canada and marketed to the Hong Kong Chinese diasporas there. Back in Hong Kong, the cake-baking function proved so popular that it became standard on all mid-range and high-end models. As of November 2007, twenty-three percent of all Panasonic rice cookers sold in the territory are equipped with a cake-baking function, whereas none of the Panasonic models sold in Japan include it. Other manufacturers have produced models with a cake button for the Japanese market, but they remain an exception rather than the norm.[49]

"Baking cake is so easy and simple."
Hong Kong, 2003.
Courtesy of Shun Hing Group

Meanwhile, the versatile rice cooker takes on an increasingly wide variety of dishes from around the world. One of the latest additions is a "Risotto" button. Decades ago, the National engineers abandoned the idea of creating a risotto cooker, because of the lack of enthusiasm shown by Italian consumers for such an appliance. Yet it was recently added, not because the Italians had a sudden change of heart but because, due to global food trends, it appealed to Asians who had developed a taste for Italian cuisine. The 2008 Hong Kong risotto model has an additional button for cooking instant noodles.

The Thai "rice ladies" have also been busy and in 2007 created a rice cooker that prepares not just instant soup noodles but also Thai fried noodles. All one has to do is put cold water and dry rice noodles into the pot, press the button, and then wait for the rice cooker to boil the water and cook the noodles until they are soft, before adding the sauce. Other Thai rice cooker models also reflect local tastes. One classic line comes in five colorful designs, including a pattern of blue elephants on a metallic silver background and a pattern of tropical lovebirds on a white background. Machiko Miyai, director of the Cooking Appliances Business Unit, confesses that she would not have chosen these patterns herself, but that is exactly why she left the planning of these cookers entirely in the hands of the company's Thai employees:

> Being Japanese, we don't know what people in other countries like. So we ask our local staff to select designs that will work in their market. After all, it is ultimately the end users who decide [whether they like our appliances or not]. Only they would know their own country's food culture and design preferences. So if we try to pick for them, we are certain to make mistakes.[50]

Miyai explains that her job is to nurture non-Japanese staff and provide a stimulating and collaborative work environment that encourages them to come up with ideas that are outside her own Japanese "box." She believes versatility and adaptability are the only way forward.

Epilogue
Made in Asia

The globalization of "Made in Japan" products is usually presented as a heroic tale whose central characters are all Japanese men: it focuses on how diligently their project teams worked, how their products created a sensation in the United States, and how their efforts enriched the Japanese economy. The NHK documentary series *Project X: Challengers* is a case in point. This show aired weekly between 2000 and 2005 on Japan's sole public broadcaster. It usually featured exceptionally dedicated salarymen, hailing them as unsung heroes who had played small yet critical roles in the Japanese postwar economic miracle. The program was immensely popular, especially among aging salarymen who had once seen, or still saw, themselves as "corporate warriors." Prior to the success of *Project X*, corporate narratives that lacked a charismatic lead character had been a hard sell. The groundbreaking weekly series, however, turned these salaryman stories into emotionally charged tales that were used by parents to impress upon their children the value of a strong work ethic. The show's theme song "Earthly Stars (*Chijyō no Hoshi*)," composed and performed by Miyuki Nakajima, stayed on the Japanese Top 100 singles chart for 174 consecutive weeks. Although not without its critics, the series established a new genre of Japanese business success stories.

The international marketing of Sony's transistor radio was featured in one of the earlier episodes of *Project X*, broadcast in 2001. The show recounted how Sony's "pocketable" radio broke into the US and German markets in the late 1950s. The opening sequence summarized the story as follows:

> The [TR-63] transistor radio became popular in the United States and Europe, not just because of its advanced "technology." Its pioneering success was made possible by the dedicated men who tirelessly fought against all odds to promote their product in foreign lands. These sales representatives traveled alone across the oceans and sold transistor radios in the United States and Europe, battling local prejudice against Japanese products; they became known as the "*samurai.*"[1]

Typical of the *Project X* narratives was the way they depicted Japan at the absolute center of this process. They described the globalization of Japanese products as a unilateral endeavor, with Japan as the origin and the West as the destination. As we saw in Chapter 3, Sony's success with the transistor radio was a wake-up call for Matsushita's Radio Division, as they also dreamed of winning New Yorkers over to the Panasonic brand; the US market was the most lucrative at the time, and thus the most glamorous. Forty years on, popular narratives relating to the early international marketing of "Made in Japan" products continue to focus on the West, ignoring similar achievements in the East.

Furthermore, the program often conflated the success of "Made in Japan" products with the success of Japan as a nation. In the episode on the Sony transistor radio, for example, the sales representatives felt that they were promoting their radio not just for their company but for their country.[2] The strong global presence of Japanese electrical appliances, and more recently of Japanese pop culture, has been a source of continuous self-congratulatory discourse in Japan. Some Japanese observers go so far as to link it directly to Japan's soft power; critics, in contrast, refer to it as "Japanization" or even "Japanese cultural imperialism." These lines of argument, however, only look at the scale of Japanese influence; they fail to consider key elements like distribution channels and the role that local intermediaries as well as consumers have played in them. The process of globalization is far more complex than a one-sided push on the part of Japanese manufacturers with consumers in the West as their target.[3]

In 2005, when the Japanese version of this book, *Onajikama no Meshi* (Eating Rice from the Same Pot), came out, some reviewers likened it to a *Project X*-style take on National/Panasonic. In fact, this inquiry into how Japanese rice cookers were introduced to the Hong Kong market started with a conviction that it would result in a different story from those generally featured in *Project X*. It was also motivated by a desire to examine the globalization of "Made in Japan" products from a less Japan-centric perspective. It soon became evident that this "minor" appliance originally targeted at Japanese housewives enjoyed an altogether more elevated status in Hong Kong. What emerged clearly from the research was that the synergy that existed between the Japanese rice cooker team and its Hong Kong intermediary was the determining factor in the successful localization of this humble kitchen appliance and its eventual domination of the Hong Kong market and beyond. The process was not unilateral but multidirectional, multifaceted, and above all collaborative. Japanese rice cookers found their way along Chinese and other transnational networks to Asians worldwide.

This account of the rice cooker's globalization is truly one of cross-cultural teamwork and of being able to accept the validity of a point of view different from one's own. Far from being Japan-centric, it involves a culturally diverse cast of characters: an enterprising Hong Kong intermediary whose insistence on catering to the needs of the local population led to the development of rice cooker models for Chinese consumers; Thai "rice ladies" who worked diligently to develop a cake-baking model that has never really taken off in Japan; and Iranian consumers who cook their rice to a golden crust by adding oil to the pot, an unthinkable act for most Japanese rice purists. By examining how the rice cooker went global via Hong Kong, one begins to see that, far from being the result of a one-sided push from Japan, it is the fruit of a complex interactive process involving local product distributors, consumers, and "rice ladies."

The heroic tales of Japanese commercial victory may boost national pride, but they overlook the contributions of non-Japanese men and women to the globalization process. One could say that the National rice cooker success story is not simply a case of "Made in Japan" but more accurately a case of "Made in Asia."

Who's Who at Matsushita

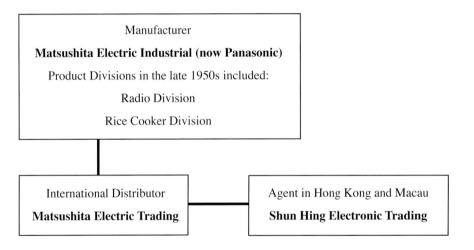

Manufacturer
Matsushita Electric Industrial (now Panasonic)
Product Divisions in the late 1950s included:
Radio Division
Rice Cooker Division

International Distributor
Matsushita Electric Trading

Agent in Hong Kong and Macau
Shun Hing Electronic Trading

Matsushita Electric Industrial
Matsushita Electric Industrial was rebranded Panasonic in 2008.

Mr Konosuke Matsushita	Founder	
Mr Kunio Nakamura	President of Matsushita Electric Industrial	2000-06

Matsushita's two brands are:

National	– mainly used for home appliances, 1927–2008
Panasonic	– mainly used for audiovisual products
	– introduced as a brand name for the US market in 1961
	– used for all products sold outside Japan from 2003 onwards and for all products sold in Japan from 2008 onwards

Rice Cooker Division, 1958–2002
Cooking Systems Division, 2002–06
Cooking Appliances Business Unit, 2006–present

Directors
Mr Tatsunosuke Sakamoto   1st Director, 1958–68
> As the first director of the Rice Cooker Division, Sakamoto pursued his ambition to take the National rice cooker to the world, and worked hand-in-hand with William Mong to develop a Hong Kong model.

Mr Yoshiaki Sano   3rd Director, 1982–89
> Sano invented the classic rice cooker switch in 1962 and spearheaded the development of an international model. While head engineer of the Division in 1978, he hired the first female specialist to join his R&D team; she would later come to be known as a "rice lady."

Ms Machiko Miyai   11th Director, 2006–present
> Miyai joined the Rice Cooker Division as the third National "rice lady" in 1983, and went on to become the first female director to oversee an entire product line at Matsushita.

International Sales Team
Mr Yūki Ogasawara   1962–75
Mr Takekazu Nishiwaki   1968–89
Mr Masayuki Nakano   1987–2004

Research and Development
Ms Takako Kuroda   1st "rice lady," 1979–82
Ms Tomoko Sasakura   Overseas Products Planner, 1990–2004

Radio Division
Mr Keiichi Takeoka   1950s
> Director of the factory that manufactured the PL-420 radio. He went on to become president of Matsushita's subsidiary in the United States.

Mr Kiyoshi Nakane   1950s
> Radio Division's Product Planning Department Head – executive in charge of international product development

Mr Shuzo Imamura   1950s
> Head of the Radio Division's Technical Department

Mr Hisashi Kusugami   1950s
> Technical Engineer

Matsushita Electric Trading

Matsushita Electric Trading ceased to be a separate unit when it was absorbed by Matsushita Electric Industrial in 1988.

Mr Arataro Takahashi	Chairman, 1955–83
Mr Shozo Iimura	President, 1970–82
Mr Tsuneo Jinnai	Senior Managing Director (*Senmu*), 1952–60
Mr Takayoshi Yamamoto	Managing Director (*Jyōmu*), 1950–66

Hong Kong Hands

Mr Shoichiro Koyama	1956–70s
Mr Junichi Ukita	1959–63
Mr Misao Naka	1962–82
Mr Kyoichi Yoshioka	1978–2003
Mr Toyofumi Hirata	1987–present

Chronology

1859	Nagasaki becomes an open port.
1868	Meiji Restoration.
1894	A plague sweeps through Guangdong Province.
1894–95	Sino-Japanese War.
1896	The Hongkong and Shanghai Banking Corporation opens its first Nagasaki branch.
	William Mong's maternal and paternal grandfathers move from Guangdong Province to Nagasaki in the mid-1890s.
1898	Birth of Mong's father Mong Kwok-ping in Nagasaki.
1902	Birth of Mong's mother Wong Fa-yuk in Nagasaki.
1914–18	World War I.
1918	Konosuke Matsushita founds Matsushita Electric Industrial.
1922–23	Anti-Japanese movements in China cause Chinese merchants in Nagasaki to go out of business.
	Mong's parents get married in Guangdong Province and move to Hong Kong.
November 7, 1927	Birth of William Mong Man-wai in Hong Kong.
mid-1930s	Mong's father resigns from Mitsubishi Corporation and starts a company specializing in trade with Japan.

1935	Matsushita Electric Trading is incorporated in Japan.
1937	Japan launches a full-scale invasion of China.
1941–1945	Japan occupies Hong Kong for three years and eight months.
1946	Mong leaves Hong Kong for China to further his studies.
	General MacArthur's occupation headquarters categorize Matsushita Electric Industrial as a *zaibatsu* and force Matsushita Electric Trading to severe all links with its parent company for nearly five years.
1948	Mong returns to Hong Kong following the outbreak of civil war in China.
1949	Mong leaves for Japan and enrolls in a primary school in Tokyo to learn Japanese.
October 1, 1949	Establishment of the People's Republic of China.
1952	Mong sets up the Shun Wo trading company.
August 15, 1953	Mong starts business with Matsushita Electric Trading and changes the name of his trading company to Shun Hing Hong.
October 1953	The Bank of Tokyo opens a Hong Kong branch.
December 25, 1953	A major fire in the Shek Kip Mei squatter area leads to the construction of Hong Kong's first public housing estate.
1954	National ships its first thirty vacuum radios to Hong Kong.
	Konosuke Matsushita entrusts Mong with the exclusive rights to the distribution of National products in Hong Kong.
	Mong becomes engaged to Serena Yang Hsueh-chi, the daughter of a Chinese businessman in Kobe.
1955	Toshiba introduces the automatic rice cooker in Japan.
	The television, washing machine and refrigerator, collectively referred to as the "Three Sacred Treasures," become icons of modern Japanese living.
	Sony launches its portable transistor radio.
1957	National exports its first rice cookers to the United States.
September 1958	National sets up its Rice Cooker Division.
April 1959	The royal wedding of Crown Prince Akihito and Michiko Shoda dramatically boosts ownership of a television set in Japan.

December 1959	National introduces a rice cooker with a built-in heating element; Mong imports his first twenty-four rice cookers to Hong Kong.
1959	The first international shipment of National refrigerators leaves for Hong Kong.
	Japanese-American George Nozawa becomes the agent for National rice cookers in the western United States.
1960	The National rice cooker team begins development of an international model in collaboration with Mong.
	Mong and his associates launch a series of cooking demonstrations to promote rice cookers in Hong Kong.
	Shun Hing Hong changes its name to Shun Hing Electronic Trading.
November 4, 1960	Daimaru, Hong Kong's first Japanese department store, opens its doors.
1961	The international model makes its debut in Hong Kong, Singapore, Malaysia, and Thailand.
early 1960s	Japanese businessmen relocated to Europe start taking rice cookers with them.
1962	Birth of David Mong Tak-yeung in Hong Kong.
February 23, 1962	*Time* magazine puts Konosuke Matsushita on its cover.
July 3, 1962	Shun Hing officially opens a National showroom—the first outside Japan—on the ground floor of Chungking Mansions.
November 1963	Konosuke Matsushita visits Hong Kong to attend Shun Hing's tenth anniversary celebrations.
1964	The rate of rice cooker ownership in Japan reaches eighty-eight percent.
1966	Launch of Mao's Great Proletarian Cultural Revolution.
	General Mills-Morinaga unsuccessfully promote a rice cooker cake mix in Japan.
1967	An industrial dispute sparks deadly riots in Hong Kong.
	The development of the modern container ship revolutionizes marine transportation.
	The total number of National rice cookers imported into Hong Kong annually exceeds 100,000.
	National develops a rice cooker for the Iranian market.

November 19, 1967	Hong Kong's first free-to-air television station starts broadcasting.
July 1968	Shun Hing sets up its five-person washing machine demonstration team to boost sales of the appliance in Hong Kong.
1970	Japanese TV drama *V is Our Sign* is a hit in Hong Kong.
	Japanese televisions account for seventy-eight percent of the total number of sets imported into Hong Kong.
1971	The Nixon administration discontinues the fixed dollar–yen exchange rate.
September 29, 1972	Japan establishes diplomatic relations with the PRC.
1972	Sales of Japanese refrigerators in Hong Kong overtake those of their Italian competitors.
	Forty-six percent of Hong Kong's industrial workforce is engaged in the textile industry.
1973	Matsushita opens a radio manufacturing plant in Jakarta.
	The oil crisis drives up the price of rice cookers.
1975	Forty-three percent of Hong Kong's 4.4 million residents live in public housing and almost half of the city's residents were born on the Mainland.
	Sales of rice cookers in Hong Kong plummet by more than fifty percent from 1974 to 1975 as a result of the price increase necessitated by the oil crisis.
1976	National introduces the first rice cooker with a congee-making function to Hong Kong.
Late 1970s	A Vietnamese immigrant starts distributing National rice cookers through Asian grocery stores in France.
1978	Hong Kong introduces compulsory junior high school education.
	Shun Hing sells 7,000 black-and-white televisions to the Guangzhou Friendship Store.
December 1978	Deng Xiaoping launches China's Open Door Policy.
January 1, 1979	Chinese authorities begin allowing Hong Kong and Macau visitors to enter China with one taxable electrical appliance per person per year.
March 15, 1979	A group of four manufacturers introduces a system that allows customers to pay for a television set in Hong Kong and pick it up from a designated collection point in China.

April 1979	National's all-male rice cooker R&D team hires its first female rice specialist; she would later come to be known as a "rice lady."
May 1979	National releases its first micro-computerized electronic rice cooker in Japan.
November 1979	National releases its colorful "Saishi" rice cooker in Hong Kong; it has a hinged lid and keeps rice warm for twelve hours.
1984	Nozawa Trading celebrates one million National rice cookers sold in the United States.
December 19, 1984	Signing of the Sino-British Joint Declaration.
1985	A congee-making function is added to the Saishi model for the Hong Kong market.
1984–86	In China, uncontrolled purchasing of consumer goods causes a trade deficit and leads to restrictions on the import of foreign electrical goods.
1987	Matsushita sets up a joint venture with a Chinese company and begins manufacturing color picture tubes in China.
	Immigration from Hong Kong to Canada and Australia shows a marked increase; many immigrants take their Saishi rice cooker with them to their new home.
1989	Tiananmen Square student protests.
1992	National sets up an international maintenance service for Filipino domestic workers who have brought rice cookers back from the Middle East.
July 1, 1997	Hong Kong reverts to Chinese sovereignty.
2001	National hires two Thai female rice specialists to develop localized models.
2003	National's R&D team in Thailand develops a rice cooker that includes a cake-baking function.
	SARS hits Hong Kong and causes the death of 299 people in the city.
	Matsushita announces that it will use the Panasonic brand name for all products sold outside Japan.
November 7, 2003	Shun Hing celebrates its 50th anniversary.
2006	National/Panasonic appoints its first female director to oversee its rice cooker line.
	Some 43 million rice cookers are sold annually worldwide.

Notes

Introduction

1 Japan Electrical Manufacturers' Association, "An Estimate of Global Demand for Seven White Goods 2007."

2 The "Three Sacred Treasures (*sanshu no jingi*)" of modern convenience, the washing machine, the television, and the refrigerator, were named after the three items that constitute the Imperial Regalia of Japan: a copper mirror, a sword, and a jewel.

3 From an interview with Yoshiaki Sano, Osaka, August 20, 2008.

4 Attempts were made to check the accuracy of these accounts whenever possible.

5 FAO, Food Outlook, November 2007.

6 Ohnuki-Tierney, *Rice as Self*, 134.

7 Panasonic, Corporate Profile, Panasonic Official Website.

8 Speech by Kunio Nakamura, Hong Kong Convention and Exhibition Centre, November 7, 2003.

9 The section on middle-class aspirations is based on Chapter 5, "Shun Hing in the 1970s and 1980s: Growth and Development," 81–131, that Dixon H. W. Wong wrote for an earlier Chinese-language version of this book. Building on his work, I conducted additional research and interviews and developed the story into its current form. I sincerely thank Dixon for his generosity and insights.

10 Hong Kong Government, *Events in Hong Kong, 1967.*

11 *Events in Hong Kong, 1967.*

12 Wong, "Shun Hing in the 1970s and 1980s," 81–3; and my additional interview, Hong Kong, December 13, 2003.

13 Interview with Bill Wong, Hong Kong, December 13, 2003.

14 Interview with Bill Wong.

15 Interview with Bill Wong.

16 Wong, 83–9.

17 South China Morning Post, *MacLehose Years*, 44.

18 Bill is referring to soccer, not American football.

19 Interview with Bill Wong.

20 Interview with Bill Wong.
21 Wong, 90. The show was launched in 1967 and ran for eight years.
22 The color encoding system used for television broadcasts in Hong Kong was different from that used in Japan. Japan followed the US system, NTSC, named for the National Television System Committee, and Hong Kong used PAL, or Phase Alternating Line, which had been developed in Europe.
23 Wong, 89–90.
24 *Rediffusion Television* later became Hong Kong's second free-to-air broadcaster ATV, or Asia Television Limited.
25 Wong, 90.
26 Interview with Bill Wong.
27 Wong, 86.
28 Interview with Bill Wong.
29 Interview with Bill Wong.
30 Wong, 91.
31 Interview with Bill Wong.
32 Wong, 90.
33 Hong Kong Government, *The Development of Senior Secondary and Tertiary Education*, 1.
34 Hong Kong Government, *Hong Kong* 1973, 13; RTHK, Xianggang zhi zao, zhi zao Xianggang.
35 Interview with Bill Wong.
36 Nakano, "Shared Memories," 111–5.
37 Interview with Bill Wong.
38 Wong, 92–3.
39 Ministry of Internal Affairs and Communications, Statistical Bureau, "Quantity of Major Durable Consumer Goods Possessed."
40 Hong Kong Government, *Hong Kong Annual Report* 1976, 90.
41 Tsang, Steve, *A Modern History of Hong Kong*, 193–4.
42 Hong Kong Government, *Kowloon Disturbances 1966*, 138.
43 Wong, 92.
44 Interview with Bill Wong.
45 Wong, "Conclusion," 167–8.
46 Hong Kong Government, *Hong Kong Annual Report* 1976, 181.

Chapter 1

1 Sanyo was the other brand to introduce automatic rice cookers to Hong Kong in the late 1950s. Its first advertisement to feature a rice cooker appeared in *Wah Kiu Yat Po* (*Overseas Chinese Daily*) on October 17, 1958, 1:4.
2 Interview with Lily Choi, Hong Kong, December 8, 2002.
3 Interview with Lily Choi, December 12, 2003.
4 Interview with Lily Choi, December 8, 2002.
5 From an interview with Junichi Ukita, Osaka, January 7, 2003.
6 Interview with William Mong, Hong Kong, September 12, 2002.
7 Matsushita, *Yume wo Sodateru*, 84.
8 NHK, *Project X: 7*, 230–68.
9 Partner, *Assembled in Japan*, 177–8.
10 The original Japanese advertising copy was: "*Gohan ga kagaku-teki ni oishiku takeru.*"

11 See Partner, 233–42, for the significance of electrical goods in Japan's postwar history.

12 From an interview with Yoshiaki Sano, Osaka, January 8, 2003.

13 From an interview with Yūki Ogasawara by e-mail, March 17, 2009. According to Ogasawara, Konosuke Matsushita spoke of this incident in his annual management policy speech in 1961, in which he praised the performance of the Rice Cooker Division. Ogasawara's colleagues remember that Sakamoto was in tears as he listened to the speech.

14 Fukagawa, *Kyacchi Furēzu no Sengoshi*, 61–4.

15 Matsushita Electric Industrial, *70 years of Matsushita Electric Advertisements*, 110.

16 From an interview with Yoshiaki Sano, Osaka, January 8, 2003.

17 From an interview with Junichi Ukita, Osaka, January 7, 2003.

18 *In the Mood for Love.*

19 NHK, *Project X: 7*, 253–4.

20 From an interview with Yūki Ogasawara, January 8, 2003.

21 Interview with Junichi Ukita, Osaka, January 7, 2003.

22 Interview with Junichi Ukita.

23 Interview with Junichi Ukita.

24 Interview with Junichi Ukita.

25 Interview with William Mong, Hong Kong, September 12, 2002.

26 The "door-to-door" approach was first introduced at apartment complexes in Senri Newtown in Osaka in the late 1950s, and in Hong Kong and Singapore in the early 1960s.

27 Egami, *Sekai no Ryori*, 189.

28 Interview with William Mong, Hong Kong, September 12, 2002.

29 Kadoma is approximately 30 minutes away, or two short commuter train rides, from the center of Osaka. As soon as you alight at the Keihan Line's Kadoma-shi station, you are bombarded with Matsushita staff announcements: "Good morning. This is an announcement for the staff of Matsushita Electric. Please walk on the right side of the road and refrain from smoking."

30 Kotter, *Matsushita Leadership*, 122.

31 Matsushita Electric Industrial, Official Website, "Kigyō Johō, Shashi 1933-nen." http://panasonic.co.jp/company/history/chronicle/1933-02.html. Retrieved on March 29, 2008.

32 Interview with William Mong, Hong Kong, January 16, 2003.

33 Interview with William Mong.

34 Interview with Shoichiro Koyama, Osaka, January 7, 2003.

35 From interviews with Shoichiro Koyama and Junichi Ukita, Osaka, January 7, 2003.

36 isM Shosekika Project, "Long-selling Products," 192–3.

37 From interviews with Yoshiaki Sano, Osaka, January 8, 2003; and Masayuki Nakano, Yashiro, Hyogo, November 11, 2003.

38 Interview with Yoshiaki Sano, Osaka, November 13, 2003.

39 Interview with Yoshiaki Sano.

40 From an interview with Misao Naka, Osaka, January 7, 2003.

41 Interview with Yoshiaki Sano.

42 From Shun Hing's product catalogue, 1989.

43 Interview with Takakazu Nishiwaki, Osaka, November 13, 2003.

44 From an interview with Masayuki Nakano, November 11, 2003.

45 Ohnuki-Tierney, *Rice as Self*, 97.

46 Interview with Yoshiaki Sano, January 8, 2003.

47 Interview with Yoshiaki Sano.

48 Interview with Yoshiaki Sano.

Chapter2

1   Refsing, "William Mong's Personal History," 17.

2   Tsang, *A Modern History of Hong Kong,* 168.

3   Gordon, *A Modern History of Japan,* 17–8.

4   Ichikawa, *Kakyō-shakai Keizai-ron Jyosetsu,* 217.

5   Ichikawa, 216–7.

6   Nagasaki City, *Nagasaki-shi Shi,* 460–2.

7   Ichikawa, 216–9. See also Nagasaki City, 279.

8   Zhuang, "Relations with China," 98.

9   Gordon, 49–50.

10   Ichikawa, 223–5.

11   Ichikawa, 238; Burke-Gaffney, "Thomas B. Glover," 130.

12   Wang, *The Chinese Diaspora and the Development of China,* 3–5.

13   Wang, 3-5.

14   Ichikawa, 254 and 207.

15   Refsing, 18.

16   Nagasaki City, *Nagasaki-shi Nenpyō,* 133.

17   Saito, *Kyōsō to Kanri no Gakko-shi,* 37.

18   Ichikawa, 254.

19   Nagasaki City, *Nagasaki-shi Nenpyō,* 156.

20   Wasserstrom, "Chinese Students and Anti-Japanese Protests, Past and Present."

21   Ichikawa, 251.

22   Hamashita, *Hong Kong,* 159–88.

23   Chan and Yeung, *Xianggang Riben Guanxi Nianbiao*, 104.

24   For those familiar with today's Hong Kong, Mitsubishi's offices would have been in the building right next door to Shanghai Tang's Central store, a brand famous for its fluorescent Chinese outfits.

25   Refsing, 21.

26   Refsing, 21.

27   Refsing, 21.

28   Matsushita Electric Trading, *Company Newsletter*, August 5, 1974, 2.

29   From an interview with William Mong, Hong Kong, February 11, 2004.

30   The proverb is from Sima Qian's *The Records of the Grand Historian* (史記), Chapter 69, "Biography of Su Qin" (蘇秦列傳).

31   Matsushita Electric Trading, 2.

32   Refsing, 24.

33   Refsing, 24.

34   Refsing, 26.

35   Refsing, 21-2.

36   Refsing, 31.

37   Interview by Kirsten Refsing with William Mong, Hong Kong, October 2002.

38   Interview with William Mong, February 11, 2004.

39   Refsing, 25.

40   Interview with William Mong, November 8, 2002.

41   Interview with William Mong.

42   Interview with William Mong.

43   Between the end of World War II and their relocation to Arsenal Street in 1954, Police Headquarters were housed in Oriental Building at 1 Connaught Road, Central. This location

was later occupied by the Furama Hotel and is now the site of AIA Central. From Police Museum, *Police Museum*, 46.

44 Refsing, 22.
45 Interview with William Mong, February 11, 2004.
46 Interview with William Mong, November 8, 2002.
47 Nagasaki City, 173.
48 Interview with William Mong, November 8, 2002.
49 Interview with William Mong.
50 Interview with William Mong.
51 *Wah Kiu Yat Po* [*Overseas Chinese Daily*], February 13, 1950, 2:3.
52 The Filipino movie *Fort Santiago* premiered in Hong Kong on January 15, 1950. This version of the advertisement for the movie appeared in *Wah Kiu Yat Po* [*Overseas Chinese Daily*] and *Sing Tao Daily* from February 12 to 16, 1950.
53 Interview with William Mong, November 8, 2002.
54 Refsing, 23.
55 Liao, "Kashō to Nettowāk", 140–1.
56 Refsing, 23.
57 Interview with William Mong, January 16, 2003.
58 Interview with William Mong, September 12, 2002.

Chapter3

1 Interview with William Mong, Hong Kong, January 16, 2003.
2 In 1848, when the French republic was newly established, and Germany and Italy were moving toward unification, Palmerston laid out his foreign policy in a speech to the House of Commons: "It is a narrow policy to suppose that this country or that is to be marked out as the eternal ally or the perpetual enemy of England. We have no eternal allies, we have no perpetual enemies. Our interests are eternal and perpetual, and those interests it is our duty to follow." See Judd, *Palmerston*, 88; Ziegler, *Palmerston*, 67.
3 Interview with William Mong, September 12, 2002.
4 Interview with William Mong.
5 Hong Kong, *Hong Kong Annual Report* 1953, 159.
6 Report of Sham Shui Po, Shek Kip Mei Six Villages Fire Relief Committee, ix; Carroll, *A Concise History of Hong Kong*, 145.
7 *Hong Kong Annual Report* 1953, 22; Hong Kong Japanese Chamber of Commerce & Industry, *A Twenty-year History*, 75.
8 Interview with William Mong.
9 Matsushita Electric Trading, "Company Newsletter," December 5, 1970.
10 Dower, *Embracing Defeat*, 68–9.
11 Matsushita Electric Trading, *50 Years of Matsushita Electric Trading*, 34–5. See also Kotter, *Matsushita Leadership*, 145.
12 *50 Years*, 35; "Company Newsletter," May 5, 1975, 4–6.
13 *50 Years*, 35; "Company Newsletter," May 5, 1975, 5.
14 *50 Years*, 93 and 101–3.
15 National Association of Commercial Broadcasters in Japan, Official Website.
16 Matsushita Electric Industrial, *70 years of Matsushita Electric Advertisements*, 72.
17 From an interview with Keiichi Takeoka, Osaka, January 8, 2003.
18 Matsushita Electric Industrial, 82.

19   Matsushita Electric Industrial, Newsletter *Passpost 21*, No. 48, 4.

20   *50 Years*, 165.

21   Interview with Keiichi Takeoka, Osaka, January 8, 2003.

22   Interview with William Mong, Hong Kong, September 12, 2002.

23   *Hong Kong Annual Report* 1953, 26. "Wages for daily paid artisans remained approximately as follows: skilled workmen $6.00–8.50."

24   *50 Years*, 165–6.

25   Interview with William Mong.

26   From an interview with Junichi Ukita, Osaka, January 7, 2003.

27   Interview with William Mong.

28   This section is based on William Mong's recollections unless otherwise noted. See also Matsushita Electric Industrial, Newsletter *Passpost 21*, No. 48, 1.

29   Interview with William Mong.

30   *Time,* "Business Abroad: Following Henry Ford," 55.

31   Matsushita, *Yume wo Sodateru*, 42.

32   Fukuda, *Shizuku Michiru Toki Tareba,* 223.

33   Interview with William Mong.

34   Interview with William Mong.

35   Interviews with Keiichi Takeoka, Kiyoshi Nakane, Shuzo Imamura, and Hisashi Kusugami, Osaka, January 8, 2003.

36   Interview with William Mong.

37   Interview with William Mong, November 8, 2002.

38   Interview with Keiichi Takeoka, Osaka, January 8, 2003.

39   The advertising slogan was bilingual, and the Chinese version, "Durable and economical; exquisite and stylish," made it even clearer that it was a good buy.

40   Interview with Kiyoshi Nakane, Osaka, January 8, 2003.

41   Interview with Kiyoshi Nakane.

42   Interview with Hisashi Kusugami, Osaka, January 8, 2003.

43   Interview with Keiichi Takeoka.

44   Morita, *Made in Japan,* 337.

45   Interview with Kiyoshi Nakane.

46   Interview with Kiyoshi Nakane.

47   Interview with Keiichi Takeoka.

48   "Company Newsletter," August 5, 1970, 4.

49   Interview with Junichi Ukita, Osaka, January 7, 2003.

50   Interview with Junichi Ukita.

51   Interview with Shoichiro Koyama, Osaka, January 7, 2003.

52   Interview with Shuzo Imamura, Osaka, January 8, 2003.

53   From an interview with Shoichiro Koyama.

54   Interview with Junichi Ukita.

55   In fact, this was common practice among upscale—jewelry, watch, electrical appliance—shops in Hong Kong. See Booth, *Gweilo*, 53 and 100.

56   Interview with Hisashi Kusugami.

57   From interviews with Keiichi Takeoka and Hisashi Kusugami, Osaka, January 8, 2003.

58   Interview with Junichi Ukita.
     The original Japanese sentence was, "*Sonna salaryman konjyō jya dame da.*" Although "thinking outside the box" was not an idiom in 1960, it accurately conveys Mong's frustration.

59   Interview with Junichi Ukita.

60 Interview with Junichi Ukita.
61 Interview with Junichi Ukita.
62 Interview with Junichi Ukita.

Chapter 4

1 Matsushita Electric Industrial, *70 years*, 119.
2 In 1959, Shun Hing Hong had also became the sole Hong Kong agent for Nivico (better known today as JVC or Victor Company of Japan, Limited), an audio equipment manufacturer that had been part of the Matsushita group since 1953, and was selling its products in the city under the Star brand. In 1960, following the lead of Matsushita Electric Trading, Shun Hing changed its name from that of a traditional Chinese trading house, Shun Hing Hong, to the more corporate-sounding, Shun Hing Electronic Trading.
3 Kelly, "Finding a Place in Metropolitan Japan," 195-7; Ivy, "Formations of Mass Culture," 248–50.
4 Economic Planning Agency of Japan. "Survey Report: Consumption-Demand Forecast 1958"; and "Survey Report: Consumer Trend Forecast 1960."
5 *70 years*, 109.
6 *Time,* "Business Abroad: Following Henry Ford," February 23, 1962, 58.
7 Interview with William Mong, Hong Kong, September 12, 2002.
8 Hong Kong Government, *Report for the Year* 1964, 170.
9 *Wah Kiu Yat Po* [*Overseas Chinese Daily*], November 13, Section 3: 4.
10 Carroll, *A Concise History of Hong Kong*, 140–4; Tsang, *A Modern History of Hong Kong*, 163.
11 Chiu, Ho, and Lui, *City-states in the Global Economy*, 42–3.
12 Carroll, 140 and 149.
13 Lee, *Housing, Home Ownership and Social Change in Hong Kong*, 116.
    A vast urban slum also began forming in the lawless Kowloon Walled City area. This tiny Chinese enclave in the heart of Kowloon was a former Qing Dynasty administrative outpost that had been staffed by imperial officials until their expulsion by the British, following the cession of Kowloon and the New Territories to Britain in 1898. But China refused to officially accept a change to the lease that would have made the Kowloon Walled City fall under the Hong Kong government's jurisdiction, and the authorities therefore had limited powers over what went on within its walls. Following the establishment of Mao's communist government in 1949, waves of immigrants from China poured into the Walled City, building illegal extensions and additions to the existing buildings and turning the City's squalid seven acres into a multistorey labyrinth of brothels, unlicensed dental clinics, and opium dens. From Carroll, 71 and 187–8; Yoshida, *Hong Kong Chronicle*, 7–25.
14 Lee, 124.
15 Chiu, Ho, and Lui, 36; See also Shiraishi, *Umi no Teikoku*, 127–49.
16 Interview with William Mong.
17 Interview with William Mong.
18 Interview with William Mong.
19 Interview with William Mong.
20 Interview with William Mong.
21 Interview with William Mong.
22 *Wah Kiu Yat Po* [*Overseas Chinese Daily*], April 6, 1960.
23 Cabinet Office, Government of Japan, "Ownership of Major Consumer Durables and Others— Household."

24   Matsushita Electric Industrial, *70 years*, 115.
25   Interview with William Mong.
26   Interview with Shoichiro Koyama, Osaka, January 7, 2003.
27   Interview with Shoichiro Koyama, Tokyo, November 25, 2003.
28   Interview with William Mong, January 16, 2003.
30   From an interview with Misao Naka.
31   Interview with William Mong, September 12, 2002.
32   From an interview with William Mong.
33   Matsushita Electric Trading, "Company Newsletter," April 5, 1971.
34   From an interview with Shinichiro Koyama.
35   Interview with Shinichiro Koyama, January 7, 2003.
36   "Company Newsletter," August 5, 1970.
37   Wong, "Shun Hing in the 1970s and 1980s," 91.
38   Interview with Tommy Ho, Hong Kong, September 24, 2007.
39   Interview with Tommy Ho.
40   Westinghouse ad, *Wah Kiu Yat Po* [*Overseas Chinese Daily*], May 2, 1971; Zoppas ad, *Wah Kiu Yat Po* [*Overseas Chinese Daily*], November 12, 1973.
41   Interview with Misao Naka, Osaka, January 7, 2003.
42   Interview with Misao Naka.
43   Interview with Misao Naka.
44   From an interview with Misao Naka.
45   From an interview with Misao Naka.
46   Interview with Misao Naka.
47   Liao, *Ethnic Chinese Business in Nagasaki and the Formation of Eastern Asian Business Network*, 209.
48   Hamashita, *Hong Kong*, 65–72.
49   Interview with William Mong, Hong Kong, February 11, 2004.
50   Hamashita, 155.
51   Matsushita Electric Trading, *50 Years*, 109.
52   *50 Years*, 109.
53   Interview with William Mong, November 8, 2003.
54   Interview with William Mong, February 11, 2004.

Chapter 5

1   The story of Shun Hing's China business, established as a result of the 1979 Open Door Policy, is based on Dixon H. W. Wong's work for an earlier Chinese-language version of this book. His work appeared in two sections of the book: Chapter 5 "Shun Hing in the 1970s and 1980s: Growth and Development," 101–6; and Chapter 6 "Shun Hing since the 1990s: Challenges and Responses," 144–50. Building on these two sections, I conducted additional research and interviews and developed the story into this chapter. I sincerely thank Dixon Wong for his generosity and insights.
2   Interview with Kyoichi Yoshioka, Osaka, November 13, 2003.
3   羅湖: *Lo Wu* is the romanization used in Hong Kong. In China, the same characters are transcribed in pinyin as *Luohu*.
4   Interview with Mrs Chiu, Hong Kong, August 24, 2004.
5   Interview with Mrs Chiu.
6   Interview with Mrs Chiu.

7 Wang, *Overview of China's Incoming Travelers and the Country or Region of their Origin*, 404.

8 *Wen Wei Po*, "Those who pay visits to relatives on the mainland are permitted to carry a Television, a Cassette Recorder, or a Camera etc.," December 29, 1978, 1.

9 *Wen Wei Po*, "Q&A with a Kowloon Customs Representative," July 1, 1979, 4.

10 *Wen Wei Po*, December 29, 1978, 1.

11 *Wen Wei Po*, "Handbook on Visits to Relatives on the Mainland," July 12, 1979.

12 Interview with Henry Chan, Hong Kong, August 15, 2004.

13 Wong, "Shun Hing in the 1970s and 1980s," 103.

14 Wong, 105–6.

15 Interview with Misao Naka, Hong Kong, January 7, 2003.

16 *Wen Wei Po*, December 19, 1978.

17 *Ming Pao*, January 4, 1979; *Sing Tao Daily*, January 3, 1979.

18 Interview with William Mong, Hong Kong, February 11, 2004.

19 *Wen Wei Po*, December 26, 1978 and January 4, 1979.

20 Hitachi, *Wen Wei Po*, June 5, 1979; Sony, June 16, 1979.

21 *Wen Wei Po*, June 23, 1979.

22 Wong, 103–4; and interview with Tommy Ho, Hong Kong, September 24, 2007.

23 Wong, 104.

24 Wong, 104.

25 Wong, 104.

26 Interview with Henry Chan.

27 Interview with William Mong.

28 *Wen Wei Po*, March 12, 1979.

29 RTHK, Jiti huiyi 70 nian dai 6: Qing xi Luohu qiao.

30 Neighbourhood Advice-Action Council, "Opinion Survey among Middle- and Lower-class Families on the Economic Impact of their Visits to Relatives on the Mainland."

31 Interview with William Mong.

32 Interview with Henry Chan.

33 China Travel Service (ed.), *Handbook on Visits to Relatives on the Mainland*, Summer 1985.

34 From an interview with Misao Naka, Osaka, January 7, 2003.

35 Wong, 102.

36 Wong, 145.

37 Amano, "Japanese Corporations and the Development of the Chinese Home Appliance Industry," 118-9.

38 Library of Congress, Federal Research Division, "China Trade Policy in the 1980s," Country Studies.

39 Amano, 119.

40 Wong, 146.

41 Amamo and Han (Fan), "Dynamism in the Development of the Home Appliance Industries in Japan and China," 64.

42 Interview with Kyoichi Yoshioka.

43 Wong, 150.1.

Chapter 6

1 Carroll, *A Concise History of Hong Kong*, 196; Wong, "Issues Paper from Hong Kong," 69-70.

2 Skeldon, "Patterns of Migration: The Case of Hong Kong," 69.
3 Skeldon, 69.
4 Carroll, 192.
5 Smart, "Business Immigration to Canada," 99–100.
6 Skeldon, 69.
7 The term "rice lady" is the English transcription of the Japanese *katakana* expression, "ライ ス・レディ."
8 Amano and Sakurai, *"Mono to Onna" no Sengo-shi.*
9 Interview with Yoshiaki Sano, Osaka, August 20, 2008.
10 Interview with Yoshiaki Sano.
11 Interview with Takako Suzuki (Kuroda), Tokyo, October 22, 2008.
12 Interview with Yoshiaki Sano.
13 National, *Gohan de Gochisou Sama*, 21–2.
14 National, 55–6.
15 *Oriental Daily*, March 4, 1980.
16 Chin, *Chūgoku Bijin-den*, 28–35.
17 Interview with William Mong, Hong Kong, September 12, 2002.
18 Saishi was not the only National/Panasonic product to be named after a renowned beauty in ancient China. A table-top cooker developed for hot pot and pancakes was given the name of the celebrated Tang Dynasty beauty Yang Guifei (楊貴妃).
19 「西施」花容添嬌姿.
20 *Sing Tao*, January 15, 1979, 4.
21 潮州: *Chiu Chow* is the romanization used in Hong Kong. In China, the same characters are transcribed as *Chaozhou.*
22 From an interview with Masayuki Nakano, Yashiro, Hyogo, November 11, 2003.
23 From an interview with Masayuki Nakano.
24 *Oriental Daily*, January 18, 1988.
25 Interview with Takekazu Nishiwaki, Yashiro, Hyogo, March 24, 2003.
26 From an interview with Yoshiaki Sano, January 8. 2003.
27 Interview by Dixon Wong with Kenneth Man, January 12, 2004.
28 In fact, by this time, Matsushita already had a Canadian agent who specialized in rice cookers. This is discussed later in the chapter.
29 Ng, "Communities: Canada," 247.
30 Interview with Tomoko Sasakura, Yashiro, Hyogo, March 24, 2003.
31 Interview with Tomoko Sasakura.
32 *New York Times*, "Boston's Other Japanese Pitcher," August 27, 2007.
33 Japan Airlines, *20-Year History*, 252.
34 Interview with Shigeru Yoshida, Tokyo, October 24, 2007.
35 The rate of rice cooker ownership is from the Ministry of Internal Affairs and Communications of Japan, Statistical Bureau. "Quantity of Major Durable Consumer Goods Possessed."
36 Interview with Shigeru Yoshida.
37 Interview with Shigeru Yoshida.
38 Ministry of Foreign Affairs of Japan. "Annual Report of Statistics on Japanese Nationals Overseas," October 1, 2005, 1; and October 1, 2006, 32.
39 Personal Communication with Koichiro Hioki, November 15, 2007.
40 D-Net Store, Appliances for Overseas Posting, retrieved April 17, 2008, from http://www.devicenet.co.jp/store/shop/mobile/item/kaden.html
41 Interview with Machiko Miyai, Osaka, November 16, 2007.
42 Interview with John Yao, Hong Kong, January 11, 2008.

43 Interview with John Yao.

44 UNESCO Institute for Statistics, *Global Education Digest 2007*, 137. "Asia" includes 43 countries under UNESCO's definition of "East Asia and the Pacific" (including Southeast Asia) and "South and West Asia," 202-3.

45 National Statistics Office, Republic of the Philippines, "One in Three Overseas Filipino Workers is a Laborer or Unskilled Worker."

46 isM Shosekika Project, "Long-selling Products," 195.

47 Interview with Masayuki Nakano by e-mail, May 9, 2008.

48 Panasonic Philippines, "Customer Service."

49 Panasonic Philippines. The service charge for repair of a gray-market rice cooker is listed as PHP 250 (approximately US$6).

50 Interview with a Japan Airlines Employee, Tokyo, October 27, 2007.

51 Interview with Shigeru Yoshida.

52 From interviews with Yūki Ogasawara and Takekazu Nishiwaki, Kyoto, November 15, 2007.

53 *Daily NK*, "South Korean Rice Cooker, Symbol of Wealth in North Korea," March 25, 2009, retrieved March 28, 2009, from http://www.dailynk.com.

54 Matsushita Electric Trading, *50 Years*, 178.

55 *50 Years*, 178.

56 UCLA Anderson School of Management, "Nozawa Endowment Marks 20th Year Granting Fellowships," retrieved April 21, 2008, from http://www.anderson.ucla.edu/x13868.xml.

57 From interviews with Takekazu Nishiwaki, Kyoto, November 15, 2007, and Yoshiaki Sano, Osaka, August 20, 2008.

58 From interviews with Takekazu Nishiwaki and Yoshiaki Sano.

59 *50 Years*, 179.

60 From interviews with Yoshiaki Sano.

61 From interviews with Takekazu Nishiwaki and Yoshiaki Sano.

62 Interview with Yūki Ogasawara, Kyoto, November 15, 2007.

63 Interview with Yoshiaki San.

Chapter 7

1 Samuel Lee is a pseudonym as the Japanese diplomat was unable to recall the Hong Kong Chinese student's actual name.

2 Interview with a Japanese diplomat by e-mail, April 29, 2008.

3 National, *Gohan de Gochisou Sama*, 56.

4 Interview with Machiko Miyai, Osaka, November 16, 2007.

5 Interview with Machiko Miyai.

6 Matsushita Electric Trading, *50 Years*, 179.

7 Mackey, *The Iranians*, 212.

8 *50 Years*, 179; Nakagawa, "Developing Iranian Rice Cookers."

9 FAO. 2009. "FAO STAT, Agriculture Production."

10 A letter from Yūki Ogasawara, January 2003.

11 Nakagawa, "Developing Iranian Rice Cookers."

12 From an interview with Yoshiaki Sano, Osaka, August 20, 2008.

13 From an interview with Yoshiaki Sano.

14 Nakagawa.

15 Nakagawa.

16 Interview with Yūki Ogasawara, Kyoto, November 15, 2007.

17   Nakagawa.
18   Interview with Yūki Ogasawara.
19   Interview with Yūki Ogasawara, by e-mail, March 17, 2009.
20   *50 Years*, 180.
21   Instituto Brasileiro de Geografia e Estatística, "IBGE Releases Book about Japanese Immigration."
22   isM Shosekika Project, "Long-selling Products," 197–8. Originally posted on Matsushita's official website, http://panasonic.co.jp/ism/long/suihanki_txt/index.html.
23   isM Shosekika Project, 198.
24   Ohnuki-Tierney, *Rice as Self*, 134.
25   Fields, *From Bonsai to Levi's*, 41–58.
26   Ministry of Internal Affairs and Communications, Statistics Bureau, Government of Japan. "Quantity of Major Durable Consumer Goods Possessed."
27   Fields, 55.
28   Fields, 56.
29   Personal Communication with a female writer, January 2005.
30   Ohnuki-Tierney, *Rice as Self*, 43.
31   Ohnuki-Tierney, 42.
32   Ohnuki-Tierney, 58 and 116.
33   Ohnuki-Tierney, 59–60.
34   Asia Case Research Centre, the University of Hong Kong, "Project SARS Rebound."
35   Interview with Kyoichi Yoshioka, Osaka, November 13, 2003.
36   Interview with William Mong, Hong Kong, February 11, 2004.
37   Interview with Kyoichi Yoshioka.
38   Speech by Kunio Nakamura, Hong Kong Convention and Exhibition Centre, November 7, 2003.
39   Interview with Toyofumi Hirata, Osaka, January 10, 2003.
40   Japan Electrical Manufacturers' Association, "An Estimate of the Global Demand for the Seven White Goods."
41   The prices are from Amazon.com on May 12, 2008. The Panasonic Corporation of North American advertises the 5.5-cup model for US$24.95.
42   Interview with William Mong, Hong Kong, September 12, 2002.
43   Interview with William Mong, Hong Kong, February 11, 2004.
44   Interview with David Mong, Hong Kong, July 9, 2008.
45   Interview with David Mong.
46   Interview with David Mong, February 21, 2004.
47   Interview with Elvina Li, Hong Kong, July 9, 2008.
48   More details in Nakano and Wong, *Onajikama no Meshi*, 232–5.
49   Using rice cookers to cook soup or stew is gradually catching on among the younger generation. Japanese fashion icon Norika Fujiwara jump-started this trend by announcing she had shed ten pounds by eating vegetable soup cooked in her rice cooker. But there is a catch: Fujiwara has two rice cookers, one for rice and another for soup.
50   Interview with Machiko Miyai.

Epilogue

1   NHK, *Project X*, Volume 6, 51–2.
2   NHK, 95.
3   Nakano, "Shared Memories," 120–1.

References

Amano, Hirofumi. 1995. "Chūgoku Kaden Sangyō no Hatten to Nihon Kigyō [Japanese Corporations and the Development of the Chinese Home Appliance Industry]," Kaihatsu Kinyū Kenkyū-sho Ho, February, vol. 22, 111–34. Tokyo: JICA.

Amano, Hirofumi and Ken Tei Han (Jianting Fan). 1993. "Nichū Kaden Sangyō Hatten no Dainamizumu [Dynamism in the Development of the Home Appliance Industries in Japan and China]," Keiei ron-shū, vol. 59, 59–78. Tokyo: Faculty of Business Administration, Toyo University.

Amano, Masako and Atsushi Sakurai. 2003. *"Mono to Onna" no Sengo-shi* [A Post-war History about Products and Women]. Tokyo: Heibonsha.

Asia Case Research Centre, the University of Hong Kong. 2004. "Project SARS Rebound," http://www.acrc.org.hk/sars/industry.asp?doc=airline. Retrieved May 11, 2008.

Burke-Gaffney, Brian F. 2004. "Thomas B. Glover." In *Nagasaki-ken: Bunka Hyakusen 6* [One Hundred Cultural Stories from Nagasaki Prefecture, Part 6], edited by Nagasaki Prefecture. Nagasaki: Nagasaki Shimbun-sha.

Booth, Martin. 2004. *Gweilo: Memories of a Hong Kong Childhood*. London: Doubleday.

Cabinet Office, Government of Japan. 2004. "Shuyō taikyū shōhizai no fukyū-ritsu [Ownership of Major Consumer Durables and Others—Household]," http://www.esri.cao.go.jp/jp/stat/shouhi/quarter/0403fukyuritsu.xls. Retrieved June 3, 2008.

Carroll, John. M. 2007. *A Concise History of Hong Kong*. Hong Kong: Hong Kong University Press.

Chan, Cham Yi and Wing-yin Yeung (Chen, Zhanyi and Yongxian Yang). 2004. *Xianggang Riben Guanxi Nianbiao* [Chronology of Hong Kong-Japan Relations], Hong Kong: Xianggang jiaoyu tushu gongsi.

Chin, Shunshin [Shunchen, Chen]. 2007. *Chūgoku Bijin-den* [Famed Beauties in Ancient China]. Tokyo: Chūko-bunko.

Chiu, Stephen Wing-kai, Kong-Chong Ho, and Tai-lok Lui. 1997. *City-States in the Global Economy: Industrial Restructuring in Hong Kong and Singapore*. Boulder, CO: Westview Press.

Economic Planning Agency, Government of Japan. 1958. "Shōhisha jyuyō yosoku chōsakekka hōkoku-sho [Survey Report: Consumption-Demand Forecast]," February.

——— 1960. "Shōhisha dōkō yosoku chōsakekka hōkoku-sho [Survey Report: Consumer Trend Forecast 1960]," February.

Dower, John W. 1999. *Embracing Defeat: Japan in the Wake of World War II*. New York: W. W. Norton & Co.

Egami, Tomi. 1963. *Egami Tomi no Sekai no Ryori.* [Tomi Egami's Recipes from Around the World]. Tokyo: Shufu no Tomo-sha.

FAO. 2007. Food Outlook: Rice, November, http://www.fao.org/docrep/010/ah876e/ah876e05.htm. Retrieved June 4, 2008.

——— 2009. FAO STAT, Agriculture Production, Production, Crops. http://faostat.fao.org/site/567/default.aspx#ancor. Retrieved February 21, 2009.

Fields, George. 1983. *From Bonsai to Levi's: When West Meets East, An Insider's Surprising Account of How the Japanese Live*. New York: Macmillan.

Fukagawa, Hideo. 1991. *Kyacchi Furēzu no Sengoshi* [Postwar History through Advertising Slogans]. Tokyo: Iwanami.

Fukuda, Kazuya. 2003. *Shizuku Michiru Toki Tareba: Matsushita Kōnosuke to Nihon Shihonshugi no Seishin* [Because the Time is Right: Kōnosuke Matsushita and the Spirit of Capitalism]. Tokyo: PHP.

Gordon, Andrew. 2003. *A Modern History of Japan: From Tokugawa Times to the Present*. New York: Oxford University Press.

Hamashita, Takeshi. 1996. *Honkon: Ajia no Nettowāk Toshi* [Hong Kong: Asia's Network City]. Tokyo: Chikuma shobō.

Hong Kong Government. various years. *Hong Kong Annual Report*. Hong Kong: Government Printer.

——— various years. *Hong Kong Trade Statistics*. Hong Kong: Government Printer.

——— 1954. *Report of Sham Shui Po Shek Kip Mei Six Villages Fire Relief Committee*. Hong Kong: Sham Shui Po Shek Kip Mei Six Villages Fire Relief Committee.

——— 1967. *Kowloon Disturbances 1966: Report of Commission of Inquiry*. Hong Kong: Government Printer.

——— 1968. *Events in Hong Kong, 1967: An Official Report*. Hong Kong: Government Printer.

——— 1978. *The Development of Senior Secondary and Tertiary Education*, October.

Hong Kong Japanese Chamber of Commerce & Industry. 1989. *Honkon Nihonjin Shōkō Kaigisho 20-shūnen Kinen* [A Twenty-year History]. Hong Kong: Hong Kong Japanese Chamber of Commerce & Industry.

Ichikawa, Nobuchika. 1987. *Kakyō-shakai Keizai-ron Jyosetsu* [An Introduction to the Ethnic Chinese Economy (in Japan)]. Kyushu: Kyushu Daigaku Shuppankai.

Instituto Brasileiro de Geografia e Estatística. 2008. "IBGE releases book about Japanese immigration," http://www.ibge.gov.br/english/presidencia/noticias/noticia_visualiza. php?id_noticia=1167&id_pagina=1. Retrieved February 24, 2009.

isM Shosekika Project, ed. 2004. "Rongu Selā Shōhin: Jidai wo Chōetsushita Meihin Tachi 4, Sekai Hyōjyun Suihanki Monogatari [Long-selling Products: Timeless Masterpieces Part 4, The Story of a Rice Cooker that Set the World Standard]." In *Hakken! Monozukuri Sprits* [Matsushita's Drive for Product Innovations], 192–201. Tokyo: Shoei-sha.

Ivy, Marilyn. 1993. "Formations of Mass Culture." In *Postwar Japan as History*, edited by Andrew Gordon, 239–58. Berkeley: University of California Press.

Japan Airlines. 1974. *Nihon Kōkū Nijyu-nen-shi* [Japan Airlines: A 20-Year History]. Tokyo: Japan Airlines.

Japan Electrical Manufacturers' Association. 2007. *Shiromono Kaden 7-hinmoku no Sekai Jyuyō Yosoku 2001–2010* [An Estimate of the Global Demand for the Seven White Goods 2001–2010]," http://www.jema-net.or.jp. Retrieved May 11, 2008.

Judd, Denis. 1975. *Palmerston*. London: Weidenfeld and Nicolson.

Kelly, William W. 1993. "Finding a Place in Metropolitan Japan: Ideologies, Institutions, and Everyday Life." In *Postwar Japan as History,* edited by Andrew Gordon, 189–239. Berkeley: University of California Press

Kotter, John P. 1997. *Matsushita Leadership: Lessons from the 20th Century's Most Remarkable Entrepreneur*. New York: Free Press.

Lee, James Z. 1999. *Housing, Home Ownership and Social Change in Hong Kong*. Aldershot: Ashgate.

Liao, Chi-yang [Ryo, Sekiyo]. 1999. "Kashō to Nettowāk no Rekishi no Tenkai [Historical Development of the Ethnic Chinese Merchant Network]." In *Higashi Ajia Sekai no Chiiki Nettowāk* [Regional Networks in East Asia], edited by Takeshi Hamashita. Tokyo: Yamakawa Shuppan-sha.

——— 2000. *Nagasaki Kakyō to Higashi Ajia Kōeki-mō no Keisei* [Ethnic Chinese Businesses in Nagasaki and the Formation of the Eastern Asian Business Network]. Tokyo: Kyūko-sha.

Library of Congress, Federal Research Division. 1987. "China Trade Policy in the 1980s," Country Studies: China, July, http://memory.loc.gov/frd/cs/. Retrieved March 21, 2009.

Mackey, Sandra. 1996. *The Iranians: Persia, Islam, and the Soul of a Nation*. New York: Dutton.

Matsushita, Konosuke. 2001. *Yume wo Sodateru* [Nurturing Dreams]. Tokyo: Nihon Keizai Shimbun-sha.

Matsushita Electric Industrial. 1988. *Matsushita Denki Senden 70-nen-shi*. [70 years of Matsushita Electric Advertisements.] Osaka: Matsushita Electric Industrial.

——— *Passpost 21* [Company Newsletter], May 28, 1992 and November 26, 1993.

——— Official Website. http://panasonic.co.jp/

——— 2008. "Kigyō Johō, Shashi [Corporate History]." http://panasonic.co.jp/company/history/chronicle/1933-02.html. Retrieved March 29, 2008.

Matsushita Electric Trading. *Shanai-ho* [Company Newsletter]. August 5, 1970; December 5, 1970; April 5, 1971; August 5, 1974; and May 5, 1975.

——— 1985. *Matsushita Denki Bōeki 50-nen no Ayumi* [50 Years of Matsushita Electric Trading]. Osaka: Matsushita Electric Trading.

Ministry of Foreign Affairs of Japan. 2005 and 2006. "Annual Report of Statistics on Japanese Nationals Overseas," October 1. http://www.mofa.go.jp/mofaj/toko/tokei/hojin/index.html. Retrieved June 4, 2008.

Ministry of Internal Affairs and Communications of Japan, Statistical Bureau, "Jyūyō Taikyū Shōhizai no Fukyū-ritsu [Quantity of Major Durable Consumer Goods Possessed]," http://www.stat.go.jp/data/chouki/zuhyou/20-15.xls. Retrieved April 18, 2008.

Morita, Akio, Edwin M. Reingold, and Mitsuko Shimomura. 1990. *Made in Japan*. Tokyo: Asahi Shimbun-sha.

Nagasaki Shiyakusho [Nagasaki City Government], ed. 1925. *Nagasaki-shi Shi: Fūzoku-hen* [The History of Nagasaki City: An Ethnography.] Nagasaki: Nagasaki City Government.

Nagasaki-shi-shi Nenpyo Hensan Iiinkai, ed. 1981. *Nagasaki-shi Nenpyō* [Nagasaki City Chronology.] Nagasaki: Nagasaki City.

Nakagawa, Hiroji. 2000. "Iran-shiki Suihanki no Kaihatsu [Developing Iranian Rice Cookers.]" October 16, unpublished manuscript.

Nakano, Yoshiko. 2008. "Shared Memories: Japanese Pop Culture in China." In *Soft Power Superpowers: Cultural and National Assets of Japan and the United States*, edited by Yasushi Watanabe and David McConnell, 111–27. Armonk, NY: M. E. Sharpe.

Nakano, Yoshiko and (Dixon) Heung Wah Wong [Oh Kōka]. 2005. *Onajikama no Meshi* [*Eating Rice from the Same Pot*]. Tokyo: Heibon-sha.

National. 2004. *Gohan de Gochisou Sama* [Thank You for the Delicious Rice]. Yashiro, Hyogo: National Cooking Systems Division.

National Association of Commercial Broadcasters in Japan. n.d. "What is NAB?" http://www.nab.or.jp/index.php?What%20is%20NAB%3F. Retrieved February 28, 2009.

National Statistics Office, Republic of the Philippines. 2007. "One in Three Overseas Filipino Workers is a Laborer or Unskilled Worker," http://www.census.gov.ph/data/pressrelease/2007/of06tx.html, May 29, 2007. Retrieved May 21, 2008.

Neighbourhood Advice-Action Council [Lin she fu dao hui] (Hong Kong). 1981. *Hui xiang tan qin dui zhong xia jie ceng jia ting jing ji de ying xiang yi jian diao cha* [Opinion Survey among Middle- and Lower-class Families on the Economic

Impact of their Visits to Relatives on the Mainland]. Hong Kong: Lin she fu dao hui.

New York Times. 2007. "Boston's Other Japanese Pitcher," August 27.

Ng, Wing Chung. 1998 . "Communities: Canada." In *The Encyclopedia of the Chinese Overseas*, edited by Lynn Pan, 234–47. Richmond, Surrey: Curzon Press.

NHK Project X Seisaku-han, ed. 2001. *Project X, vol. 6*. Tokyo: NHK Shuppan.

――― 2001. *Project X, vol. 7*. Tokyo: NHK Shuppan.

Ohnuki-Tierney, Emiko. 1993. *Rice as Self: Japanese Identities through Time*. Princeton, NJ: Princeton University Press.

Panasonic. 2008. "Corporate Profile," Panasonic Official Website. http://panasonic.net/corporate/. Retrieved March 29, 2008.

Panasonic Philippines, "Customer Service," http://panasonic.com.ph/csd/index.html. Retrieved May 21, 2008.

Partner, Simon. 1999. *Assembled in Japan: Electrical Goods and the Making of the Japanese Consumer*. Berkeley: University of California Press.

Police Museum (Hong Kong, China). 2008. *Police Museum*. Hong Kong: Police Museum, Hong Kong Police Force.

Refsing, Kirsten. 2003. "Chapter 2: William Mong's Personal History." In *You le sheng pai "Dian fan bao" Er qi [Selling Japan in Hong Kong]* by Kirsten Refsing, Yoshiko Nakano, and Heung Wah Wong, 17–38. Hong Kong: Hong Kong University Press.

Refsing, Kirsten, Yoshiko Nakano, and Heung Wah Wong [Xianghua Wang]. 2003. *You le sheng pai "Dian fan bao" Er qi: Meng minwei he xin xing ji tuan zou guo de dao lu [Selling Japan in Hong Kong: William Mong and the National Brand]*. Hong Kong: Hong Kong University Press.

RTHK. 2002. Jiti huiyi 70 nian dai.

    Episode 2: Xianggang zhi zao, zhi zao Xianggang [Made in Hong Kong; Making Hong Kong].

    Episode 6: Qing xi Luohu qiao [Emotional Ties across the Lo Wu Bridge].

Saito, Toshihiko. 1995. *Kyōsō to Kanri no Gakko-shi* [Competition and Control: A History of (Secondary) Schools]. Tokyo: Tokyo Daigaku Shuppan.

Shiraishi, Takashi. 2000. *Umi no Teikoku* [Maritime Empire]. Tokyo: Chuko Shinsho.

Shun Hing Group. 1993. *Shun Hing and You into the 21st Century*. Hong Kong: Shun Hing.

Skeldon, Ronald. 1998. "Patterns of Migration: The Case of Hong Kong." In *The Encyclopedia of the Chinese Overseas*, edited by Lynn Pan, 67–70. Richmond, Surrey: Curzon Press.

Smart, Josephine. 1994. "Business Immigration to Canada." In *Reluctant Exiles? Migration from Hong Kong and the New Overseas Chinese*, edited by Ronald Skeldon, 98–119. Hong Kong: Hong Kong University Press.

South China Morning Post. 1982. *The MacLehose Years, 1971–1982*. Hong Kong: South China Morning Post.

Time. 1962. "Business Abroad: Following Henry Ford." *Time*, Asia edition, February 23, 55–9.

Tsang, Steve Yui-Sang. 2004. *A Modern History of Hong Kong*. Hong Kong: Hong Kong University Press.

UCLA Anderson School of Management. 2005. "Nozawa Endowment Marks 20th Year Granting Fellowships," http://www.anderson.ucla.edu/x13868.xml, December 1. Retrieved April 21, 2008.

UNESCO Institute for Statistics. 2007. *Global Education Digest 2007*. Montreal, Canada: UNESCO Institute for Statistics.

Wang, Gungwu. 1993. *The Chinese Diaspora and the Development of China*. Hong Kong: Asia Society, Hong Kong Center.

Wang, Xingbin. 1997. *Zhongguo lü you ke yuan guo, di qu gai kuang*. [Overview of China's Incoming Travelers and the Country or Region of their Origin]. Beijing: Lü you jiaoyu chubanshe.

Wasserstrom, Jeffrey N. 2005. "Chinese Students and Anti-Japanese Protests, Past and Present," *World Policy Journal*, vol. 22 (2), 59–65.

Wen Wei Po. 1979. *Hui xiang bin lan* [Handbook on Visits to Relatives on the Mainland], July 13.

Wong, (Dixon) Heung Wah [Xianghua Wang]. 2003. In *You le sheng pai "Dian fan bao" Er qi* [*Selling Japan in Hong Kong*] by Kirsten Refsing, Yoshiko Nakano, and Heung Wah Wong.
  Chapter 5: "Shun Hing in the 1970s and 1980s: Growth and Development," 79–131.
  Chapter 6: "Shun Hing since the 1990s: Challenges and Responses," 133–56.
  Chapter 7: "Conclusion," 157–68.

Wong, Siu-lun. 1997. "Issues Paper from Hong Kong." In *Migration Issues in the Asia Pacific*, compiled by Brownlee, Patrick and Colleen Mitchell. Wollongong, NSW: APMRN Secretariat.

Yoshida, Ichiro. 1997. *Honkon Gaiden* [Hong Kong Chronicle]. Tokyo: Tokuma Shoten.

Zhuang, Guotu. 1998. "Relations with China." In *The Encyclopedia of the Chinese Overseas*, edited by Lynn Pan, 98–103. Richmond, Surrey: Curzon Press.

Ziegler, Paul R. 2003. *Palmerston*. New York: Palgrave Macmillan.

Newspapers

Ming Pao (明報), *Oriental Daily* (東方日報), *Overseas Chinese Daily* (華僑日報), *Sing Tao Daily* (星島日報), *Wen Wei Po* (文匯報).

Movie

Wong, Kar-wai. 2000. *In the Mood for Love* (花樣年華).

Index